# SEASONS & DAYS

## Books by Thomas McIntyre

*Days Afield,* 1984

*The Way of the Hunter,* 1987

*Dreaming the Lion,* 1993

*The Field & Stream Shooting Sports Handbook,* 1999

# SEASONS & DAYS

*A Hunting Life*

Thomas McIntyre

The Lyons Press
Guilford, Connecticut
An imprint of The Globe Pequot Press

The Lyons Press is an imprint of The Globe Pequot Press.

10 9 8 7 6 5 4 3 2 1

Printed in the United States of America

Designed by Compset, Inc.

ISBN 1–58574–598–7

Library of Congress Cataloging-in-Publication data is available on file

*These stories are dedicated to Bryan.*
*Someday, with luck, I hope he will have his own to tell.*

# AUTHOR'S NOTE

**For the names** of big-game animals, I have chosen not to use "s" when pluralizing them. Thus the plural of deer in this book is "deer," elk "elk," bear "bear," and so on. With the names of domestic animals, I have used "s": "dogs" for the plural of dog, "pigs" for pig. I have also used "s" to pluralize most small game; but when it came to some animals, such as the coyote, who seemed not quite betwixt or between, I went with "s," too. In addition, when I could use a masculine or feminine singular pronoun to refer to a male or female animal, I did, except when that might cause confusion between animal and human, in which case I used "it" for animals, regrettably.

**Most of these stories** originally appeared in different forms in *Sports Afield*.

"Beagle Nation" originally appeared in different form in *Petersen's Hunting*.

"Chinese Blue," "Dust and Shadow," and "The Ptrouble with Ptarmigan" originally appeared in *Gray's Sporting Journal*, all in different forms.

"Have *Gevaer*, Will Travel" originally appeared in different form in *Bugle*.

"My Life as a Turkey (Hunter)" originally appeared in different form in *Turkey & Turkey Hunting*.

"The Last Black Bear" originally appeared in different form in *American Hunter*.

"Old No. 7" and "Presbyopia, Pronghorn & Blood on the Poet" originally appeared in different forms in *Field & Stream*.

λόγοι γ όρπ αλαι οι'κατ έλ ου σι ν'ωζ καί θε οι   .   .   .
... Ancient stories relate that the gods too enjoy both participating in and watching this sport; the result is that in paying attention to these things the young who do what I recommend are dear to the gods and pious, believing that these activities are overseen by one of the gods. Such men will be good also to their parents and to the whole of their city and to every one of their friends and fellow citizens. And not only men who have had a passion for the hunt have become virtuous, but women also, Atalanta or Procris or whoever else, who have been given this pursuit by the goddess.
—Xenophon, *On Hunting*


*Now, as Horace tells us that there are a set of human beings,*

Fruges consumere nati,

*"Born to consume the fruits of the earth," so I make no manner of doubt but that there are others,*

Feras consumere nati,

*"Born to consume the beasts of the field," or, as it is commonly called, the game . . .*
—Henry Fielding, *Tom Jones*


*Digressions, incontestably, are the sunshine—they are the life, the soul of reading; take them out of this book for instance—you might as well take the book along with them.*
—Laurence Sterne, *Tristram Shandy*

# CONTENTS

Preface: To Kill . . . xi

The Bandtail Above All . . . 1

The Geography of Dove . . . 7

Delta New Year . . . 13

Ghost Town, Ghost Bird . . . 19

Beagle Nation . . . 27

Northbound . . . 35

The Ptrouble with Ptarmigan . . . 43

Days on the Water . . . 49

Not a Goose Story . . . 59

My Life as a Turkey (Hunter) . . . 65

The Teachings of Don Pepé . . . 75

The Fire in the Beast . . . 83

Cross Strawberry Creek Mule Deer Liver: A Recipe . . . 93

Winter Is a Greater Hunter Than Men Will Ever Be . . . 97

Bucks of Summer . . . 105

The Perfect Deer . . . 111

Presbyopia, Pronghorn & Blood on the Poet . . . 119

Elk in the Highwood . . . 125

Tour de Caribou . . . 137

An Improbable Animal . . . 145

A Kodiak Moment . . . 153

Grizzlyland . . . 161

The Last Black Bear . . . 173

Goin' 'Gatorin' . . . 183

Have *Gevaer*, Will Travel . . . 193

Czechs and Balances . . . 203

Around the World in 7mm: A Tale of Two Caledonias . . . 211

The Cuban Flu . . . 221

Chinese Blue . . . 233

"A Suggestion of Grace and Poise . . ." . . . 245

Old No. 7 . . . 259

Dust and Shadow: A Short Story . . . 271

Afterword: . . . Or Not to Kill . . . 283

# PREFACE: TO KILL

**At sixteen I** killed a barren-ground caribou bedded on Alaska tundra under a lead sky. I bellied to the rim of the basin where he lay and shot him through the lungs with the rifle I had borrowed from my father. The caribou shuddered and rolled onto his side, his big-hoofed legs stiffening, his heavy-antlered head sinking to the ground. I rose and bolted another round, setting the safety. Pink blood frothed from his nostrils, and as I walked to him he gasped, drowning. While I watched, the big hooves began to kick and the round staring eye turned from deep ice-water clarity to opaque bottle green. The caribou stopped shuddering. I still trembled . . .

The Spaniard José Ortega y Gasset is the modern philosopher most overworked by hunters desperate to sound literate. A cranky, somewhat more than elitist, existentialist critic of "mass man," Ortega y Gasset was also staunchly republican (as in Spanish Republic). Although it has been quoted to the brink of cliché, his book-length essay, *Meditations on Hunting*, was the twentieth century's most luminous examination of the hunt. And what *Meditations* made clear is that at the end of the day, after the spotting and the pursuit and the stalking of an animal, "The hunter is a death dealer."

Hunting is, indeed, about death. Or more precisely, killing. Killing is what makes the hunter (animal and human) different from every other walker in the woods. Not that this always explains the kill to the satisfaction of our friends, especially those of the more doctrinaire environmentalist stripe, or often to our own family. Sometimes not even entirely to ourselves.

The killing I'm talking about is, of course, the legal killing of wild animals in the hunt, not homicide, or the hunting of "armed men"; the killing in hunting is not murder or human combat incognito—assuming one is relatively free of pathological impulse. Hunters are excruciatingly inarticulate about why they kill or what it is like to do so. Part of it is very much a case of like trying to tell a stranger about rock 'n' roll, but also because, as Ortega y Gasset says, hunting means "accepting reason's insufficiency." The desire to hunt, and ultimately kill, comes from a place well before consciousness and words, so that when it arises today it does so almost always outside articulation. Most hunters can't even say when it began for them, but some still try.

At age four I walked into the small dark den of my father's best friend's house. Both men worked in aerospace, the industry just then starting to be the big tit of the Southern California economy. On the paneled walls were the heads

of a deer, an elk, and a wild boar. There were also the head of a red African forest buffalo and a pair of perfect rose-ivory tusks, my father's friend having taken
all his savings, cashed out his wife's life-insurance policy, and gone to (then)
French Equatorial Africa to kill an elephant at thirty yards in dense jungle.
None of these were things that would ever hang on the avocado-painted walls of
our home, and it was incomprehensible to me that they could be found anywhere in tract housing in suburban Los Angeles County.

In later years there would be walking behind on the desultory hunts for
farm-raised pheasants set out by the state of California and shagging birds during the once-a-year San Joaquin Valley dove shoots that my father approached
as social duties rather than outings, "outings" implying being let loose, my father in his life never entirely prepared for that. I went on thinking, though,
about those heads and those tusks and the kind of country where they might be
found, until I was old enough to shoulder my own shotgun. Then I went on
thinking about them some more.

The summer I talked my father into letting me go up to the Talkeetna Mountains in Alaska, taking the rifle he owned but almost never used, was the summer of 1968, of Chicago and Soviet tanks in Prague; but unlike most of the rest
of my overindulged generation (who claimed to want either to storm the barri-
cades or play a guitar just like ringing a bell), all I wanted was to kill something,
as they say, "bigger than me." When I looked at the caribou, at the top of Denali
beyond, and at the sky above, I realized that everything around me in the hunt
was bigger than me. It was bigger than the caribou, too. Bigger than both of us.

Killing is the most incomprehensible part of the hunt, to a large extent because we have almost no widespread experience of the reverential or even pro-
saic forms of killing anymore, no longer even slaughtering our own livestock.
The writer Reynolds Price said, in one of those plummy soliloquies National
Public Radio dotes on broadcasting, that "death has become almost the last obscenity, the single thing we're loath to discuss in public"—which only points out
how rarely Mr. Price must get out of the house. If anything, we are further
steeped in the cult of death than Aztec high priests, from talk of "living wills" to
"doctor-assisted suicide" to the "right to die" (it's really more an obligation, isn't
it?). Death is now not just proud, but dern-near haughty. It is killing that is the
true unnamable, and as such it is what everyone, while feigning repulsion,
wants a glimpse of—but only at a sanitized, plastic-wrapped remove. Make no
mistake, people watch "reality" shows about law enforcement because of the
carny barker's pitch that there might be a killing to be seen on the inside, just as
fans perch in the stands at stock-car races craning to see a crash-and-burn (as a
service to its readers, the Web site of the *Washington Post* offered an interactive
map charting the course and the details of the career of the D.C.-area sniper; one
of the highest-rated, and ethically most obtuse, *60 Minutes* episodes televised a

man's euthanasia, live on tape). This is prurience. Killing is real, and real killing makes no allowance for voyeurism.

What is killing in the hunt like, then? Is it fun? Is it wicked? Most important, is there anything sexual about it?

Bull, bed, belly, shudder, stiffen, gasp, tremble—what other conclusion could there be than that killing must be all about sex? This is possible to conclude because (aside from the Freudianization of all human behavior, and the view of some that the hunt is a form of "rapism"), hunting and sex can seem to be practically the final natural acts. Not for nothing is sex vulgarly characterized as the "wild thing"; for nearly all of us sex is the last bivouac in the wild, our only first-hand experience of it anymore. So sex is the template we, knowing no better, place over all wild experience, forgetting that there was once for humans, and still for animals, far more to it than that. Sex in the wild is an intense but infrequent, seasonal activity, and only one of many natural acts, much more time taken up by gestation, birth, nurturing, feeding, gathering, divination, migrating, hiding, fleeing—and killing. It is a hangover of modernism to want to see everything as sexual (and a shibboleth of the postmodern to pronounce the sexual criminal), but killing is not a division of sex; in the wild it is its own entirely separate bureau.

Is it fun, though?

The correct answer given by the more enlightened hunter of the day is that he takes no pleasure in killing. He does it solely in pious acknowledgment of the cost of his food, or as a last-ditch, unavoidable, altruistic, pain-filled, conservation tactic ("thinning the herd"). Which is all, if you'll forgive me, more than passing strange. Very few people in the industrialized world are hunters for any other reason than personal choice; far from bumming out its participants, hunting is, in the words of another Spaniard, Felipe Fernández-Armesto, in his history of food, "an attractive way of life, which still exercises a romantic appeal for some people in sedentary and even urban societies: thousands of years of civilization seem insufficient to scratch out the savage under the skin . . ."

What about real "savages," the indigenous hunters for whom killing is something more than a style-of-life option? Any smiles to be found on those people's faces? What experience I have had of such hunters has shown me a willingness to display something akin to sacred delight after a kill is made: Why wouldn't there be, when a kill can provide food, clothing, craft material, even objects of veneration, all in one bundle and with one pull of a trigger or release of an arrow? Beyond the human realm, watch those Sunday-night wildlife documentaries. See the cheetah run the Thomson's gazelle to ground, or the croc roll in the river mud, the wildebeest calf in its toothy grin? Detect much solemnity, let alone remorse in such killing? There won't even be crocodile tears.

Do I hunt for the joy of killing? No, I hunt to hunt. I could find far less tax-
ing means of satisfying an obsessive love of killing, had I one, than by hiking for
miles through chaparral to shoot a plateful of quail.

Killing does give me pleasure, though, sometimes great pleasure, when I kill
well. I believe this is the raw response to good killing by those who love to hunt.
I know of nothing we do, without coercion, that is not ultimately rooted in pleasure, however postponed or sublimated or lofty. Denials of the pleasure inherent
in killing are probably less heartfelt than they are hunters' P.C. means of throwing an increasingly denunciatory public off the scent.

Does this make it wicked?

In his NPR essay, Price, quoting a line from the Roman poet Horace—"*Feast,
then, thy heart . . .*"—counseled that unless "a heart craves blood and cruelty, its
owner should feed it lavishly." What Price did not explain was in what way blood
equates to cruelty, and why it is wrong to feed with blood—certain kinds, anyway. Blood can be holy, sacrificial, celebratory, and yet not perforce cruel. Some
of the most profound cruelties involve the shedding of not a single drop of blood.

In our ever-more denaturalized world, though, we can recognize nothing in
spilled blood but heartlessness. This is not the fault of blood so much as of our
stunted perception that makes us want to put faith in the chimera evoked by a
phrase like "cruelty-free." Never mind that it is most often employed as a mar-
keting slogan for cosmetics or a goad for extorting donations for animal-rights
causes; it represents a genuine desire (perhaps to deny that "savage under the
skin"), although one that fails to account for the fact that each second of sentient
existence rides on (or at the very least, owes a tremendous debt to) an innate bow
wave of cruelty from which we are powerless to extract (or forgive) any living
creature, including ourselves. None of which is to say that blood/killing cannot
be cruel in and of itself.

In true hunting, though, cruelty is never the object and is either inadvertent
or the result of inexperience. Good hunting means good killing. Good killing
means having the skill, knowledge, and empathy to be able to inflict a wound
upon an animal that will take its life swiftly, honorably, and with a minimum of
pain. When an animal is killed well, to use (who else's?) Hemingway's words, all
of him will race all the rest of him to the ground, leaving the hunter with almost
no opportunity for regret. Bad killing—fumbled, prolonged, obviously painful—can fill a good hunter with physical sickness, both for the unintended cruelty,
and for the dishonor done the animal. Bad killing, though, to paraphrase
O.y G. one last time (for the time being), exists only at the expense of good killing.

There was a time when good killing mattered, when men were expected to
be good killers. There is D. H. Lawrence's hoary chestnut, referring to James
Fenimore Cooper's *Deerslayer*, about how the "essential American soul is hard,
isolate, stoic, and a killer." What is never quoted is Lawrence's next sentence: "It

has never yet melted." Maybe not in Lawrence's day; but since then the essential postmodern American soul, at least that of sensitized man, has turned into nothing less than a sump of goo.

Killing has never been the exclusive route to manhood (or personhood), but neither has an out-of-hand rejection or irrational ignorance of it. If you want to know what today's American man's soul is thought to be like, you can see it foreshadowed in Woody Allen's nebbish Alvy Singer in *Annie Hall*, a character whose breathtakingly comprehensive catalog of passive-aggressive anxieties and puerility included an inability to kill not only a lobster but also spiders, all his twitchy neuroses inexplicably meant to be endearing. It's endearing (barely so) only so long as it doesn't come down off the screen. It would then become clear that it is not only killing that such a soul is incapable of but all too often trustworthiness, commitment, self-sacrifice, and courage, as well. (Since September 11, and subsequent events, this benign view of a cuddly impotent manhood may be beginning to lose some favor.)

I kill, and try to kill well, because it is difficult, involves moral and ethical reflection, compels me to look directly at death—and life—and is an authentic thing in a grotesquely inauthentic world. This next is the part antis and humanitarians guffaw at loudest, but when I swing my shotgun onto a rising pheasant, in that instant able to see the diamond glint of his eye and each iridescent feather of his cape, it is in a sense an unconditional dedication of myself to him, with nothing then mattering more or anything else as real.

An end to good killing will not mean a healthier environment, merely one too weakened to sustain any longer the most ancient of nature's processes. (What about animals vital to "biodiversity" or ones that are endangered? That's easy: Good killing means not hunting such animals.) In a way, it's like the refusal of the "environmental movement's leading intellects" to bear children because they consider that the "most humane thing" to do. It is an attempt to prove a negative, that the world is enriched because a child does not exist, when all that is verifiable is that the world is one child fewer. A natural world without human hunting is irremediably impoverished.

Within his environment all of a caribou's life—all of the life of the caribou I killed—is an anticipation of the hunter, the killer, in whatever shape he assumes. If not me, then the grizzly or the wolf pack or winter, no animal going gentle into any good night (of them all, death by hunter may actually be gentlest). And yet the caribou was never afraid of dying, not even conscious that he was going to die, never once discussing it in public. If able to be told about it, he probably would have shrugged, if caribou shrug.

Standing beside the body of a dead caribou, the trembling ebbing, I wondered at the thing of killing, which now seemed small, and hardly sorrowful. Against the sweep of the tundra, against the snow of Denali, against the curtain of light that would fill the night sky, it *was* small. Almost anything I could see was bigger than killing—this kind of killing. It made death itself, even my own someday, seem small, too, and insignificant, hardly worth mentioning. Killing gave me that.

Would I have felt that without having killed? There is no way now for me ever to know.

I have a young son who knows his father as a writer, a man of both bad jokes and bad moods, a sometimes mystified churchgoer, a hunter, and an occasional killer, among other things. Not all these are necessarily what I would like him to know his father as, but I do hope he knows that when it comes to the killing part, his father tries to do it well. I think it's important that he knows that killing well, if you are going to kill at all, does (or did once) matter—even if he only knows it through memories I pass on to him. Would I wish him (or a daughter, if I had one) to be a killer himself someday, if he wanted? The right kind, in the right world—to be sure. Will he grow into such a world? I wish I could say, but I worry enough about it to hope he does not come to love killing as much as I have in case he will have to set it aside, or be prohibited from ever taking it up. Would a world without such killing be better, more cruelty-free? Has the scratching out of any natural thing ever made the world better, more cruelty-free?

Really?

# Chapter 1

*He hunted into the light and wind. The sun through the firs gave no warmth. The shadows were black.*

*Looking into the light, he saw the flare of backlit fur. Crossing through the trees, the fur moved like something carnivorous. That meant one of three.*

*Not grizzly—a bear did not hide; and a cougar showed only tracks. That left the fewest, wolf.*

*He crouched to sight beneath the limb line. His heart beat and the tip of his tongue, caught between teeth, numbed.*

*The wolf, circling for scent thirty yards upwind, was a smoke drift. When it stopped, lowering its muzzle to sip the ground currents, he could see it was a big silver dog. Lifting its head, the wolf looked at him.*

*His heart beat harder and he wanted to hide his eyes; but the gold wedding bands of the wolf's irises seemed not to see him, or if seeing not to care, and he could only watch.*

*In the moment before the last moment, the .30–40 leveling, the cold of the wood stock against his face, there was the memory of an old Piedmontese he'd known who accounted it the very worst kind of luck to wish anyone "good hunting."*

*"In bocca al lupo!" Fall into the jaws of the wolf, he said.*

*In the last moment, a leather-gloved thumb on a hammer's polished spur, there was a question: What kind of luck must it be to fall into the eyes of the wolf?*

# THE BANDTAIL ABOVE ALL

*. . . the pursuer cannot pursue if he does not integrate his vision with that of the pursued. That is to say,* hunting is an imitation of the animal.

—José Ortega y Gassett
*Meditations on Hunting*

**Our proper pursuits** vary. They are, in that final analysis, whatever means something to us. I do not know what yours are, but mine begin with something as simple as a bird, a bandtail pigeon. On second thought, there's nothing simple about bandtails.

Please do not confuse the bandtail with the pigeons that infest cities. The bright lights hold no allure for the bandtail. That fowl you see puffing lickerishly in parks and on the ledges of office windows is the rock dove, a refugee from the Old World, where—in Iraq, for example—it has been a domesticated animal since 4500 B.C. It has now simply gone feral and is a common jackanapes—host to enough diseases to warrant a warning label.

The bandtail is a genuine Pacific Coast bird, though it wings as far east as New Mexico; and when you see flights of them wheeling out of dense mists you are filled with expectations of sea and granite, fir vistas, and the desire for an onshore breeze to clear the sky. The birds are blue-gray in flight, but if they catch the morning sun just so their breasts can flash like new pennies. When you kill one you can see closely the black tail band and white neck crescent and corn-colored beak, the feet with long, curved black claws for perching, and the pale violet head and breast. And after so many years of hunting his delicate cousin the mourning dove, you are always surprised at how large the bandtail is.

After a few twelve-year-old Jamesons, I once shouldered my way through a Portland, Oregon, fight crowd to shake the hand of Floyd Patterson as he made his way to the dressing room from the ring following six rounds of hitting at will somebody called Charlie "Emperor" Harris. As I tried to take the former champ's hand I found that mine would not reach around his. In spite of my whisky courage, that startled the hell out of me. You are startled, and sobered, in much the same way when you pick up the body of a bandtail. The deception comes from the apparent effortlessness of his flight. The flight of a green-winged teal, for instance—a bird of comparable size—seems to match his weight as he works as hard as he can to stay aloft: One missed beat, you are certain, and he would plummet. Yet each wing beat of the bandtail surges him through the air with the greatest of ease—his wings like sculls sweeping through water—and when he is dead you cannot quite believe that a bird as large as that flew so high, so straight, and so fast.

The best way to pursue bandtails is to "get on top of something": Few birds will surmount him, as he does not relish the company of strangers in his sky. The aesthetics of bandtail hunting demand snow (and if you are a city boy from south of the Tehachapis, snow can be as exotic as unicorns) and plenty of mast crop such as acorns, piñon nuts, salal berries, and the Boschian red fruit of the madrone tree. The most obvious advantage of all this feed is that if the birds simply aren't coming in to it, or are so high they resemble a tactical air strike, you can at least forage to your heart's content.

When you reach the top of that "something," you will have done well to have brought along a full-choked shotgun and magnum loads, and you should let the bandtails take their time to circle in low enough. They will come in bustling flocks, and you will have to kill them thoroughly. In the parlance, the bandtail is famous for "taking a lot of lead": The way some folks are notorious for holding their Jack Daniel's Old No. 7, the bandtail is notorious for holding No. 7½, or even 6, chilled shot. He will sag when you fire, and there will be a puff of feathers where the shot has hit; but then he will shake it off the way a boxer shakes a punch and, setting his wings in that unmistakable way that tells you he is dying, he will sail away from any chance you will ever have of finding him, to fall dead beneath a bush three canyons distant and be eaten by a predator more worthy than you. And you will sag a little also as you endeavor to evaluate precisely what brand of low-life you are for having done such a thing to an animal who supposedly means something to you.

Then another bandtail will spiral in and you will fire and he will drop along that perfect parabola of mortality—so exquisitely sad and beautiful a thing that it transcends all remorse—and because you will be hunting in rough country you will have to scramble to find him lying still and warm in the salal or with his wings spread across a deadfall fir. You will stare at him for a moment before slipping him into your game bag, and for just a moment nothing else in life will be of much consequence. There will be a brief intermission from the din of memories of lost love, fears of where the money is going to come from next, and questions of whether you are at all who you think you are that usually fill your head to distraction. You won't pitch your shotgun into the ocean just yet, but promise yourself that if you ever wound another pigeon and cannot find him you will (or at least give it serious consideration). And hope it never comes to that.

It is a puzzler, all right. You will have killed him because you loved him—or at least had profound respect for him. Not destroyed him, only taken his life. That is the hardest thing to grasp, but it is what has to be grasped if you are going to hunt him, or venture to tell me I may not.

Even if the understanding eludes you, drop by sometime. If I have any band-tails in the freezer I'll crack some out for you and broil them up, painting the breasts with clarified butter and a sprinkling of salt and paprika. As you slowly chew the dark flesh, you may begin to taste a wildness that can only be found beneath the darker fronds of memory, and you may come to see what I mean.

You will have to pardon me, though, if at the shank of the evening I take down my over-and-under and depart from you. I will travel through the night until I find a high place and climb until everything else is below me. My nostrils will flare like a horse's and be filled with the smell of pines and snow. By the time I stop, my heart will be thundering and the alveoli of my lungs will have expanded to their supposed tennis court of surface area. It will not be dawn yet, but my night vision is good, and I will find a pinecone and pry out some piñon nuts. I will have to remove my gloves to crack them and get at the sweet white kernels. As my fingers ache, my sweat chills, and the cold knifes through my beeswaxed boots, I am likely to wonder (possibly in terms somewhat larger than just this mountain or just this morning) what in the hell I am doing here all alone, watching this dark sky. Then at shooting light there will be a bandtail on the wing, looking for all the world like a cross between an F-15 and the image of the Paraclete. And as I track the clear line of his gyre, I may have an answer after all.

# Chapter 2

*December 13, 1872: Theodore Roosevelt, fourteen, wearing his first pair of spectacles and carrying his first gun, a 12-gauge Lefaucheux side-by-side, kills his first bird, a warbler, on the banks of the Nile a few miles south of Cairo, Egypt.*

# THE GEOGRAPHY OF DOVE

**I was trying** to remember the places doves have led me in this life. It doesn't seem possible that a couple ounces of bird would be capable of leading anyone anywhere, even in a flock—but it's either that or they have been tailing me all this time. I'm inclined to believe that it must be the former.

Where they first led me, at the age of eleven, was across a barbed-wire fence and into a pasture of turkey millet where I stood with my 20-gauge hugged against my chest, watching the sun burn its way above the Sierra's jagged crest. I could smell the San Joaquin Valley soil warming beneath my sneakered feet; then I saw a mourning dove in flight. For the first time in my life I swung a gun at a bird on the wing and fired. And saw a bird die. I walked to him and picked up the first game animal I had ever killed. Yes, I whooped some, but there was another thing, too, some other feeling, that I have been trying for the past four decades to put my finger on, that made that dove, whom I eventually made myself slip away in my too-long game bag, seem to weigh in my hand far in excess of what one could ever have suspected.

For two decades I returned to that part of the Valley each season to hunt doves, even though the changing face of agriculture there made the hunting less and less what it once was. Unchanged in their essence, though, were the dove hunts themselves, with their abiding rituals of ice and whiskey in a motel glass for the ride out to the restaurant and the noisy dinner the night before opening day; the cool hum of the air conditioner in the dark motel room when I was too excited to sleep ("journey proud," southerners call it); the predawn shuffling out to the car and the sight down the row of motel rooms of all the other dove hunters—strangers to us, yet all of us brought to this Valley by the same little bird—shuffling out; and the fast drive on the straight, unlighted country road through the smell of fresh hay out to our friends', Mary and Elmer's, ranch, where we drank coffee and ate doughnuts before heading out to the field or pasture or dry sinking basin, wherever Elmer has seen doves in August's last days.

Our morning shoot was the year's first test of our wingshooting skills—sometimes the skills worthy of praise, others pitifully poor, or at any rate that's the way the doves made them seem. Then it was back to Elmer's to pluck and clean the birds in the shade of a tall cottonwood in his yard, the men having that first, always-best cold beer of the hot day, the children curious as to its taste (in time my curiosity would be satisfied, and about the whiskey, too), the dogs

waiting patiently, like supplicants anticipating the auguries, for somebody to lob
them a delicacy sorted out of a dove's entrails. In the late morning Mary called
us in for eggs and pancakes and Portuguese sausages, and more eggs and pancakes and Portuguese sausages. An afternoon siesta followed; then the late-
afternoon shoot in the blistering heat; more doves to clean; and in the warm
evening, in Mary and Elmer's cool adobe house, one of the world's truly grand
farm dinners of blood-rare roast beef, garden tomatoes, and red onions sliced together in vinaigrette sauce, roasted buttered potatoes, cold milk, pie, and vanilla
ice cream—in an era of "dietary obsession" when nutritional zealots seek "sacred"
foods to "burnish their characters, extend their powers, prolong their lives" (just
like cannibals always have), the honest-to-God farm meal is fast becoming an
anathema; yet one wonders why so many of the egg-meat-bread-butter-and-
potato-eating farmers one has known have all managed to live so damn long.
Taking it all, those dove hunts were for me a fixed point in the changeable
course of a year, a landmark to steer for. Coming at the start of the hunting season, they were my New Year's Day.

There have been other places doves have led me. Once, I found them on the
Njugini River in southern Kenya. I was shooting sandgrouse (a grouse-shaped
member of the dove-and-pigeon family, high fast-fliers coming in from over the
yellow thorn trees to collect water in their breast feathers), birds quite foreign to
me. I never really know what to think when I first kill an animal that is foreign
to me; there is something so *impersonal* about it. But the sandgrouse were coming in energetically, and hunting strangers—especially plump, gray, darting,
swift strangers—is an awkward moment we just have to adjust to. Then some
doves appeared in the morning light—don't ask me which one of the several
hundred varieties; they were just unquestionably doves—and after I'd taken a
few of them, things were all right again and I wasn't feeling socially maladroit
anymore. It was like rounding an unfamiliar corner to find home waiting
ahead.

In another September I walked off an airliner in Memphis, Tennessee, following doves, and heard my bear-hunting friend Fred, of Ripley, Mississippi,
who had come to fetch me, announce, "Well, Tom, I had my choice of three
dove hunts we could go to, so I settled on the one with the best party!"

Down in the Delta country of Mississippi the dove hunting itself proved only
fair to middling that year, and the weather turned out to be some of the hottest I
had ever experienced. The party afterward, though, at the shotgun house down
by the Sunflower River, where the doves were barbecued to a T, a mighty fine
rock 'n' roll band played long into the night, local luminaries with names like
Doug, Louie, Jimmy, and Blinky were in attendance, along with lovely and gra-
cious southern ladies too numerous to mention (invitations promised "Bloody
Marys and apologies" for the following morning), and the whiskey flowed con-

vivially, was indeed one of the best parties in my memory, though something of a disappointment to those who had been present at the previous year's festivities—those having been capped by a rousing good fistfight involving a fair percentage of the male attendees and lasting for what seemed hours. Oooh, but you should have been here last year, son, more than one partygoer informed me, tapping his jangling bourbon glass against my sweaty shirtfront. One must never underestimate the positive effect a good party will have on one's regard for a dove hunt.

Leading, then, even as I was getting my lead on them, is what doves must have been doing to me all these years. And as they lead me into my fortieth season as a hunter, I realize that there is more to it than merely the states and countries and continents. Another sort of geography has been involved. As I look back on it now, I see that where those small grayish birds have led me, ultimately, is from childhood to adulthood to middle age and beyond.

I'd like to think that doves will continue to be there, leading me along the rest of the road as far as it runs.

# Chapter 3

*Climbing the wild boar trail from the bank of the dry river, I flushed the Valley quail. The birds beat their wings with furious burrings, scaling off between the cottonwoods and through the December-afternoon light. I followed, clambering over deadwood last winter's runoff pushed up among the standing trees, moving through green grass covered by leaf fall. Reaching the brush pile I thought the birds had flown to, I stood. The birds flushed again, one at a time at a distance to my left, back toward the riverbed. Most were out of range, or flying low, keeping the trunks of trees between themselves and me. I walked toward the river and a quail flushed right, going behind a sycamore before I could fire, then another got up left, and I swung back and fired, and the bird fell to the white gravel of the river. I broke the side-by-side without looking, marking where the bird fell, hearing the cork-pop of the empty hull ejecting, then the hollow click of the new high-base 7½ dropping into the chamber and the deep clunk of the action closing. By then I was to the bird, just one out of an entire covey rise. There was nobody around, not even a dog, to lay claim to it. Only me.*

# DELTA NEW YEAR

**It was between** Christmas and the first of January. Most years this is a time for planning which New Year's Eve party to leave early from or deciding whose house to drag oneself to the next day to watch the bowl games. This year, though, it would be a time for going into the Delta with Fred and his young son Freddy B. It would be a time for staying in Fred's cabin at his old hunting club in Oxberry Bayou, going after ducks with a farmer friend of his in flooded rice fields in the morning, hunting deer in the club's hardwood timber in the afternoon, and drinking some whiskey in front of the fire at night. It would, in short, be a time for ending the year right for a change.

We made the long drive south from Ripley to Grenada County with the three of us in the cramped cab of Fred's small Jeep pickup—and with a sneak boat lashed to the roll cage and two big net bags of decoys, shotgun and rifle cases, shotgun and rifle shells, waders, duffels, sleeping bags, a portable tree stand, and ice chests piled high in the back. As we rolled across the Tallahatchie Bridge, the stars were cold and sharp in the black sky, and Muddy Waters was coming out strong on the tape deck—Fred, as we neared Oxberry, exuberantly yanking his duck call from where it hung on the rearview mirror and accompanying Muddy's blues harmonica with it. When we arrived in camp late that night, we asked Mr. Buck, the camp cook, to awaken us at 4:30 A.M., but as a precaution I set my travel alarm clock before turning in. I needn't have bothered.

Mr. Buck's fist hit the cabin door and he called out, "It is exactly four-thirty! You want one egg or two?" at the precise moment my alarm sounded the next morning. Ten minutes later we were in the brightly lit kitchen of the camp's main bunkhouse, eating eggs and bacon and corn bread and drinking hot coffee. Fred had warned me ahead of time that there had been so little rain in the fall, he had serious doubts whether there was a wet pothole to be found anywhere in all the counties of Grenada, Tallahatchie, Leflore, Sunflower, and Bolivar put together. But Fred's friend Bob's rice fields might have some water in them and we might just find a greenhead or two there.

It was still dark when we entered the Delta at the edge of Bob's land, the line of demarcation between hill country and alluvial flatland a gently sloping ridge, like a low dune at the rim of a great becalmed lake of soil. I was riding up in Bob's pickup, and as we came over the ridge and the headlights streamed out into the predawn darkness where there was nothing rising up anymore to catch them, Bob said to me, "Well, you have just come into the Delta."

We separated there from Fred and Freddy B. and drove around on the levees to one of the far fields near a brake of tall willow trees. Unloading the sack of dekes, Bob let me out, then reversed the truck several hundred yards back up the levee and out of sight, the lights going out like birthday candles. As he came walking back in the half-light, I could hear the flapping of his rubber chest waders long before I could see him again.

The water reached to our calves as we waded out into it, breaking through the skim ice and trying not to suck down in the softest spots in the muddy bottom. Fred had been wrong; there was at least one wet pothole in the Delta, and when we reached the middle of it in the rice field, we tossed our dekes out into it.

"What we really ought to have are a couple of those little layout boats to lie in," Bob said with a shrug, then kicked out a place for himself in the ice and sat down. I glanced hopefully around for a dry spot but, not finding one, sat down beside him in the mud, the frigid water washing up around my hips.

The dawn was beginning to seep across the surface of the pothole when the first black shape of a greenhead set into the spread, breaking the pink glassiness of the water. From my sitting position I tried to swing on him. He rose straight up and swept himself into the receding band of night to the west as I fired. All I could see then was an afterimage of red flame; all I could hear was the duck's wings carrying him off into the dark.

As the sun climbed, it seemed only to grow colder as we sat in the wet field. Skeins of ducks wheeled and passed high above; but not even Bob's calling could bring them down to us, and they disappeared noisily behind the willow trees. Looking around, we saw ducks setting in at the opposite end of the rice field. You cannot make a duck land where he does not wish to, so we got up, collected the dekes, and headed for the truck so we could go to *where* the ducks wished to.

Now the cold really hit me and I began to shiver till it felt as if my bones would rattle against one another. My gloves were wet and the stock of my shotgun was caked with mud. We climbed into the truck without pulling off our waders, smearing the gray Delta gumbo on the seat, and followed the levee around to where the ducks were, the heater in the cab adjusted to "Equatorial" the entire way.

Fred and Freddy B. had one pintail between them when we waved them over. We set out all our dekes in the water by the levee and made blinds for ourselves by burrowing into the tall weeds. After sitting in what was more ice than water, to have dry weeds on a firm dirt bank to lie in while a yellow winter sun poured down on me was like being offered a scepter and a crown. Then the ducks came.

How many flights did Bob and Fred call in? Three? Four? Five? All I know is that, lying there with my shotgun drawn up beside me and the weeds pulled over me, I would peek out from under the brim of my camouflage hat and see the mallards swinging by overhead. With each swing they would pass lower, until I could hear their whoosh as they came by.

"Next time," Fred would whisper with a rasp around his blues duck call clenched in his teeth. Then he'd start blowing on it again, making all the metal leg bands on the lanyard chime.

They came in from the east, crossing in front of us, their colors bright. We let them touch the water in the midst of the dekes before rising up.

"Only drakes now," Fred called as the ducks flared, and I locked onto a greenhead and fired, watching the big bird fold up and fall with his orange feet pedaling and his glossy-feathered head thrown back. I waded out to where he lay. As I hefted his warm body and watched the beads of water roll off his belly, I turned and saw Fred smiling out at me from the weeds. In his blue eyes—eyes as cold blue as a wolf's above a bushy buffalo hunter's mustache—I could see that killing the ducks was the least of it for him. For Fred, calling those birds down from the sky was everything. The rest was aftermath.

Late that afternoon, while Mr. Buck was cleaning our birds for the munificent sum of fifty cents apiece, Fred took me into the hardwoods. (Later, Mr. Buck would nonchalantly allow as how it was a good time of year to present a man with a tip; and remembering that Parchman figured in Mr. Buck's biography, I was eager to give him a little something.) I had my .45–70 slung over my shoulder as I followed Fred between the trees. He halted and knelt to look at a deer trail. He pointed out a tree and said for me to make my stand there. Then he disappeared, his portable tree stand on his back and his '06 in his right hand.

I sat at the base of that tree that afternoon, watching the light leave the timber, listening to a dog running, thinking: There certainly are a number of different things you can do between Christmas and New Year's. You can always stay in a city somewhere and go to too many parties and drink too much with people who are never going to have the slightest comprehension of what it is you do with your life, or of how hunting could possibly mean so much to you that you would gladly travel halfway across a continent just to spend a day or two with one of the few of your friends who understands perfectly. Or you could spend it as I now was, hunting hard all day with that friend and going to bed early in a piney-smelling cabin in a silent forest in order to be up early the next morning to go at it again. Sitting there, I could only hope that next year was going to turn out one-tenth as well as this one was ending.

At last light I heard Fred fire once. Standing, I slung my .45–70 back over my shoulder. I started toward the shot, then heard Fred call out. I met him dragging a fat, sleek whitetail doe over the fallen leaves.

We would be going a little farther afield tomorrow, trying to pack as much into the waning year as we could. When we returned to camp and got the deer hung up, we asked Mr. Buck to wake us in the morning at four. This time I didn't worry about a clock.

# Chapter 4

*[The male sage grouse] first inflates the air-sacs which line his neck until they assume alarming proportions, meeting in front and frequently engulfing his head; the tail with its spiny feathers is spread to the utmost and pointed skyward; then the gallant pitches forward and casts off for a belly-buster slide over the ground, not without much assistance of propulsive feet. As a result of this ridiculous dryland swim, the feathers of the breast are worn off at the tips till only the quills protrude. These ragged quillends, in being forced over the earth, produce a mild roar which passes for an aria by Caruso with the gray lady in the sagebox. La! but it is absurd! Do you suppose— now do you suppose we ever make such fools of ourselves?*
—William Lea Dawson, *The Birds of California*

# GHOST TOWN, GHOST BIRD

**The night's final** shooting stars showered the far western rim of the Great Basin, trailing yellow fire as they flared toward this cold desert without touching it. A September dawn would tint California's eastern side where meltwater rivers flowed to no ocean. At the end of the dusty washboard road my friend Charley and I traveled down, there would be Bodie with its badmen's ghosts and its ghostlike sage grouse. Taken together, the two were not always easy to sort out.

In a not-quite daylight, Charley and I reached the California State Historic Park at Bodie, eighty-five hundred feet up on a hilly plateau of sagebrush. Shooting was prohibited within the boundaries of this once most unbridled gold camp—praised in its day for having the widest streets, the wickedest men, and the "worst climate out of doors"—so Charley and I turned south out of town, following another stretch of dirt road a mile or so to a long sage ridge above a green meadow. The part about the climate, at least, still held. When we got out of Charley's car this summer's morning we were in bulky down jackets and beginning to shiver in the sharp wind; yet well before noon we'd be in shirtsleeves and sweating freely.

We hunted hard for an hour, sweeping the "sage." We were not actually hunting in true sage at all. True sage, the kind that gets sprinkled into sausage meats and poultry stuffings, is an herb of the mint family and a native of the Mediterranean region. For hundreds of years, perhaps longer, folk doctors brewed sage teas as specifics for loss of memory and to increase wisdom. Having no such lofty properties to boast of, silver-gray sagebrush is merely a North American foliage that smells like sage but is related to the daisy. The only thing sagebrush seems to be good for is providing feed and habitat for sage grouse and other wild animals. Therefore, I would gladly sweep every leaf of sage from every *cuisine* in Provence–Alpes–Côte d'Azur in exchange for one acre of Great Basin sagebrush.

Hunting in it, however, was still a chore for Charley and me. Neither of us owned a light-footed bird dog, and these giant grouse are invisible unless stepped on. We walked a steady pace—driven as much by the predawn cold as by hunting instinct—the brush tugging at our cuffs.

The sun began to glimmer off the sawteeth of the high black cordillera of the Sierra Nevada in the western distance, reddening the snow-filled troughs still

lingering along the faces of those "Snow-White Craggy Mountains." Charley and I halted now, warmed by our walking, wondering if that far-off sound we heard was the wind or a coyote. Suddenly, standing as still as if they had been waiting there a very long time, wanting to know why we had not recognized their presence sooner, a herd of mule deer was a hundred yards from us, heads turned, watching us over their powder-white rumps. As they turned back and ambled away, we turned also and saw the sun start over the taller line of hills to our east. Their tops were above nine thousand feet, but from here they were only hills.

The sunlight flowed down the west-facing hillsides, unveiling old tailings and toppled gallows frames where the earth was gnawed by mine shafts. From where we stood we could also see the sun filling the little pocket in the hills where Bodie lay, like the tide running in under a grounded wreck.

When Bodie lived, it was the hardest town west of Natchez-under-the-Hill. Any genuine "Badman from Bodie"—who in mythical shape was sicced, in lieu of the bogeyman, onto little kids by nineteenth-century mamas—must surely have been someone to contend with: Whenever some "curly wolf" out of the surrounding territory wanted to know just how tough he really was, he'd saddle up and ride into Bodie to find out, and more often than not was rewarded with a pine box for his exertions. In its prime between 1878 and 1881, the town was reputed to have had "a man for breakfast" every day as the result of gunfights, stabbings, ambushes, holdups, and simple cussedness. This reputation was well enough founded for one arrival in '79 to report that during his first week in town six fatal shooting matches were carried out—a truce being called for Sabbath observance. A small girl, upon hearing that she and her family were moving from nearby Aurora, Nevada, to the flourishing new mining town, is said to have closed her bedtime prayers by adding, "Good-bye, God; we're going to Bodie!"

Waterman Bodey, a gold-fevered New York Dutchman, is believed to have first found ore on the site of the town that bears his misspelled name in July 1859 while hunting rabbits. Before he could capitalize on his discovery, a snowstorm buried him one night a few months later as he struggled unsuccessfully to reach his cabin. For the next fifteen years meager livings were dug out of the ground by the town's small population, until in the mid-1870s rich strikes at the Standard and the Bodie mines began drawing miners from throughout the West's gold fields. By 1881, twenty-five million dollars in gold and silver had been taken from Bodie Bluff. The town by then could boast four newspapers, three breweries, two banks, a volunteer fire brigade, a Chinatown, hotels, saloons, and some sixty bordellos. The population stood at roughly fifteen thousand hardy souls variously employed as miners, launderers, bartenders, undertakers, union organizers, claim jumpers, stage robbers, hired gunnies, thimbleriggers, and soiled doves. Law and order was fitfully maintained by vigilance committees, but to their credit only a single lynching is on record. It must (or maybe should) have been a twenty-four-hour Peckinpah movie and a perfectly lovely place in which to reside—as long as you managed to survive mine cave-ins, blizzards, bad whiskey, assorted venereal diseases, and getting shot in the face without provocation by hombres with names like "Rough and Tumble Jack."

Then the strikes played out and Bodie's mining stocks crashed in 1883, sending the town into an eclipse from which it never emerged. Until 1932 Bodie remained, in the cold dry air of its high plateau, one of the best-preserved wooden ghost towns the West had to offer. It was in that year, though, that fire razed two-thirds of the business district. Yet much of the town still stands today, and since the early 1960s the state has operated it as a historic park.

Now Charley and I gave up on finding any grouse on this south ridge and moved back past Bodie and out to a higher ridge running west of town. We left our jackets in the car, started at the bottom of the ridge, and wove up through the sagebrush and dust. Here, unlike on the other ridge, we began to see grouse sign: clean small heaps of dry elongated pellets of pure sagebrush. We heard sporadic, distant gunfire from other hunters as we climbed; but after a difficult hour, which had taken us a little over halfway up the hillside, we stood waist-deep in brush and panted like the retrievers we should have owned. We agreed to swing wide and head down to the car (and there call it quits); but when I turned I saw out of the corner of my eye the white flashes in the morning sun of grouse breasts as a covey flared up and landed on top of the ridge above us. I told Charley and he simply shrugged and we started the hot climb back up again to grouse habitat.

The sage grouse selects that habitat with some care. First of all it must be within a mile or so of a stream or wet meadow. After finding water, the sage grouse must then find low, sparse sagebrush for his hens to nest in, then thick cover, along the edge of his wet meadow or stream, in which his hens can brood their chicks in the summer. For winter range—grouse flocking together in large numbers in late autumn—he requires south slopes and rocky, windswept ridges where the sagebrush will be kept clear of snow so he can feed. But more than anything else, in the spring the cock must have his traditional strutting ground, or *lek,* in a sagebrush clearing with good visibility. Here he parades and postures and puffs with the other cocks to the delight (or indifference) of the hens—the males occupying specific mating areas of the lek in accordance with hierarchical rankings ranging from the lone master cock to subcocks and guard cocks, all the way out to those forlorn fellows lurking on the edge of the breeding ground like eunuchs outside a harem window.

A master cock may put on his courting performance year after year from within the very same ten-foot-in-diameter "primary mating area" in the lek. If the performance lives up to its advanced billing, a master cock may breed forty hens a day. An ornithologist like William Lea Dawson may call the entire spectacle absurd, but there is no arguing with success.

In the sage grouse's life the role sagebrush plays cannot be overemphasized. While chicks will feed on crickets and grasshoppers for a time, the adult bird's diet is almost exclusively herbivorous, with up to 75 percent of that diet being composed of sagebrush—and in the winter that figure rises nearer to 100 percent. The reason is that the gizzard of the sage grouse is a soft membranous sac (unlike the strong, muscular, seed-crushing gizzards of more adaptable fowl); and while capable of great distension, it cannot reduce plant material more demanding than the tender shoots of sagebrush, or the forbs in meadows. Yet even on such a seemingly restricted diet the cock sage grouse may reach eight pounds and is second only to the wild turkey in size among our upland game birds.

For the hunter on foot in open sage country, these second largest upland game birds will often manage to keep moving all day, out of range, making a long and challenging chase for that hunter. And they are not above taking flight a hundred yards in front of you. It is also my experience that when the sagebrush is heavy, or the birds have just landed from a flight, they may hold tight and get up only when you chance to be within a few feet of them. (I once spent ten minutes circling and circling within six feet of a wounded bird I was searching for, only to have him get up, with a sound like the thudding top rotor of a Sikorsky helicopter, as I was about to step on his tail feathers.) And while they are very hard to see on the ground, when they get up they are not easy to hit and kill, sometimes taking both barrels of magnum-loaded No. 4 chilled shot before going down. For birds as big as they are, they can also too readily be missed; but then you have the privilege of seeing them make their long, stiff-winged, cruciform sails far out over the yellow-blooming sagebrush and blue lupine, the chill wind whistling off the tips of their extended primaries.

Where I glimpsed those birds landing was in a jumbled pile of pale stones on the ridgetop. When Charley and I got to within a couple of hundred yards, I suckered him into climbing above and around the rock pile and coming down on top of the birds, while I would go up just a little farther and block the route he'd push them down through. Charley agreed, suckered not in the least, knowing he would have a better chance anyway from above of getting the kind of jump shooting he dearly loved.

After ten minutes of climbing, Charley came out behind the rocks and found a sage mesa spread before him. Working his way along the edge of it to where I sighted the grouse, he carried his 12-gauge Wingmaster at the ready. Reaching the spot, he saw no birds; but when he took a few more steps, a single grouse got up, only five feet in front of him. He fired, drawing feathers, then pumped and fired again, the bird dropping like an origami figure falling from the hand. Reloading, he started for the bird, then realized the unlikelihood of just a single being here. He moved forward alertly, prepared to walk up more birds; and when he was almost to the dead grouse, four live ones flushed. Two more hollow, booming shots, and another bird fell. The rest sailed over the edge of the mesa and past another pile of rocks. I saw them coming. They drifted by like paper kites dropping. I pulled up on the rear one in line and fired twice, watching him flutter and fall after my second shot.

Charley and I met up and carried the heavy, warm birds down from the ridge to the car. We put away the empty shotguns and cleaned grouse. (Sage grouse can be skinned but will also pluck as easily as a dove—though in either instance they should be drawn quickly to dispel any strong sagebrush flavor.) Charley happened to have the medicinal fifth of gin lying with the bald spare and oily rags in his trunk, and happily located a bottle of Rose's lime juice, too, to keep it company. Forgoing cocktail shakers (and glasses), we had post-hunt Kamikazes in the early morning, gargling together alternate sips of lime juice and gin, smearing blood and feathers over the glass of the bottles as we handed them back and forth. We would soon have to find some water to rinse the drawn and featherless birds in. Then we would marinate them in red vermouth overnight and tomorrow part them like chickens on a cutting board, dredge them in flour and brown them in onions and butter, roast them in their marinade and whatever else came to mind, and then eat their dark, dense, but tender meat as we drank crisp white California wine. For now, though, we dropped them into the ice chest, capped the bottles, and moseyed into town for one last look, and to walk off the cocktails before the drive out.

We walked through town along the weathered boardwalks. Passing the false-fronted buildings with the dusty relics of a different time—chipped enamel, tarnished brass, cracked wood—seen dimly through the dirty windows, I wondered on which street old "Rough and Tumble Jack" finally met his fate. Charley and I walked on, leaving the town behind as we headed for Boot Hill.

As we crossed a sagebrush-dotted green meadow, we saw a large covey of sage grouse (off-limits to hunting inside the park) stepping nervously away from us. I thought of what ephemerids these birds must be—like all upland game birds, their population cannot be meaningfully reckoned in terms of a fixed number but rather in terms of upward and downward yearly trends: One or two disastrous hatches and they could flare out like this dawn's shooting stars. Their dependence on sagebrush, the shrub disappearing from the West, also made them vulnerable. Then I realized that where these "Cocks-of-the-Plains," "valiant sons of the desert," and "grizzled veterans of the wormwood" (as Dawson stirringly titled them) were stepping was among rusty ore cars and splintered wagon wheels, over the barren foundations of long-gone hurdy-gurdy houses, and across the graves of miners who never struck it rich, spreading their spiked tails into the desert rose, blossoming on top of not-very-ancient human ruins. That's when their ephemerality seemed not nearly so profound. As we drew up on Boot Hill, the grouse whirred low into the thin blue air ahead of us.

Segregated outside Boot Hill's consecrated ground stood a lone tombstone marking the grave of a whore who'd stayed around too long with the miners who never made a strike of their own. Inside the cemetery Charley and I wandered from chiseled marker to chiseled marker with minor curiosity, contemplating whose beloved wife lay here, which native of Ireland had gone to his reward there, considering all the dead lying where they could not, short of the Judgment, whir away either high or low into any blue air. Then I halted at a bright white stone and read my own name cut into it and decided that was as deeply as I wanted to get involved in this particular saga of the West. I told Charley it was time to get out of Dodge.

Later we stopped along a rocky channel of swift, clear meltwater running through a canyon, Jeffrey pines and piñons clinging to the cool walls above us. We rinsed the birds, our hands throbbing as we kneaded the cold river. There was probably a law against rinsing drawn sage grouse in California's trans-Sierra streams. Not that me and Charley gave a damn: We were, for today, bad men from Bodie.

# Chapter 5

*The hare will suddenly jump up and attract to itself the barking and crying of the hounds as she runs away. The hunter should call out as the chase begins: "Tally ho! Well done, clever dogs!" And he should run with the pack, twisting his clothing round his hand and holding up his stick in the direction of the hare, but not get in front of her; for that is useless. The hare quickly slips away, ceasing to be visible, and usually goes round again to the place where she was discovered. Then he should shout after it, "Strike, boy; Strike! Strike!"*
—Xenophon, *On Hunting*

# BEAGLE NATION

**Along with a** written constitution and universal suffrage, there are few more distinct symbols of democracy than the beagle. Czars may run wolfhounds, but presidents, especially nominally populist ones, would do well to keep beagles. Lyndon Baines Johnson—in between shooting Hill Country whitetails while a uniformed Air Force colonel perched on a stool in the corner of the shooting house, the briefcase containing nuclear launch codes on his lap; or having a Pearl too many and herding cattle in his armored Continental as Secret Service agents jogged valiantly alongside—was perhaps most famous for a photograph of him lifting one of his beagles by its floppy hound ears. No other single gesture could have more clearly revealed the gawky Texas ranch kid in Li'l Abner overalls, a single-shot .22 in hand and beagles running a rabbit in a circle back to him, lying at the core of the leader of the Free World.

The beagle is actually an ancient Old World breed, and hardly a plebeian one. Far enough back, wild wolf-dogs were first domesticated by hunters to help them raise "suspicious game," as Ortega y Gasset termed it. This is what is known in Greek as *cynegetics* or hunting with dogs, and it is also used to describe the entire art of hunting (which, I guess, would make us all officially "cynegeticists," next time anyone asks). Bringing the dog into the hunt is also what Ortega y Gasset describes as "the only effective progress imaginable in the chase," because it links one natural hunting instinct (the human's) to another (the dog's). As early as the eras of classical Greece and Rome, hunters were linking up with beagles, which are believed to descend from the otterhound through the bloodhound. (One of the earliest of all hunting book was *Cynegeticus*, or *On Hunting*, by the fourth-century B.C. Athenian historian Xenophon; and it deals primarily with beagling, nets being used to capture the prey.) By the time of the Crusades, the beagle had been well established as a hunting breed and is considered the ancestor for all hunting hounds.

The name "beagle" may derive from the Celtic word *beag*, meaning "small." The fourteenth- and fifteenth-century kings Edward II and Henry VII kept packs of "glove" beagles, while Queen Elizabeth had "pocket" ones, the names describing their relative sizes. The somewhat *louche* district of London known as Soho got its name from the cry "*Soho!*" that beaglers made when a rabbit was put up by the dogs, back when this area was royal hunting land.

As the aristocracy's interest shifted to foxhounds, the country folk of Britain were more than happy to keep on with their beagles for sport and provender. It was only natural that when many of those same country folk came to America, they brought their beagles along for similar purposes. Even though the beagle was not "recognized" as a unique breed in the United States until 1884, the dogs had undoubtedly been here far longer. Over the years, hunting beagles in America were bred for shorter and shorter stature (perhaps in response to the smaller size of the quarry here, cottontails, versus the practically enormous European brown hares; or because cover was much denser and tighter to the ground, unlike the fairly manicured farmlands of Britain), until today a good rabbit dog is under thirteen inches high at the shoulder.

Beagles are, like Bruce Springsteen, born to run. Letting a pup nose around in the briers till he puts out a rabbit is about all it takes to start one, after basic obedience training. That's the other democratic thing about them: Nobody needs to do any fancy training, no steadying to wing and shot, no hand signals, no need to make them "honor" another dog. Let's make all the pointing and re- trieving people mad as hell by saying that it is sometimes hard to discern whether their gun dogs are, when they lock up on point like they just touched the third rail on the subway track or have to wait, trembling, for the fetch com- mand after a bird goes down in a shower of feathers, really having all that much fun out there. Perhaps they are; but I defy anyone to suggest that when a beagle is "chopping" after a rabbit or worrying a dead one on the ground, he is having anything less than an absolute blast! And hardly a man is now alive who is im- mune to the dog's infectious joy. With all due respect to the late Charles Schulz, no stranger to beagles, happiness is not a warm puppy, but a hunting beagle.

Anyone who hunts with beagles, whatever his social or economic status, is blue collar at heart. That's another democratic thing about them. There is defi- nite working-class cleverness, maybe even slyness, to hunting with beagles. A good beagler is reminiscent of Robert Frost's "Hired Man," who never stood "on the hay / He's trying to lift, straining to lift himself." Anyone who hunts rabbits with beagles knows that it is simply an easier, more enjoyable, *better* way than hunting without beagles. Someone who prefers to spend a winter day all alone, jumping up and down on a spreading juniper bush, then hopping off to pick up his shotgun and load it before trying to get a shot at a fast-disappearing rabbit, rather than letting an ecstatic pack of beagles circle that rabbit back to him, is hunting at least partially to prove something, not for the pure pleasure of it.

I say "pack" because even a hunter with a single beagle is part of a pack, formed by his dog and himself. Nonetheless, beagles do better associating and hunting with others of their own kind, so a responsible beagler soon realizes that he is not likely to have just one dog for long. The pack mentality of beagling also makes it hard to be a genuinely arrogant hunter. No matter how good you may think you are at recognizing rabbit cover, or your prowess as a shooter, or even your talents as a trainer and breeder, it's still the dogs doing the lion's share of the work. The beagles, in the jargon of beagling, ultimately "account" for the rabbits, while there are times, as after too many unconscionable misses in a row, met by curious head tilts from the dogs, when a hunter can feel like a no-account.

Another interesting thing about beagling is that it isn't always just rabbits whom dogs may be accounting for. Certainly, the quarry of choice for beagles and beaglers is the cottontail. There are a number of primal moments that a hunter needs to see in order to have completely hunted. Ducks, webbed and maple-leafing into the dekes, would be one. A big whitetail, rutting, coming out of the timber with his rack held high is another. And a third is a cottontail, pursued by beagles, making that sweeping, inexorable circle back to where it started. (There is likely some behavioral or "ethological" explanation for this, maybe having to do with the rather limited dimensions of the rabbit's neocortex. It's always seemed to me, though, that the rabbit has determined to disregard Satchel Paige's dictum about not looking back, and, seeing something that might in fact be gaining on it, decides to get back down the rabbit hole without further adieu.)

As intrinsic as cottontails are to hunting with beagles, they are, as I said, not the only manner of beast a beagle is capable of putting out of cover. This is something the wily beagler will take full advantage of, hunting with his dogs where and when he can legally take other game, as well, believing two grouse, three quail, and a pheasant in the bush could be worth a cottontail in the hand, if the pack has a chance of flushing them, too. And then there are the things you would never expect to be flushed.

One afternoon a couple of winters ago I went out beagling in Arkansas after a morning duck hunt. The beagling was a little slow, but we did put a few rabbits to flight and busted a bobwhite or two into the air under the gray sky. Then the dogs entered another of the thickets scattered out over a large pasture, and four of us spread out around the edges of the cover.

The barking, when it began, was different this time. It was somehow—what?—more urgent, more furious, not from chasing something straining to get away as much as it sounded as if the beagles were barking at something facing them, perhaps bayed up, but that they knew better than to try to grab.

"Bobcat," the dogs' owner pronounced.

Now we all crouched and peered hard into the thicket for a sight of the dogs and the cat; but when they came out, it was from the far end of the thicket, beagles and bobcat disappearing into a long row of brush before we could even get a

look. Not before we heard the sound, though, of the dogs running down the
brush line, giving mouth.

We followed, and after several hundred yards the dogs were silent. The quiet
of the winter day seemed suddenly unnatural without barking. I turned, not
knowing quite why, and looked back down my side of the brush line. The bobcat had managed to double back and was seventy-five yards away, walking away
in the soft sand outside the brush in a swaying, high-backed, downhill-sloping
easy stride. I shouted for the others, and the cat broke into a run. We trailed it
back into the same thicket, and this time the dogs' owner and one of the other
hunters followed the sound in, looking just a little like a pair of Jim Corbetts off
to deal with another man-eater. In a minute or so there was the sound of a shotgun over the baying of the beagles, and directly a very happy hunter came back
out, carrying a long, heavy-pawed tom, his first bobcat ever.

While strange things do happen on beagle hunts, they are in addition to the
experience that brings so many of us, across so wide a spectrum of society, back
to the rabbit brush again and again. It's the rabbits we come back for, and the
dogs. Neither cares about who or what you are other than, for varying reasons,
whether you are a good hunter or not. And beaglers themselves feel pretty
much the same way: The only thing that matters is that you love rabbits and
you love dogs.

Down in Mississippi a few winters before the Arkansas trip, I was out on another post-duck-morning rabbit hunt on land owned by the duck club where I
was a guest of one of the members. This was '90s Mississippi, not '60s, but the

member, and the other owners of the duck club, were unquestionably white, as well as white collar. When they wanted to put on a rabbit hunt, though, they knew the best beagle pack around belonged to several black men who worked at the nearby mill.

There was never any question about the black men hunting "for" us. They would be hunting with us, the duck-club owners letting them use their land in exchange for the beagle men letting us all share the benefits of their dogs, democratic and free-market, all in one. When they showed up with their beagles, nobody seemed to notice much that they were carrying J. C. Higgins pumps or wearing shower caps for rain gear, while the other hunters had on Barbour coats and over-and-unders broken in the crooks of their arms. The only thing anyone noticed was the game little red-black-and-white dogs, as sleek-coated and shiny as otters and aching to be turned loose. And then what was noticed was all the rabbits they chased out into the muddy fields for us, one after another, at one point a dozen or more out of one big clump of johnsongrass growing up around a pump head. The barking of those beagles was a music we could all understand. Then we had enough rabbits hanging from our game straps, and it was time to stop.

We divided up the rabbits, shared a few beers, shook hands all around, and said good-bye, until the next time. It was probably not a big thing, as moments in democracy go. But even if it was only something small, it was still good, just like rabbits and beagles.

# Chapter 6

*Both Grouse & Ptarmigan populations are influenced by weather. Adult birds require a high level of Protein in their diets to lay eggs & in turn the young must have high Protein to survive. It takes hot summers with high air temperatures to produce the Insect life needed to create & maintain a high native Grouse & Ptarmigan population. It seems very possible that the high in the Sun-Spot Cycle & the Grouse Cycle could be one in the same. The Snowshoe Hare Cycle is another which may follow the Sun-Spot Cycle. . . .*

*Willow Ptarmigan are found in Open Mountain Valleys & in Mountains that are rolling & gentle. At times in the Cycle they get into flocks of 2–3 hundred. In the late fall the males cackle at dawn & are an excellent Alarm Clock.*

*—In a Letter from a British Columbia guide and outfitter*

# NORTHBOUND

**For the first** cartographers to lay eyes on it, that trackless north country must have seemed a land forever to remain uncharted. Not until 1907 was the first reliable map of the northern interior of British Columbia published—the crowning achievement of the Oblate missionary Father A. G. Morice. (This priest managed—during the course of parochial and exploratory treks through the seventy-thousand-square-mile expanse of wilderness that was his parish—to take the first accurate measure of the land, using only a compass, chronometer, aneroid barometer, sounding line, and the oral reports of Carrier Indian hunters and guides.) Even today—though it is hatched with dirt roads cut through by government bureaucracies, timber companies, mining corporations, and various small-time laissez-faire-capitalist enterprises—the interior, north of where the maintained dirt road ends in the outpost of Manson Creek (itself four hours north of where the tarmac plays out in the village of Fort St. James), appears in road atlases as so much *terra incognita*.

There are times of the year, though, when only terra incognita will do. In the fall I often want to go lay eyes on some "unknown land." It might be a seasonal change in body chemistry that makes me migratory, or maybe it is that the weather is cool and still dry and right for traveling. For whatever reason, in one particular fall I needed remote northern country to go into, to "get away from it all," and so chose the Omineca Mountains, across the Pacific-Arctic Divide, to hunt grouse in. Ruffed, Franklin's, and blue grouse, and willow and white-tailed ptarmigan—the variety pack of Tetraonidae—make their homes in that country, yet grouse seem to have been, in all the rich history of the northern interior, among the least of reasons for venturing into its fastness.

It was beaver, whose pelts could be stretched into circles flat as drumheads and bundled off east and across the Atlantic to be made into felt hats to grace the heads of fashionable gentlemen, that brought the likes of Alexander Mackenzie and Simon Fraser (no less intrepid explorers by being equally intrepid merchants) into the interior—as beaver brought so many other like men to the Mountain West of all North America.

Mackenzie and Fraser's North-West Fur-Trading Company's *engagés* were the first Europeans into British Columbia's northern interior, the first to erect trading posts in it, and the first to give it an English name other than "Unexplored"—the Scots Fraser calling it, after his homeland, New Caledonia. (Some years later I'd find myself in another "New Caledonia," but that story will have to wait.) The North-West Company in time combined with the ubiquitous Hudson's Bay Company, and by 1836 the amalgamation was such a going concern in the area that, according to Father Morice's detailed accounting in *The History of Northern Interior British Columbia (Formerly New Caledonia)*, "67,510 salmon; 11,941 of the smaller fish, plus 781 sturgeon and 346 trout; 2,160 rabbits; 153 ducks, 10 lynxes, 8 marmots, 3 porcupines, 1 swan . . . and 14 dogs" were used as provisions for the many employees of the numerous trading posts in a single twelvemonth—not counting, of course, an unrecorded number of horses who were also eaten.

In 1855 gold became another reason for venturing north into the interior, and it remains one today, with some people coming in with full-scale mining operations, and others with just the fever and a grubstake (and sometimes with just the fever), even though every worthwhile claim was staked long ago. They still come north to trap for furs, but also now to log and to guide and to hunt moose, caribou, mountain goat, wolf, black bear, and grizzly. One or two came in fulfillment of a messianic purpose. And not a few come for the naive reason people have always headed into the northern wilderness to live—the notion that somehow, by going as far north as they can get, they will outdistance whatever was chasing them "down there": an idea not without a certain appeal. But all too often, by the first January their cabin is only half built, the kids are croupy, the chain saw has cashed it in, and whatever was after them down there must have hidden under a tarp in the back of the ten-year-old pickup and hitched along.

Which is why I intended to be in this north country for only a few days in the fall simply to hunt grouse. To live successfully in the North, you need a firm purpose to your being there—not merely some indistinct quest for wholeness— or the North, not easy to begin with, can turn bleaker than anyplace you could have left behind: The country cracks greenhorns like they were thrift-store china. But even without a firm purpose, if you go for only a short visit, and pick your spot well, it can still work. Bearing that in mind, I wrote to several guides in the northern interior, asking them what they knew about grouse. One replied.

The outfitter, whose name was Larry, got my letter in late August as he was setting up his spike camps in time for the season's hunts in the Cariboo Range. Someone's wanting to come north strictly for grouse seemed a bit addled to him at first; but, scratching his balding head under his green cap, he noticed that the return address was California, and that explained it—as it explains so many other strange phenomena these days and into the foreseeable future.

Taking time out from raising tents and trailing up pack animals, he sat down and wrote in blue ink beneath a letterhead with a mountain on it: "I have hunted Grouse myself & guided for them, usually with Big Game, for over 25 years. I am a naturalist & an avid bird watcher. I have trapped & lived in the Back Country since early manhood."

Warming to the letter writing, he went on to explain, in that headlong prose peculiar to outdoorsmen, the natural history of grouse, telling me about their life cycles and sun spots and how the call of cock ptarmigan would wake him in the fall. If for you, far south in some city, the morning had begun with white noise coming from a clock radio, this was the kind of letter that would leave you wide awake. I wrote back, telling Larry to expect me in the northern interior of British Columbia in mid-October, when I would do some grouse hunting.

I have noticed that a fault of too many westerners (American and Canadian alike) is their low esteem for the intelligence of grouse. "Fool hens" is what they call them, and belittlingly describe ways to catch them with hand loops, or tell of how they shot an entire flock, one by one, out of the branches of a pine with a small-caliber rifle—how one season they killed and canned scores and scores of them (bag and possession limits be damned), those silly birds that simple to knock off. What is never brought up is how long into the season it was possible to wreak such havoc, or how far ahead of the hunter the birds started rising up after a while, or how deep in terra incognita these birds were found. What is hardly ever brought up is that the grouse is a bona fide wilderness dweller who, like the caribou, the grizzly, and the mountain sheep, cannot long tolerate men.

When, in mid-October, I came north to Fort St. James—with the old log buildings of the Hudson's Bay trading post still on the shore of Stuart Lake, and with the low quiet voices of Indians in the neon cafés—I found that the western opinion of grouse was little different there. My guess would be that only a small minority of the grouse killed in the northern interior are taken shooting-flying with shotguns. The vast majority are killed incidental to big-game hunts or by passing motorists brandishing .22s out truck windows at the sight of the birds picking up grit along the road shoulders. The grouse are so famous for being at-tracted to the warm open spaces the roads provide for them in the dense timber that when I told a resident of the Fort I was northbound to hunt birds, he as-sured me that the drive up would offer excellent opportunity for sport. As it turned out, while his appraisal might have been accurate for the opening day of the season, it had nothing to do with the conditions to be found in mid-October: Even if one were up for a little road hunting and ground sluicing, the grouse along the shoulders had been shot at (quite illegally) by about every timber faller and tool push who passed by, and were as jittery and flighty as quail. These birds would have to be *hunted*.

From the Fort, I rode farther north in the weekly mail truck to Manson Creek—the neo-sourdough at the wheel telling me how he'd downed his moose the Sunday before last, about a mile back into the woods behind his house, and was able to return for it, driving a skip loader from the lumber mill, and carry it out whole. Larry met me in Manson, and as we drove even farther north into the backcountry to his cabin, he revealed himself to be a man who had known from his boyhood that the only thing that would satisfy him in this world was to be a hunter and fur trapper in the wilds of British Columbia, and who in his "early manhood" quit the prairies of Alberta to buy a trapline around Germansen Lake in the Omineca Mountains. He still remembered, with some nostalgia, his first two winters up here when he had not seen another human until the thaw. Now he could say, with a twinge of bitterness, that he had neighbors within fifteen miles, year-round.

It had been snowing when we left Manson—Larry saying that of all the country around in any direction, including north, winter came to these mountains first, and did not leave until weeks after spring had come everywhere else. (But with this sun-spot cycle, he added, the weather seemed to be changing every which way, with the winters turning warmer and wetter and the animal herds ebbing and flowing all over one another's ranges.) Now, as we drove along the shore of Germansen Lake, the sky was blue and untouched. We stopped once to saw up a poplar a beaver had felled across the road, and after three hours of driving from Manson we turned off onto a pair of ruts running across a frozen meadow and climbed up to log corrals and cabins set at the foot of a mountain—Larry pointing out to me, as we pulled up, a northern shrike chasing a hapless whisky jack into the pines.

A set of moose antlers was nailed to the roof over the porch of Larry's cabin. Around the cabin and back into the woods were scattered the low houses to which his pure-blooded Eskimo sled dogs were tethered. Their bloodcurdling howls echoed through the trees as we got out of the truck, but once you let these hundred-pound animals off their chains and into the cabin, they would try to climb into your lap and lick your face. Larry said they were the only means of transportation he had in the winter to get around his trapline; and when he was out on the trail at sixty-below, he would bed down at night with bull caribou hides wrapped around his sleeping bag, and his team huddled around him—sleeping as snug as a bug until all the animals erupted in a snarling dogfight at the stroke of midnight.

After supper, Larry led me down to my cabin, telling me not to be concerned about the possibility of a young local grizzly nosing around, then wished me a good night's rest. Inside my cabin I lit the lamp and wondered what I would do without country like this—populated by trappers and sled dogs; where even a nighttime visit to the privy could have the makings of a bear story—to get away to. I wasn't in California anymore, Toto.

Holding that thought, I cupped my hand around the lamp chimney and blew out the light.

The Franklin's were in the pines below in the morning. As I carried my shotgun through the spongy wet dimness in the trees, Larry beside me said that sometimes all that had to be done in hunting Franklin's was to stand still in the forest and they would begin calling out, announcing their whereabouts. Today, though, the birds burst out of the branches near the tops of the trees with no cries at all. Killing a male, I held him, seeing the inky darkness of his feathers, the white spotting on his breast, the fierce redness of the comb above his eye. Fool hen, indeed. We hunted on.

The ruffed grouse, Roger Tory Peterson writes, is "usually not seen until it springs into the air with a startling whir." As we hunted ruffs through the long shadows slanting over the leaves on the ground in a poplar grove that afternoon, I saw his point. Jumping them out of what seemed no cover whatsoever, we followed them deeper into the grove, rising them up again and again as I shot and Larry gathered the downed birds. He told me that in winter these birds would dive beneath the snow at night for insulation, and in the morning they were always exploding into the air from beneath your snowshoes. Wolf were quite partial to grouse, he said; and once he'd seen a big silver dog leaping ten feet into the air to catch a grouse on the wing.

In the northern interior of British Columbia, the sun never finds its way much above the level of the treetops anytime of the year; and by two-thirty in the afternoon in mid-October the light has gone golden in the sky. Larry and I had some traveling to do to be back in camp by dark, so we packed up the birds and headed in. At twilight in his camp, Larry cleaned the birds, showing me the highbush cranberries, clover, and rose hips in the crops of the ruffs, the bundles of pine needles in the crops of the Franklin's. He would tack the wings out on boards to dry, using them as lynx flags over his trap sets, where the dangling wings would catch the eye of furbearers.

We ate mountain goat steaks for dinner, and in the next day's gray morning with our hot coffee had mountain goat liver. Then, saddling two horses—mine a twelve-hundred-pound gelding named Bucky—we rode up the mountain to find ptarmigan and the winter.

Down at Larry's cabin light rain fell, dripping from the moose antlers; but as we climbed, the rain turned to snow piling up in heavy "whisky jack blankets" on the bent fir branches. On the trail, though, we could still mark the signs of pine martens, weasels, rabbits, wolf, and a track Larry was unfamiliar with, but which I took to be the biggest mule deer track I had ever seen. He thought it was a bit far afield for mule deer, but said that, with the weather change, he wouldn't question it.

After climbing two thousand feet on horseback, we crossed the timberline and came out in rolling draws where moose had cropped the willow bush as flat-topped as ornamental shrubbery. Ahead of us in the bush bobbed the black-eyed heads of a flock of willow ptarmigan, whiter than the snow around them now that all their summer plumage was gone. Swinging off Bucky, I drew my 12-gauge from the scabbard and loaded it. Larry held the horses' reins while I crept toward the birds. When I got up on them, seven black-tailed birds flushed, fanning out like a stud-poker hand. After I emptied both barrels, two bright birds lay on the fresh snow, making it look dingy in comparison. I carried the birds back to Larry, and he told me his last story, that while he had once seen a wolf catch a ruff, another time he had seen one of these white birds outfly a peregrine in full pursuit of it.

"'Old Haggle-Bird of the North,' they're called," Larry said—for their incessant cackling. He placed the birds I gave him into his day pack.

Tethering the horses, we had to climb higher on foot, to the broken rock up on the mountainside, before we found any white-tailed ptarmigan—birds slightly smaller than the willows. The snow, drifted in the shallow gulches, crested above our knees, so we used the long grass poking above it to locate the ridges we could travel on. Nearly at the crest, with the sun weak on it, we found the whitetails perched fat and round on bare snow. They flushed in front of us and I fired. While I removed the empty shells from my gun, a bird died with his white wings outspread as if embracing the snow. I picked him up, and we rode off the mountain.

For dinner that night we ate grouse—the meat of the ruffs as fine as that of any pheasant, and the Franklin's and ptarmigan's wild and dark. Afterward I said good night to Larry and, oblivious to the prospect of bear, crossed the brittle snow, past the shapes of dogs sleeping and horses shifting from hoof to hoof in the corrals. In the cabin I lit the lamp again and adjusted the wick so it would not smoke. Then I built the biggest fire I could fit into the Favorite Box 25 stove and hung my damp socks and jacket behind it and sat staring into its open door. When the fire had burned all the way down, I got into my sleeping bag and blew out the lamp.

In the darkness I could feel the cold seep back into the cabin. I tried to remember everything. There were Larry's stories and the walking and the riding and the Franklin's and the ruffs and the willows and the whitetails all flaring up. The only thing I hadn't found were blue grouse. There were some out there, though, where no one was able to find them in this remote northern country I did not know what I would do without. I'd have to come back.

I had the memories packed up to carry down there with me. Now I set them aside so I could sleep, lying in my sack of feathers with my head to the north, to the Arctic Sea where the rivers flowed and where, beyond maps, the light of the aurora came down upon the pole in red and yellow and blue and . . .

# Chapter 7

*There is one other species of bird that normally lives on the tundra but sometimes flies out onto the sea ice—the ptarmigan (Lagopus mutus). Especially during the spring and summer, ptarmigan land on the ice up to a mile or so offshore, leaving willow leaves and tracks among the rough ice as evidence of their presence. Eskimos hunt ptarmigan on the land whenever they have a chance, but they do not bother to look for them on the ice.*
        —Richard K. Nelson, *Hunters of the Northern Ice*

# THE PTROUBLE WITH PTARMIGAN

**The classic British** grouse hunt is a matter of bespoke tweeds and bespoke guns. It is stone shooting butts, loaders at the shooters' elbows, and beaters marching abreast, flailing the heather with white flags. Gentlemen draw numbers for shooting position, carry dainty silver flasks in the side pockets of their jackets, and having dressed for dinner, try not to pass out between the fish and the meat. Grouse hunting in Britain commences on the, ah, Glorious Twelfth of August. In northern Québec, though, it is more like the Glorious Twenty-fifth of August to the Regrettable Thirtieth of April, more about hunting than shooting, and a good deal less complicated, even though it involves a bird bafflingly called ptarmigan.

I've never fully understood the name. According to the *Oxford English Dictionary*, its first appearance in the language came in 1599, referring to the varying grouse of the Scottish mountains, the rock ptarmigan, *Lagopus mutus*—the same rock ptarmigan found at altitude circumpolarly, including in the northern latitudes of this hemisphere. The word is said to have come from the Gaelic *tarmachan* but to be of unknown origin.

In fact, *tarmachan* derives from *termagant*, "Termagant" being, of course, the vociferous and tumultuous deity whom Christians of the Dark Ages invented for the Mussulmen (who recognized no such god) and who was a stock character in the moralities, allegories, farces, mystery plays, puppet shows, *fantoccini*, and like diversions of the day. So, "termagant"—one who is loud and boisterous—and "ptarmigan"—a bird that clatters up with a cacophonous, not-entirely-melodious cackle. That part of the name is perfectly understandable. What will never be completely clear is, Why the "p"?

"P.Q." —as in way up north in the P.Q., the Province du Québec—is rather more clear. Because this is where one goes to look for ptarmigan, first to Kuujjuaq (once Fort Chimo) at the base of Péninsule d'Ungava, then another forty miles northwest by Beaver over rock and tundra and stunted spruce and crystal-filled potholes to land on the water below the long log main building of a lodge on Diana Lake.

Diana is one of the chain of lakes, falls, rapids, and braids that make up the Dancelou River between here and Ungava Bay. Mostly, this is considered a place of caribou and brook trout, char, and salmon. As much as any of these, though, it is country of the willow ptarmigan, *L. lagopus*.

Aside from molting to white in winter, the prime difference between the willow ptarmigan and the red grouse of Britain, *L. scoticus*, is the refreshing absence of formality attached to it. Ptarmigan hunters carry guns built by those renowned firearms artisans Browning, Remington, and Ithaca. They dress in bespoke denims and caps with bugproof veils to keep out the blackflies. And they walk.

My hunting companion Bob, our faithful guide and antagonist Ed—an irascible (some might even say termagant) wildlife artist and consummate sportsman—and I would walk out of our tents in the long row of wall tents behind the main lodge and, crossing a few hundred yards of spongy tundra, begin to hunt ptarmigan. There were still blueberries and crowberries out on this last day of August, and shortly there were ptarmigan among the berries. The rusty-backed birds were just starting to turn white, their bellies and feet (feathered to the talons, as if covered in spatterdashes) permanently that color. These birds were as eager to take wing as the inmates of an aerophobia ward at the state hospital; but without benefit of beaters, or even a dog, we managed to chase them down and coax them into the air.

I don't know about driven birds, but it has always seemed to me that the most interesting aspect of any upland bird's flight is the flush. Only by walking up a bird do you get to see and hear the real pyrotechnics of wingshooting, the rest merely trajectory. This is particularly so with the flush of ptarmigan, especially if three or four or more birds make up the flush. Then it is like one of those starburst fireworks detonating just above the earth, the birds strobing brown and white and cackling in chorus as you set your feet and bring up your gun, swinging on the closest bird then trying for a second as the first is Catherine-wheeling to the ground.

After hunting our way around the hill behind camp, then crossing the lake and hunting out the peninsula on the other side, we had put up enough ptarmigan (and one gawky two-year-old black bear, last seen churning east across the tundra) for us to have nearly a limit apiece—as heavy a load of plump birds, anyway, as we cared to carry in our sagging game bags.

Back at the lodge, Bob and Ed chose to pluck and gut their birds in the usual way; but Jean-Claude the camp cook (if "camp cook" is an adequate term for a chef who used to prepare dinner for Charles de Gaulle) knew how to treat game birds better. Having lived in America for many years, and loving to hunt and fish, he worked each season at the lodge, all to be able to get out every other day with his rod or gun. He dreamed of someday having the chance to cook "beezon" as the Indians did, talking constantly about the sanctity of aged game. He had gone on for so long about the way "zhe flavor iz in zhe featherz," that when I got back to the lodge with my birds I had him show me how to draw them in the French manner. With their intestines pulled out, but their lights, livers, and hearts left in, the birds were then left to "hang" for a day or two before being wrapped up, plumage on, and placed into the camp freezer.

One night, some of the ptarmigan failed to make it to the freezer; and when Jean-Claude had completed his work on them, the darkly flavored meat fell

from the bones. Luckily it fell only as far as the bed of sautéed fresh wild mushrooms (Jean-Claude having hunted them down on one of his afternoon outings)
covering the plate. Swirling a glass of rather good red table wine, I wondered
why anyone bothered with traveling to Scotland to eat a grouse.

During the week at the lodge, we would alternate shooting days with fishing
ones, the brook trout fishing utterly laughable, in the sense of Bob and my being
unable to stop laughing at our inability to find a single pattern the ravenous fish
would not gang-tackle. (There was a Double Humpy of mine that performed
only indifferently and that Ed mocked ferociously, but not ferociously enough,
apparently, to preclude his borrowing it from me one day when he'd run out of
flies.) The ptarmigan hunting was sort of funny in the same way, too.

Traveling by freighter canoe down the Dancelou, we often saw flocks of the
birds standing right on the bank, gawking at us, looking like clusters of mesmer-
ized tenpins. Eventually, we simply picked a place to land and started hunting.

Spreading out across the tundra, we headed toward some island of stunted
spruce half a mile away. We always seemed able to put birds out of such islands,
unless we jumped them before we ever got there. Then it was a footrace, one of
flushing birds, shooting, retrieving, then chasing after the rest of the flock that
had flown off a quarter mile and landed and begun running through the fields
of bare granite. Within an hour we would have enough birds (or be out of shells:
On one hunt I managed to double on the very last two shells I'd brought out that
day) and would either head back to camp or see if we could find a place to put in
another hour of catching trout—if we *had* to.

Jean-Claude came out with us on our last day, delirious as always to be out of
the kitchen and on the tundra with a shotgun—so he could shoot more wonder-
ful things to bring back to the kitchen. This hunt was nearly a mirror image of
our others, but somehow none of us was left with a sense of monotony.

Our game bags were already almost full when we went after the biggest flock
we had seen on any hunt. There were fifty or sixty birds together on the ground,
bobbing along. We chased them for some three or four hundred yards, trying to
get them into the air; but they seemed adamant about remaining earthbound.
Finally, some of them must have lost their heads and flushed, and with them
went the rest of the flock in waves. When they did, I found myself too far off to
one side, having hoped to perform a flanking maneuver on them, and so, out of
range, could only watch and listen.

As the first birds rose up and Bob, Ed, and Jean-Claude began to shoot, it was
more like Tombstone than Balmoral, the hunters firing, chasing, reloading, firing again, mixed in with the noise of the shotguns the distinct sound of hefty
ptarmigan thudding onto the tundra. After the running gun battle, seven or
eight birds lay on the ground. We picked them all up and started back toward
the beached canoe.

Jean-Claude and I were crossing through some brushy spruce when we kicked up a small flock at our feet. We emptied our guns and nothing fell, but I saw the last bird I shot at give a shudder. The flock beat their wings hard straight away for 150 yards, out over a flat of tall green marsh grass, then banked and sailed left, heading for the cover of more rocks and spruce. When the rest of the flock wheeled, though, the bird I'd shot at kept going, alone, flared and stalled, splashing down into the grass where I marked it.

Jean-Claude had been watching the rest of the flock and hadn't seen the one who dropped.

"Come on, Jean-Claude," I said, "help me look for a bird."

We hiked directly toward the mark, Jean-Claude asking every dozen paces, "Iz it here?" As we crossed the marsh, water halfway up our gum boots, Jean-Claude had stopped asking, "Iz it here?" convinced that I had no idea what I was doing. Then there was white, like a crumpled handkerchief lying in the tall grass. There was also brown mixed in with the white. As I reached down to pick up the warm bird (and hold it like a magician pulling a rabbit out of a hat, for Jean-Claude's amazement), I had a feeling of how much it mattered to have found this last bird on this last hunt of the last day, and not to have left it lost. It was that all-important final detail that shaped the way you remembered things, especially things like a good hunt.

"I cannot believe you made a retrieve zhat far," said Jean-Claude, looking from the bird back to where we had shot.

Even though it was the last night, we did not dress for dinner then, either. We did remain conscious through all the courses, though, and later found ourselves in the guides' tent with a hardly mellowed Ed, Jean-Claude, a couple of the other guides, and the lodge's owner. We lacked port or cigars, but did keep finding un-usual fluids in a large cardboard box filled with variously shaped bottles and set in the middle of the tent's plywood floor. Rummaging by candlelight through the box's contents at approximately 11:30 P.M., Jean-Claude cried out something— "*Sacre bleu!*" or "*J'accuse!*" —and leapt to his feet, clutching a bottle of Grand Marnier by the neck as if performing a magic trick of his own. He was out of the tent at a lope, telling us as he went to be at the lodge kitchen by midnight.

So at the stroke of twelve we trooped into the kitchen just as Jean-Claude was flaming an enormous plate of crêpes suzette, the blue sheets of fire like the au-rora that blazed overhead in the night sky. And that was the final final detail of the hunt: us standing around, eating sweet warm crêpes, sanctified birds in the freezer to carry home on the Beaver in the morning, and the subarctic dark pressing itself against the lighted windows of the lodge. August 12th was long past, but I doubted that it could have been any more glorious than hunting ptarmigan, inexplicable "p" and all.

# Chapter 8

*Angel:* México lindo.
*Lyle Gorch: I don't see nothin' so* "lindo" *about it.*
*Angel: Ah, you have no eyes.*

—The Wild Bunch

*Poor Mexico, so far from God and so close to the United States.*
—Porfirio Díaz

# DAYS ON THE WATER

**Five rivers and** arroyos, the San Carlos, Pilón, Purificación, Corona, and El Charón, were once splayed fingers leading to the Río Soto la Marina and the sea. In the 79,829-square-kilometer state of Tamaulipas—whose northern panhandle boundary lies along the Río Bravo, the land widening and turning south to fill the region between Atlantic water and the Sierra Madre Oriental, known locally as the Sierra Gorda, reaching to over thirteen thousand feet at its highest peaks—these rivers in the past drained the center of the Gulf Coastal Plain of Mexico. Now in this temperate mesquite-and-grassland country just this side of the tropic, there is a lake where no lake stood before.

Over a hundred thousand acres of land were covered by the dammed-up waters of Lake Vicente Guerrero, supplying five billion cubic meters of water annually for modern practices of irrigation. Back in the year and month of my birth, some twenty years before the lake was born, A. Starker Leopold surveyed the waterfowl of this Soto la Marina River system and found neither blue-winged teal nor green-winged, gadwall, shoveler, canvasback, nor pintail. Thirty-one years later in a late February, I went to a lodge on the lake to hunt these ducks, which, along with widgeon, cinnamon teal, and other species, the water now draws there in great number.

When I first met the patrón of the lodge—a moneyed Texan who kept a Mexican partner somewhere—he wore a safari hat and stood at a fourteen-inch band saw in the wood shop he had constructed behind his large apartment at the lodge, roughing out the form of a teal from two blocks of sugar pine bolted together. As he worked he told me how he'd always wanted to hunt over a set of decoys handmade by himself and one morning the previous spring had arisen and taken up a chunk of wood in one hand and a paring knife in the other and set out to carve a duck. An hour later he had produced little more than a blister big as a walnut and decided he was going to have to receive professional training to learn really how a duck was carved.

"Fourteen thousand dollars later," he said, making a long story not merely short, but truncated, "I was in the decoy business." He pulled the wood away from the blade and eyeballed the line of the belly, then put it to the blade again, sawdust floating into the air. He could now carve ducks of extreme detail and no small amount of grace. Besides turning out his decoys, he'd built a sprawling lodge on raw scrubland on the lake's shore, hunted, fished, and scuba-dived

intensively throughout the world, and went so far as to keep bobcat and mountain lion as house pets. He was a man with a whim of iron.

The first morning on the lake was cold enough for a wool sweater. The afternoon before, after my arrival, I shot with the patrón in the drowned
mesquite timber up the flooded Río Pilón, and the shade had been welcome.
The shooting was slow and I sat on a low dead limb, my feet floating in my
waders on the muddy water as I listened sleepily to the warm wind in the high
tules around me, rattling like sabers. Now as the guide Rogelio ran by memory
across the predawn lake to the Río Purificación, the wind had a bite that kept
me wide awake.

There were Rogelio and I in our boat that morning, with two other Mexicans, one another guide and the other there to help set out the decoys and beat
the swamp to stir up the birds, in a second boat. We rode until there was not
enough water for the boats' drafts, then got out and waded through soft mud
into a shallow lagoon hidden by tules. There was a blind there made of dead
moss draped around old snags with a bare wooden bench placed inside for a
seat. As the Mexicans set out the decoys, I could see ducks lifting up far out
across the low dead trees. Then the Mexicans were gone, and I waited.

When I heard the Mexicans again, they were hooting and defaming the
ducks as they waded around me at a far perimeter. One of the guides stayed
with the boats and beat the side of his as he shouted. Then the ducks were flying. I crouched as they come toward the blind, and rose up as they started to set
into the decoys. The Mexican No. 6 shells banged hard in the 870 and the ducks,
mostly shovelers and teal, began to drop. I shot fast for two hours until it became
too warm for a sweater, then the gray-haired Mexican who was not a guide
came to collect me. He wore chest waders smeared with dry gray mud, and
when he saw the ducks I had taken he was pleased. He strung them together
with a length of twine and counted out loud in Spanish, using a piece of stick to
draw the number for me on the back of his hand when he was done, the numer-
als showing momentarily white on his brown skin before fading. I had killed a
dozen or so (well inside the limit), and that was enough for the morning.

Before the afternoon hunt we ran on the lake down past the Río Purificación.
Then we came back to the shallow water, and I waded in to the same seat again,
smelling the sulfur my feet sucked up from the bottom. As I approached the
blind, I saw ducks getting up from the set; and as I came out from behind some
tall trees, a blue-winged teal flew low at me. I crouched and jacked a green plastic shell into the chamber, and when I stood and fired, the duck tumbled almost
to my feet.

The afternoon brought in fewer birds and was in a way more pleasant. There
were more pintails and widgeon, and as I looked out across the dead scrub trees,

the trunks banded black by the old high-water mark and the bare branches above bleached osseous white, I had time to watch the ducks come slipping through, wheeling and banking without touching a twig. When the gray-haired Mexican came for me at dusk, he again counted the ducks, now fewer, and because I knew Spanish, though badly, he asked if I would be speaking with the patrón that evening.

I told him yes, and the Mexican asked me please to say to him that he, the Mexican, said the patrón was a great man. I promised, wondering exactly what the hell century I was in here.

The name "Tamaulipas" is said to derive anciently from a Huastec word, *Tamalihopa*, meaning "place of the olives." The Huastecs were a Mayan-speaking coastal people considered to possess the highest degree of cultural development among the aboriginal tribes inhabiting Tamaulipas. They were mound builders and growers of cotton, but confined themselves primarily to the basin of the Guayalejo-Tamesi River in the south. The interior of the state, which for the first two centuries of their occupation of Mexico the Spanish found too desolate even to contemplate populating, was originally the territory of the nomadic Indians the Aztecs named the Chichimecs, meaning roughly "lineage of the dog." This was not the slander it might at first seem, since many of the rulers in the Valley of Mexico readily claimed Chichimec blood, perhaps in the same manner in which on St. Patrick's Day all politicians are Irish.

Still, the Chichimecs were ultimately thought a most barbarous lot by the Aztecs. They had a language shared by tribes possibly as far removed as California, and up into what is now Texas and Louisiana, but they insisted on painting their faces and bodies, wearing the skins of animals and sandals made of yucca fiber, and living in caves. With bows and arrows they hunted rabbits, peccary, deer, and birds—nearly anything except roadrunners, which they protected because they fed on rattlesnakes. They speared and trapped fish on the rivers and gathered fruits, berries, roots, and peyote from the "Hill of the Air," which would inspire them to perform lengthy celebrative dances unaccompanied by any musical instruments other than the hallucinogenic ones blowing rhythmically through their brain cells.

The Chichimecs were not an aggressive people, unless called upon to defend what they saw as their land. The Spanish, who knew that land simply as the coast of the Mexican Gulf, and later the province of Nuevo Santander, never encountered any hostility as they passed through it with their salt caravans en route to the Laguna Madre. The Chichimecs were represented by numerous tribes in the basin of the Río Purificación. One, at what is now the southern edge of the water of Lake Vicente Guerrero, was named Los Ojos de la Tierra, the "eyes of the earth."

As we headed into the lodge after sunset, I felt the night hurrying toward me across the water from the east, the night a cool wind. We bounced heavily in the chop, and Rogelio now wielded the beam of a two-hundred-thousand-candle-power light over our bow to find a channel cut through the dead trees. Ducks and coots clattered away in the light as we ran at them, and the branches of the trees twisted up whitely out of the dark, arboreal specters.

That night in the lodge's trophy-hung "Safari Bar," I conveyed the Mexican's message to the patrón and ate filleted duck breasts wrapped around jack cheese and deep-fried. Later I sat alone in the darkness on the second-story patio outside the bar, watching Orion and a waxing moon, listening to the cries of coyotes.

I hunted the same blind one more time the next morning. As we ran up to the place I would begin to wade from, Rogelio caught in the light a big bull canvas-back swimming. A live canvasback always looks more like a decoy of a canvas-back, more like some of the patrón's handiwork, than a decoy does, but my mind was actually elsewhere. Yesterday afternoon when we had run down to the Río Purificación before the shooting, we visited the town of Old Padilla on the flooded bank of the Río. As we approached it, we saw the empty church on the lakeshore and a long building with an archway running through its middle and ornamental turrets of pink stone topping the facade.

"*Mi escuela*," Rogelio said with pride.

The school was now some way out into Lake Vicente Guerrero and looked as if it had been cut adrift after being abandoned by all hands—the *Marie Celeste* of primary education. The water reached to the ledges of the glassless windows, but I had no way of knowing how much more might lie beneath the surface. Nothing else of Old Padilla showed above. I had never seen a town buried by green water before.

The province of Nuevo Santander did not become the state of Tamaulipas until Mexico gained its independence from Spain. The Mexican War of Independence was a fitful uprising stretching over more than a decade from the "cry of Dolores" on September 16, 1810, until the Plan of Iguala, the Mexican Declaration of Independence, in 1821. During this time, various republican leaders came to the fore to achieve often spectacular, though short-lived, successes in the field, only to have to meet the members of their firing squads at the dawn of a later day.

It was not until a military coup brought a liberal government to Spain, and the church and gentry of Mexico came to fear the confiscation of their property, that Augustín de Iturbide, a royalist and former officer of the army of Spain responsible for suppressing many of the preceding revolutions, was able to unite the country's many factions and establish Mexico as a constitutional monarchy under a European prince, with a national congress and a junta of regents to which he was elected president. His presidency was predictably brief for a man of Iturbide's ambitions; and on July 21, 1822, at the age of thirty-eight, he was crowned the first emperor of Mexico since Moctezuma's successor, Cuautémoc. The state of Tamaulipas was alone in voicing opposition to the coronation.

Iturbide's ascension could not prevent the resurrection of republican senti- ment. At the same time a wave of crime broke out in the newly freed nation. Iturbide reacted to these threats to his rule by muzzling the press and dissolving the congress. New revolutions sprang up, and he was forced to abdicate and go into European exile.

Not even a pension given him for life could persuade Iturbide not to return to Mexico to offer it his aid when he received word that Spain meant to invade his homeland. He sailed from England unaware that the new Mexican government had decreed him a traitor should he ever set foot in the country again. He landed on the coast north of Tampico in July 1824 and wearing a bandanna to mask his face, rode toward the town of Soto la Marina, near which he was, in spite of his disguise, recognized and arrested by troops of Tamaulipas's military commandant. Marched to the state's provisional capital in Padilla, where the state congress was in session, he put his case before them and was answered with a swift order of execution.

On July 19, having confessed his sins to a priest three times and having asked that the gold coins he carried in his pocket be dispersed to the riflemen after his execution, Iturbide knelt with bound arms in the plaza of Old Padilla and re- ceived a volley of shots to the breast. The site of the death of the former emperor, El Libertador of Mexico, as his tomb would read when his body was later moved to Mexico City, was marked for many years in Padilla by a monument, until in 1971 the water of Lake Vicente Guerrero reached to cover it. The green water I'd seen the day before.

The second morning at sunrise I made a triple on baldpates, the three ducks falling one after another. It was the end of the season, and the birds had grown decoy-shy. I killed a few more and left for a new place for the afternoon.

Going to the new blind built on a shore of deep green pasture where cattle grazed, I waded beside the wood posts of an old fence. Looking up, I saw hun- dreds of ducks rising from the grass where they had been feeding. They flared out over the distant dead scrub and began to settle into the water beneath it.

In the blind of tules on the shore there was a crate for me to set my shell boxes on. It was very hot, and I rolled my hip waders down around my calves in seven- league fashion to keep cool. The ducks came back over in ones and twos, and it was pure pass shooting that afternoon. They were all American widgeon, and when I killed a duck I immediately retrieved it and brought it into the blind to lay it on the wooden crate in the shade. When it was time to go, I had four or five of the white-headed birds lying on the box—more than enough to make a good day's hunting. Pulling up my waders, I headed back to the waiting boat with the sun going down behind the Sierra Gorda at my back. I saw in the water ahead of me the moon reflected, while in the wake my feet left the twilight glowed.

The next, the last, morning was cool and gray. Before my plane left, I had time to take my bait-casting rod and go out with a fishing guide to try to catch some Florida bass, which the lake now produced. We ran for half an hour to where there was submerged structure and trees, and the *guía* attached the clips from his electric trolling motor to a black car battery and began to tow us around the shore of the lake with a soft whir.

Vicente Guerrero, for whom the lake was christened, was a young mixed-blood muleteer from the town of Tixtla near Acapulco. In the early days of the War of Independence his courage, extensive knowledge of southern Mexico gained from his travels with his mule trains, and fierce hatred of the *gachupines* ("the wearers of spurs," as the Spanish-born officials and landowners were contemptuously known) elevated him to the command of the revolution's southern front. Over the long course of the war, Guerrero remained an intractable guerrilla chieftain for the republican cause. Taking to the mountains when he had to, he overcame not only dysentery, an outbreak of smallpox among his troops, a bullet wound through both lungs, and military setbacks, but also a viceregal offer of a pardon and a governmental sinecure if he would only abandon his revolutionary activities. These he would never forsake.

After Iturbide, General Antonio López de Santa Anna (who had first gained battlefield experience as a young officer in the Spanish wars against the Huastecs, and who would rise up again and again to gain control of Mexico during the first thirty years of the republic) made the great warlord Guerrero the second president of Mexico in 1829, only to have him deposed and, on February 14, 1831, executed. In 1833 when Santa Anna took power as president in his own name for the first time, he declared Iturbide—whom he had also betrayed—a national hero and had his portrait hung in all of Mexico's public offices.

I fished a crank-bait lure in Lake Vicente Guerrero. In two and a half hours I caught and released thirty bass, one a three-pounder, and had a big female twice that size up to the boat before she threw the hook. It was time to go.

As we started back I asked the guide if there were any *tigre*—jaguar—around.

"*Sí*," he said, nodding with vigor. "*Y léones, y muchos venados*," he added, holding two fingers at each side of his head to mime "deer."

That would have been something, I thought, to have been here in the days before the lake—although also before the ducks and the bass—and been able then to hunt *tigre* along one of the river canyons, waiting on a stand above a tethered peccary, an Indian with Chichimec blood tugging the beeswaxed braided-horsehair cord of a *pujandero*, the jaguar call made from a gourd to imitate the grunting roar of a male *tigre*, as night fell.

I suppose it is only natural to think of past days, but those are not the days we now have. This lake, named for a dead muleteer and covering the place where an emperor died, had taken some things, but left others in their place, and you lived in the days you had in the best way you could.

As we made for the lodge and the plane, a hawk of a species I did not recognize stooped onto the water and lifted a coot off it. He carried it to the yellow rocks on the shore, where he killed it. As the raptor mantled his prey and began to feed, he took no notice of our passing.

# Chapter 9

*The hunt went on for weeks, as did the rain. When the rain stopped, there were only mudholes to drink from. He ate hard biscuits and slept on the ground, his horse tied to his saddle, until prairie wolfs came and spooked the horse and the saddle into the darkness. Buffalo were missed, some wounded; others charged. One night, as they lay in four inches of water, his astonished guide heard him saying, "By Godfrey, but this is fun!" and meaning it.*

*By September 20, 1883, he had moved across the North Dakota Badlands into Montana Territory. There, age twenty-four and a New York State legislator, Theodore Roosevelt killed one of the last good buffalo bulls remaining on the High Prairie with a single clean shot and abandoned himself to dancing around the huge beast.*

# NOT A GOOSE STORY

**Jim and I** (as opposed to me & Joe) had been wading the beaver marsh all morning. The long grass was bent by frost, there was ice in my mustache, and my feet felt good and cold in my hip boots. So far we'd jumped half a dozen ducks. Jim managed to kill one teal; I managed to fire not even a shot. Which was fine.

The dense morning fog began to lift by the time we meandered across the marsh and came to stand on the bank of the New Fork, watching it run clear and chill with deep pools holding brown trout. Jim started to move on but then pointed into a stand of cottonwoods on the other side of the river. I looked where he aimed his finger and saw the brown hillock of a Shiras's moose cow rising up among the trees.

"She's one big old cow," Jim said admiringly. "You kill her back in there, though," he added, sinking off once more into the marsh, "the only way you're getting her out's with a knife and fork."

Jim L. lived at the foot of the Wind Rivers. The view from his living room soared away forever to shining peaks. There were sheep and elk back in there, and moose, antelope, mule deer, ducks, geese, and trout down here. Here and there were bear.

I met Jim, and his brother-in-law, also Jim, and that Jim's brother Jerry, down in the Caribbean. They had gone to fish and hunt and have a good time for themselves; I had gone to see if there was anything to be written about it. I went to many places to see what there was to be written about them, making what passed for my "living" telling others where I had been and what I had seen. Sometimes the going got to be too much of a good thing, as in this October when I found myself between terminals, between one too many jet aircraft and those places I went to make that living—with even more of the same ahead of me—so that this October had come to look more like that "damp, drizzly November in my soul" than the *dandy* early fall it ought to be. I had a little time in the vale between the terminals, though; time enough to go someplace and do some things whose only recommendation for me was that it was where I wanted to go and what I wanted to do. Going whaling was pretty much out, but I could go to Wyoming. And not have to tell a soul.

That was why Jim and I were slogging around in that essentially aqueous solution of the Cowboy (actually "Equality") State on that frigid morning, trying to frighten assorted members of the family Anatidae into headlong flight so we might kill and eat them. And the best part was this: No one told me to come here; I didn't have to tell anybody what I saw; I was here to find no "angle"; my only reason for being here was because it was where, *precisely*, I wanted to be today.

So we went on crossing ponds behind the dams of beaver and sank to the tops of our waders in green bogs; had mallards we were trying to put a sneak on vanish into thin air; and watched plumes of steam rise off the river like the breaths of a hundred men, with absolutely no ulterior motive. As we headed back to the truck, we saw a pair of honkers beating away from us in the blue sky, and I thought happily: There goes the goose story; *¡vaya con Dios!* As we put up our unloaded guns, Jim was downright apologetic about the shooting. He needn't have been; I was also *doing* precisely what I wanted.

We drove down to the Green River where it ran beneath high cliffs at the back of Jim's wife's family's ranch. As we bounced across the bottomland, jacksnipe and four-point mule deer bucks got up in front of us. Jim had high hopes for the fishing, wanting to show me a good time. But when we reached the river it was an unseasonable two feet too high and cloudy as dishwater. We stood on the rocky bank under the warm fall sun, our spinning rods dangling listlessly. Then, as we went on standing, a raft of one dozen Canada geese floated placidly around the bend like carefree river holidayers and rammed smack into us. We gawked at them clamoring and flapping over our heads, their bellies seeming close enough to brush the down with our fingertips, the shotguns securely back in the pickup. (I told you, I wanted to shout at them, there will be no *goose* story!) We began to fish.

We made long, vain casts into the current. Moving upriver, we slathered across the slick stony bottom but found, everywhere, the news was the same. Jim the Wyoming lad was used to running water that lay between the banks of a river as limpidly as if a crack squad of world-class glaziers had puttied it into place and polished it to spotlessness with vast white cotton hankies. He was also used to a mess of trout, right now. Me, I was used to no such thing. When Jim saw a river as unnaturally high, muddy green, and basically unfishable as this one in *October* of all months, he quite rightly trudged out of it after three casts and reclined upon the nearest gravel bar, idly flicking over smooth pebbles with his index finger. Me, I went on standing in the river, flicking out my sparkling French-manufactured lure, neither killing time nor injuring eternity, just trying to get as much out of this deal as I could. In a while, though, to make Jim feel better, I pretended I was disappointed, too, and left the river behind.

Later (this time having brought along the shotguns, too), Jim and I fished a jeweled string of tiny beaver ponds that held cutthroat. Only it wasn't holding them today. Which, again, was fine. After all, this was just between me and no-body else.

The canyon where the ponds lay coiled ascended to snow and was garnished at its foot with aspens starting to turn. We broke down our rods and headed back in the pickup. Then in the last beaver pond, on the far side of the aspens, we saw a flock of young mallards. Laying down our tackle, we took our shot-guns and stalked the ducks as if they were quail. They rose off the water and quacked out over the sage, and I downed one for my three shots while Jim neatly took three for his. They were too few to make any kind of *real* waterfowl story, but were fat and warm in our hands and would be as tasty as all get-out.

Afterward, in the Eagle Bar in La Barge, a time-honored saloon very much in the glorious middle of nowhere—a saloon built of antique wood, patronized by even more antique cowpokes, and decorated with a water-stained print on the wall depicting the gallant (and addlepated) Last Stand of George Armstrong Custer and the men of the Seventh, a print that must have been hot off the presses mere weeks after the incident—Jim and I sat on stools and sipped beers, our waders turned down like buccaneers' boots and spattered with duck blood, the cleaned birds lying cool outside in a fishing creel. Some coot who said he'd spent his life in a "kerosene orchard" leaned into the bar beside me and rested his chin in his hand in a pose resembling that famous one of Proust's (if the ele-gant Marcel had taken to wearing a sweaty old Stetson, going about Paris in need of a shave and leaving most of his teeth at home, soaking in a glass to rinse out the madeleine crumbs), and asked where I got the red police braces holding up my green woolen britches. Grand Junction, Colorado, I answered, remem-bering a cloudy day a decade before when I had also gone hunting solely for the sake of *going hunting*.

"Colorado's where I'm from, too," he said, seeming to tip me the wink on some profound secret, then drifting off down the bar. Jim and I finished our beers and started to leave, but the barmaid, unbidden, brought us two fresh ones.

"What," we asked, "is this?"

She pointed to a tall stranger framed by the waning sun pouring through the big front window, a fellow a-dazzle in white dry-cleaned western wear, pump-ing hands and slapping backs for all he was worth.

"Just bought the house a round. I think he's running for something," she con-fided with a shrug.

"But I don't even live in Wyoming," I confessed (not then, anyway).

"That's okay, honey. Just drink your beer. I won't breathe a word."

Four days later—two of those swallowed by a blizzard of horizontally pro-pelled snow—I was south of Rawlins, hunting pronghorn with the other Jim and his brother Jerry. And I didn't have to breathe a word about it to anyone, either. There were times to lay eyes on shining peaks, cast a lure made in France into a running river, try to touch a wild goose, or chase a pronghorn antelope on the prairies for no better reason than that those were what there was to be done. And not telling about them could be as important, maybe more, than telling, to keep the heart from running dry.

In an interval of snow-brightened light between the shadows of two airplane terminals, then, I once upon a time saw a great herd of antelope run along the rocky floor of a wide canyon, then start to turn up to the high ground where I waited. There was a big buck, his long horns black as ebony wood, bringing up the rear; and as he galloped onto the top of the ridge, I raised my rifle . . . and someday I might tell all about it. But not today.

# Chapter 10

*In the dark, the Spanish fans of palmettos rattled, and he tried not to imagine the black forms of alligator bellied out of the ranch canals. Ocean reefs ground to sand lay underfoot, and yesterday's rain had run through it like water through a spout, leaving stars above. A sharp smell of pig was in the soft air. The herd of night-rooting wild hogs ahead caught his wind and ran, squealing and grunting.*

*"Damn." The word was whispered, to himself.*

*The east–west trail was gray, a trace of light on closed eyelids. The hunting tree was three hundred yards west, the roosted birds a hundred yards beyond that. He reached the tree, squinted for snakes, and set up.*

*The small birds were not singing yet, but he did not need to wait for them before he owl-hooted this morning, or to hoot at all. He could wait for a tree gobble.*

*A gobble never seemed a happy sound, not like small bird's song. Like an elk's bugle, too much rode on it, for the turkey. It was a sound that thrilled like almost nothing else, though. When the first gobble knifed the stillness, it sounded much closer than a hundred yards. His answering yelp would have to be right.*

*In the early light he saw the palmettos looked nothing like Spanish fans.*

# MY LIFE AS A TURKEY (HUNTER)

**There was a** time when it seemed beyond dreams to hunt one, let alone four of a kind. Two (human) generations ago, no more than half a million wild turkey were in the country—and a generation before that, less than a tenth of half a million. In California where I grew up, there had never been a native wild turkey, unless you counted an extinct near-species, *Parapavo californicus*, whose asphalt-preserved bones showed up periodically among the bric-a-brac of Late Pleistocene camel, mastodon, mammoth, sabertooth, pygmy antelope, and the stray hunter-gatherer extracted from the ooze of Rancho La Brea on Los Angeles's Wilshire Boulevard. When I was young, to see a turkey anywhere wasn't merely an event—it was a landmark.

I saw my first in the early 1970s out where so much of our fauna is encountered, on the interstate. This interstate was carrying me through the Texas Hill Country, and I was over in the passenger seat, dozing, my head lolling against the window, little saliva bubbles pearling my lips. I am not sure I can recall who I was with or where I was going, but I remember the early-morning light wedging itself under my eyelids, and my lifting them in time to see, strutting just beyond the guardrail in the hardscrabble terrain, what looked like machines made from mica. Only they weren't machines or mica, and I knew what they were in an instant—without ever having seen a live one before. I sat up so fast to look around, I nearly put my skull through the roof. But they were gone.

I saw them again on the big island of Hawai'i as I hunted feral goats, sheep, and pigs. Coming off blood-colored volcanic ground wormed through with lava tubes and overlaid by war trails marched on by the feather-cloaked ghosts of ancient Polynesian warriors, I walked into rolling green country like the Coast Ranges in spring in central California. Many of the island's protected native nene geese waddled around guilelessly; and when I topped a grassy rise, a flock of big birds detonated in front of me. For a moment I thought they were nene, but no, no. Geese did not make an agitated *purrt, purrt, PURRT*, when they flew, and were incapable of getting airborne "with the rush and whir of a shell," as the Missourian Mark Twain described it. Only wild turkey did that, and this time, as the huge fowl volplaned heart-stoppingly away, I was even able to recognize them as Rio Grande turkey.

It was a fascinating thing back then to realize that wild turkey were exceptional not only by existing (even in comparison with rare geese), but by coming in an assortment of exceptionalities. It was possible, it seemed, not just to hunt wild turkey, but to hunt four distinct subspecies—Rio Grande, Merriam's, Eastern, and Florida (or Osceola)—without ever leaving the forty-eight contiguous United States. This feat even had a quintessential American name—a Grand Slam.

When I first started hunting wild turkey, though, in the early 1980s, I was not so much focused on a particular subspecies as I was on taking a turkey, pure and at least somewhat simple. By that time the wild turkey population of California, where I still lived, had gone from fossilized remnants to upward of a hundred thousand live birds, established primarily through the transplantation of Rio Grande turkey wild-trapped in Texas. A hundred thousand offered even me some possibility of killing my first turkey, even when my calling skills were so rudimentary that I ended up jumping one in the Shasta foothills on a rainy April day, the two of us bumping into each other on a grassy ridgeline. I remember the gnarled smooth-burgundy-barked arms of the madrone trees; the almost artificial, patent shine of their green leaves; the red head of the two-year-old Rio bobbing up as our eyes met; the stiff pendulum swing of his beard as he burst skyward; and my raising the dripping pump and pressing the safety button then slapping the trigger as the muzzle swept ahead of him. Yet I didn't count that as my first *real* wild turkey—being more of a roadkill, or trailkill. My first real wild turkey I killed for my wife.

We weren't married yet, but affianced and enjoying the blissfully delusional interlude during which couples are disposed to indulge each other's whims: hers for movies in French; mine for chasing living things up and down hills at ungodly hours of the morning. She came out with me into the actual central California coastal mountains before dawn on a late-March day, and we hiked down to a place above a canyon where I had roosted Rios the night before. She was outfitted in a camouflage jumpsuit, gloves, hat, and veil—different from the one she would later wear. I had my camo, too, and for some reason an eleven-pound Spanish Laurona 10-gauge double with thirty-two-inch barrels. We set up at the base of a Valley oak, sitting at a right angle to each other; and as we waited for the light to come into the sky, I whispered to her about the importance of not moving when the bird presented itself.

When there was light, I slipped the diaphragm call into my mouth and managed to keep from gagging long enough to make a soft yelp—like the one I'd practiced interminably at home while listening to an instructional cassette—and with a sensation akin to horror received an immediate gobble back. It was sheer beginner's luck, and reminded me of the first time, up in a clear-cut in Oregon, when I'd tried using a predator call and had a bobcat step out in front of me—and then gotten the yips so bad I couldn't even steady the sights on it. I didn't tell my wife-to-be any of that; I just took another blind stab and yelped again, and the turkey

gobbled again, closer, as if it were all part of the Great Cosmic Plan. He was coming, as inexorably as fate, and there was virtually nothing I could do to screw it up.

He was another two-year-old and popped out of the canyon, bisecting our
angle. I gave as soft a yelp as I could, and twenty yards from us he began to fan
and puff and drum and spit and dance. He was to my right, and it did not look
as if he were going to move around in front of me. I would have to twist to the
side to make the shot. I waited for him to turn away with his tail spread before I
moved, but I also wanted him to go on dancing, so my betrothed could see the
spectacle. After several minutes of his displaying, he turned away, and I turned
toward him, almost toppling over from the weight of the shotgun. Then he
turned back and broke strut and I killed him with the right barrel.

I was up and running, whooping as I bounded toward the still-flapping Rio gobbler. I let him stop thrashing, then hoisted him by his spurred, crustacean legs.

"*Did you see that?*" I yelled, unable to resist puffing and strutting a bit myself.

My fiancée was looking directly forward from her seat on the ground at the
base of the tree. Now she lifted the mesh veil and turned her head toward me.

"I heard it," she offered.

"*Heard it?*" I asked, the gobbler transmuting into burdensome weight.

"You told me not to move," she said.

"Not your eyes," I said. "You could have moved your eyes."

She then established the template for all connubial discussions and negotia-
tions to follow by declaring flatly, "You didn't say that."

We married anyway.

Having taken the Rio Grande in California, I started considering the other
three wild turkey subspecies outside the state. I don't think I was as interested in
them for the sake of collecting a Grand Slam as I was in undergoing as many of
the variety of turkey-hunting experiences as I could. And that led next to Merriam's, and to a rifle.

I had a friend in Montana in those days, shortly after my marriage. He knew a
place out on the Musselshell where we could hunt mule deer, sharp-tailed grouse,
and Merriam's turkey. He recommended that when I obtained my deer tag, I
should also get one for turkey. That sounded fine to me, and I asked him about
bringing along a turkey shotgun. What for? he asked; I already had my deer rifle.

At this formative stage of my turkey-hunting career, the notion of using a
rifle to reduce a turkey to possession ranked right down there with dynamiting
fish. I vocally objected to it on the grounds of its evincing a distinct lack of
sportsmanship. On the phone, my friend responded with a prolonged silence,
before saying, "Just bring the damn rifle."

(The Merriam's, by the way, was named for Clinton Hart Merriam—1855–
1942—but not by him. Merriam, chief of the U.S. Department of Agriculture's

Division of Economic Ornithology and Mammalogy, later to become the Bureau of Biological Survey, and ultimately to turn into the U.S. Fish and Wildlife Service, was the arch "splitter" when it came to classifying species, finding new ones behind every tree. At one point, he used slight variations in skull formation to determine that eighty-six distinct species of grizzly existed. It fell to ethnographer and natural historian Dr. Edward William Nelson to name the large southwestern subspecies of turkey after Merriam—otherwise, Merriam might have come up with a dozen different ones on his own.)

Again through transplantation of wild turkey (this time from Colorado and Wyoming), the Merriam's populated the Yellowstone drainage of southeast Montana. And that's where my friend and I meant to hunt in late October.

My qualms about letting my deer rifle do double duty on turkey were based on the assumption that wild turkey just *hung around* at a couple of hundred yards, outside shotgun range, and would let you pot at them at will with a rifle, leaving, if you connected with a high-velocity bullet, not much more than could be spooned into a Dinty Moore can. Such qualms existed until my friend and I stumbled across a flock of fall birds on the side of a snow-covered hill and tried to chase them down. We were reasonably fit, and we must have pursued those turkey all-out over four ridgelines before we ended up halted on the last one, never having caught sight of the birds—who didn't fly but only ran—again. We blew and sweated when we stopped, and my friend turned to me, an eyebrow raised, and said only, "Not sporting with rifles, huh?"

A couple of days later, driving out to hunt mule deer from the ranch where we bunked, we spotted a line of turkey running through the pines and snow, and we piled out of my friend's pickup. We ran forward, and my friend bellied down with his .257 Roberts and centered a gobbler in his crosshairs. He was shooting one of his own painstakingly crafted handloads, so it must have come as a bigger surprise to him than to me when all he got for his troubles when he pulled the trigger was a deafening click. I was sitting in the snow, deferring the first shot to him, when with a certain amount of disgust he shouted at me to shoot.

The birds were strung out in the trees, and I marked the biggest gobbler in the back. I was shooting a .270 Weatherby Magnum, by no stretch of the imagination an appropriate turkey gun; but the gobbler stopped and looked at me, out at seventy-five yards, and I hit him with the 150-grain Nosler Partition at the base of the neck and didn't waste an ounce of his twenty-four pounds—dressed weight—of meat.

I gave that Merriam's to my friend for his Thanksgiving; since then we've drifted and don't talk anymore. That's the thing about life and turkey hunting: They both go on.

The Eastern I remember best came at a time when I was crippled, literally. When the Achilles tendon snaps during martial-arts practice, it does so with a sound audible to all the other veteran blackbelts on the tatami mats, who react with a collective shudder—which tells you for sure, in case you didn't know, that you are properly fucked. That was the sound my left one made once, just before Christmas; and for the next several months I was confined to a walking cast and crutches while I waited for the tissue to regrow. By April it had come back to where I could get around with a cane and without a cast, and I was ready to hunt turkey, again.

Another friend had a small spoil-bank farm out in Indiana, and invited me to join three of his hunting buddies and him there for Eastern turkey. I was coming from the West (Wyoming now, instead of California—which, as we all know, is beyond the West), and they from the East. I reached Indiana and the farm on the night before opening day; the friend and his buddies did not, their flight weather-delayed, forcing them to overnight in a hotel in Pittsburgh. There was nothing for me to do, after the farm's caretaker showed me the best blind, but to get up the next morning and hobble out to it alone with my semiauto 12-gauge, a single turkey decoy, and my triple-glass slate call.

As I walked with my cane and shotgun down the dirt road toward the blind, I flushed a woodcock that rose with the crack all too reminiscent of a tendon snapping. The blind was a bunker, built out of stout logs and draped over and around with camouflage netting, and easy to find. I put out the jake decoy twenty-five yards to the south of the blind, then climbed inside, careful to find a place to rest my recuperating leg.

Turkey hunting is, for the most part, waiting. Unlike hunting deer from a stand, though (where all you *can* do—absent rattling and grunting, which are options—*is* wait), with turkey hunting you are obliged to do something—to call. And once more, unlike deer, you can often tell if you're doing it right when the turkey answer back. Though not always.

When the first small songbirds started to sing, I scratched the striker across the sanded surface of the slate call to give a yelp. And almost at once I had three gobblers, scattered around me, calling back. That's where they stayed, *scattered*. Through the early morning I yelped and received gobbles in return. I heard the birds moving through the trees, but they were moving back and forth, not coming. By nine o'clock they had stopped, probably gone off with hens. I had nowhere in particular to go, so I sat, every quarter hour scratching out another yelp. I looked up and down the road, but the only thing I saw resembling a turkey was the decoy to the south. By ten-thirty I was ready to head for the barn, or farmhouse, anyway. Then I looked north one more time.

He came out of the trees where he'd been moving back and forth in the morning before setting off to breed. He was back now in the open forty yards away, head down and carried forward, his beard dangling to the ground like a length of hawser. He remembered that he had heard a hen calling here earlier, and there

was what looked like a jake in the territory of the call. He was coming for the jake or the hen (whichever he met first). I watched him through the camo netting. Assuring myself his attention was on the decoy, I got the shotgun up and resting on my knees, pointed at the opening of the blind where the turkey would cross.

It took him a very long time to close those forty yards; when he came in front of the blind's opening, sixteen paces from my gun, I didn't even have to yelp to make him stop; he did it all on his own. When my friend and his buddies finally arrived that night, he was waiting to greet them, tagged, registered at the game-check station, dressed, and hanging from a beam in the cool darkness of a shed, twenty-two pounds, with ten and a half inches of thick black beard.

The turkey I waited longest for was the Osceola. Found only in peninsular Florida, it was named for the storied Seminole war leader. (Though Creek by birth, and never a true chief—but Crazy Horse and Geronimo never were, either—the original Osceola waged a two-year, Vietcong-style war against the U.S. Army, exacting a toll in lives from that army that ran into the thousands, and a cost in treasure that came to some sixty million 1830s dollars. In the end, Osceola was captured through subterfuge and died of a bad throat—the military doctor who treated him severing his head after his demise, embalming it, and hanging it on his disobedient young sons' bedsteads at night as a rather grisly object lesson.)

I was lured to central Florida so often by the Osceola turkey—the lightest-weight and darkest-winged of the subspecies, and the only acceptable excuse for being lured to central Florida—I figured I spent more time in the area than an

Irish Traveler after hurricane season. Over the better part of a decade of hunting Osceola, the closest I ever got to bagging one was a rushed shot I fired at a long-beard that shock-gobbled at the late-morning hoot of a real owl (at half past seven, late for an owl), then came charging down a sandy road in response to one yelp from me. I had my decoy too far out this time, forty yards in the direction the turkey was coming from; and when the tom checked up at the decoy, and I felt myself full-up with Osceola fever, I jerked the shot and watched him fly, thinking, *Aim*, butthead—or at least *point!*

At long last I hired a professional Osceola guide in Osceola County. The guide, Jim, had been leading hunters to Osceola turkey for more than twenty years, and when I took mine with him, it could have seemed almost anticlimactic—if it hadn't been for the seven or eight years of frustrating Osceola hunting that had gone before. My ten-year-old son was with me (had it been so many years ago, before he was even born, that I had killed that Rio Grande with his mother?) and the afternoon prior to the hunt we scouted a couple-of-thousand-acre ranch Jim had leased the hunting rights to, finding more than enough gobblers to show us where to set up in the morning.

Before light, Jim and I made a blind in the thick bare roots of a Spanish-moss-draped Spanish oak, and fashioned a seat behind us in a thicket of palmettos where my son could see and we wouldn't have to worry about young-boy fidgets spooking turkey. For a decoy, Jim had a full-body mount of a once-living Rio jake, set out thirty yards in front of us. Just after full light, from four hundred yards away, a hen left the timber and crossed the open green pasture to walk up to the jake and circle him, preening, mindful (as mindful as turkey get, in any case) not to look at him and appear anything but aloof, while the jake somehow managed to ignore her enticements.

The botanist William Bartram, who composed a surreal chronicle of his journeys in 1770s Florida, described turkey gobblers expanding "their silver bordered train" as they strutted around the "coy female," the "deep forests seeming to tremble with their shrill noise." The forests weren't exactly trembling that morning, but there were gobbles, and with Osceola that is a sound you have to get up mighty early in the morning to hear: On spring days in Osceola County, the temperature can climb into the nineties by midmorning, pushing the birds into shade and silence; it also created an atmospheric phenomenon, as the sun heated the ground and drew up the moisture, in which the humidity-thickened air muffled gobbles—Jim said he'd seen more than one gobbler at a hundred yards, stretching out his quivering head and opening his beak, and not hearing a thing. That also meant that gobblers couldn't hear yelps after about eight o'clock in the morning, so trying to find them after that was slightly problematic. More than almost any other subspecies of wild turkey, then, it was necessary to know the patterns Osceola followed to anticipate where they would be early in order to be able to hunt them well. Jim knew those patterns.

That morning Jim yelped every ten or fifteen minutes; and ninety minutes after daybreak a nine-inch-bearded gobbler came walking in from our right toward the posthumous jake. When he was almost to the decoy, Jim said to take him. I covered his head with the muzzle of my semiauto 12.

Behind me, as the gobbler collapsed—beating his wings involuntarily against the ground with a dry flapping—Bryan, having seen the whole thing, whooped as I had whooped for that Rio long before. Now I had my four of a kind, my Grand Slam. That was only a name, though, for something that did not exist without having been given a name. I'd hunted all four subspecies of the United States' wild turkey, not because they constituted a "Grand Slam," but because they had been there to hunt; and I would go on hunting them because they would be there in ever-increasing numbers, *to* hunt. That was worth whooping about, whatever you called it. "Turkey hunting" sounded about right. Like life, you called it as you saw it.

# Chapter 11

*[The ocellated turkey's] gobble is utterly unlike that of Meleagris and may be written phonetically as "ting-ting-ting—co-on-cot-ziti-glung," the last note having a bell-like quality. Some Mayan hunters stalk the gobbling males, but this is said to be a difficult feat in the tinder-dry forest of spring. The trick of calling gobblers with a hen call apparently is not known. . . . Ocellated turkeys are surprisingly fast on the wing, and I recommend hunting them as one of the finest sports to be had in North America.*
—A. Starker Leopold, *Wildlife of Mexico*

# THE TEACHINGS OF DON PEPÉ

**Breaking trail, Mito** raised the machete as if lifting his hat, then let the blade fall, its weight, velocity, and edge shearing the vines and branches. It looked perfectly smooth and effortless, the steel ringing like a chime—announcing I was hunting Mexico again.

There are easier lands to hunt than Mexico. The bureaucracy can be Kafkaesque; travel difficult and not without physical hazard; amoebic disease may be at swim in the next sip of water. Set beside this is the fact there are things to be seen in Mexico that can be seen nowhere else. And that one can come to love hunting there.

The machete's chime reminded me of that, and also of the last note of the "song" of one of those things to be seen only in Mexico, the ocellated turkey gobbler, the rest of whose spring mating call defied imitation or comparison: the croaking of large atonal arboreal amphibians accompanied by John Cage–prepared pianos? Once heard, though, it was remembered, even if like some secret oath it may not be repeated.

The ocellated (*Agriocharis ocellata*) is the second of the world's two species of wild turkey—the other the unfortunately named "common" wild turkey (*Meleagris gallopavo*) found throughout North America, including Mexico. Another name for the ocellated is the Mayan turkey, while the Maya themselves called it *Cutz*.

A. Starker Leopold in his *Wildlife of Mexico* called the ocellated turkey, an inhabitant of the Yucatán Peninsula, "one of the finest game birds of Mexico," adding, a bit self-consciously, "and for that matter, of North America." The first time I laid eyes on a live one, I saw his point.

On a February day in a private menagerie on a large hacienda outside Mérida, Yucatán, a beardless gobbler trotted back and forth in his wire-caged pen. His breast and back feathers were coppery, wings brown, white, iridescent green, and barred black-and-white. Gray tail feathers were spotted with peacock "eyes," or ocelli (giving him his name); his needle spurs longer than the rays on a vaquero's silver rowels. Oddest was a knobbed head of naked turquoise skin, covered with glowing orange wartlike caruncles. Hell, this could be the finest game bird in the *world* (or at least the most spectacular); and if I'd had any doubts before, I was certain then that I had to hunt one.

Even before I had seen one in the flesh, though, I had already decided where I would go to hunt this most Mexican jungle fowl (familiar to me from bird books), this bad acid trip with plumage, and with whom I would hunt him. It could only be in Campeche state, and with my old friend Don Pepé.

I'd gotten to know Don Pepé some years earlier on the road to ruins. Before light one winter morning we left his Snook Inn along the Champoton River, heading toward the Mayan ruins at Edzná, bound for a maize field to hunt white-winged doves and red-billed pigeons.

Fog was in the air; and as it turned to a cottony apricot through the window of the old VW van, Don Pepé, sitting beside me on the bench seat in the back, declared, "This is something in which I disagree with Shakespeare.

"'Tis the very witching time of the night,' does not Hamlet say at midnight?" continued Don Pepé, waving toward the dawn glowing through the fog. "But *this*, I think, is the true witching time."

The outline of Don Pepé's life owed much to the bewitched vagaries of twentieth-century history. A World War I baby boomer with a League of Nations' lineage—German-Lebanese-Spanish-Mayan—his birth in Vera Cruz had been eventuated by a series of turns that began with the diversion of the ship his mother and grandmother had been sailing from Europe to Buenos Aires in August 1914, and their subsequent separation from the rest of their family until the Armistice. Married five times, himself, and father of ten, Don Pepé had been quoting Shakespeare, Churchill, and similar luminaries for over fifty years, often while dining with guests and friends.

A perennially trim gourmand, he regretted his lack of an ability to eat till bursting. Whether at the inn or the camps he set up in the jungle, the *selva*, my (or your) dinner with Don Pepé could include stone crab claws, stuffed squid, *real* red snapper, *mole con pollo*, butterflied whitewing breasts marinated in sour-orange juice and seared on a griddle, black beans not of this earth, homemade habañero salsa, cold sliced vegetables in vinaigrette, and fresh chilled fruit from pineapples to melons, papaya slices the size of platters, and ones not likely to be seen off the peninsula, such as the sapodilla tree's persimmony *zapote* (with a seed like a large shiny black beetle) or the date-flavored *mamey*.

Between meals, Don Pepé guided and outfitted in the *selva* of Campeche. In the past he went after puma, ocelot, and jaguar (hunting them with his clients in a deceptively languid-looking manner—with shotguns and buckshot while recumbent in hammocks suspended above tethered goats); by the time I knew him, the game list included peccary, brocket deer, doves, pigeons, ducks, snook, and his favorite, his "children," tarpon. The ocellated turkey, though, remained his most sought-after game.

That first time I hunted with Don Pepé, we remained in the open maize field, trying to hit the seemingly slow-sculling and large wild pigeons and definitely missing the tumbling and yawing whitewings. I kept thinking of the *selva*, though, and the ocellated turkey that lived in it. It was the *selva* that Don Pepé had always loved, especially as a place to walk and to find coolness in the heat of the day, which in late April came soon after sunrise.

In the late April when I came to hunt ocellated turkey, Mito, one of Don Pepé's guides, and I listened at the edges of fields before light; and if we heard no singing by the time the sun was up, we moved into the shadows of the *selva* ourselves. Following trails and washed-out roads, sometimes having to cut a way with the machete, we tried to jump an ocellated turkey or searched for the coin-sized tracks (*pecas*) of brocket deer, for which I also had a permit, and mostly found the larger tracks of peccary and whitetail.

On the *selva* floor we saw partridgelike tinamous (actually tiny rheas, New World ostriches, said to express a rather liberal view of family values by mating in threes). In the trees were toucans, crested guan, parrots, woodpeckers, and motmots—"clockbirds" who strip the filaments from the shaft of their central tail feather almost to its tip, then swing it like a pendulum as they perch. Far to the south in tall ramon trees we even saw the same "little men" a band of Kiowa reported seeing after traveling deep into Mexico long ago, the "men" howler monkeys. (These refrained from pelting us with their feces, as they were known to do. Perhaps they recognized Don Pepé.)

And once we did see an ocellated gobbler, already in flight through the trees.

Coming out of the *selva* onto a dirt road, we almost always found a *campesino* on his one-speed bicycle, his long-barreled, rusty, officially illegal single-shot 16-gauge slung across his back. Such hunters' motto was "*Parajo que vuela, a la cazuela*": The bird that flies ends up in the pot, which, considering the general lot of the Mexican peasant, is hard to take exception to.

Finally, one dawn on a falling-down hacienda called Quisil, we heard a gobbler singing in a hilly hardwood thicket across a cut and blackened cane field. (Calling, as Leopold said, is rarely used by Mexicans for ocellated turkey, the hen's call a soft whistle that carries only a very short distance. Instead, the traditional method in Mexico for hunting ocellated turkey, in spite of what Leopold said, *is* to stalk them.)

Mito and I crossed the field, dew holding down the black ash, and crept through the vines and thorns, sweat from the humidity soaking into my camo. It was a small thicket, but it seemed to take forever to move silently through it as the gobbler sang. Then Mito froze, moving one finger toward a tree.

I stared for several seconds before I saw a dark shape in the limbs. I slowly raised the 12-gauge and waited.

The *macho*'s knobbed head lifted, and he looked around. Then he flapped to the ground. The brush was not very thick here, and the bird would be gone in an instant. I moved the muzzle to cover his head and neck, took the gun off safe, and squeezed the trigger.

Wings beat on the ground instead of the air as Mito sprinted forward, slipping like smoke through the thorns that ripped and tugged at me as I followed. When I reached him, Mito had the bird; and all I could do was stare at something as strange and beautiful as I had ever seen in the wild.

Mito placed the turkey in the burlap bag he carried, and we made the long hike back to the van where Don Pepé's eldest son, Jorge, waited, reading a paperback Western written in Spanish. When we met back up with Don Pepé that morning, he smiled with some pride at the gobbler and said, "This is the gift we give our friends."

The world-record ocellated weighs only twelve and a half pounds with spurs just over two inches. My gobbler was an ounce or two under eleven and a half pounds with one-and-three-quarter-inch spurs. Rather than determining if he qualified for record classification, though, we did something far more appropriate, skinning him and letting the chefs at Don Pepé's inn find a place for him in *la cazuela* and turn him into an exquisite *mole con pavo ocelado*.

On the drive back to Mérida past old Spanish fortifications, Don Pepé, dressed in a white guayabera and with gaunt-shanked old man's legs sticking out of Bermudas, took the wheel of the van. His fifth wife, wearing a hearing aid bought out of an outdoor catalog (intended to enhance hunters' ears, but a bargain compared to one prescribed by a doctor), reached over from the back to feed him cold peeled wedges of zapote. As Don Pepé drove he told me of his inventions he never patented (adjustable-speed wipers, "heads-up" aircraft instrumentation); the woodscraft he had learned (such as his conviction that yellow hammocks repelled insects because they were the color of fire, which, of course, all animal life abhorred); his acquaintance with space-flight (and let's not forget *Vergeltungswaffe zwei*) *meister*mind Wernher von Braun; how El Diablo himself got the drop on him one night in a hut in the *selva* when Pepé could not get to his pistol; and how some people shared a "radio channel" in their heads over which unique ideas and insights were transmitted simultaneously around the globe (or as Melville put it, "Genius all over the world stands hand in hand, and one shock of recognition runs the whole circle round"). Glancing at an overpass and seeing laughing boys holding a four-foot iguana aloft, as if to hurl it down on us, I realized that in Mexico "magic realism" was not merely a literary genre. You only had to look at the ocellated turkey to see that.

In the city I shook hands with Don Pepé outside a small hotel built around a fountain. He handed me a box with the skinned and salted pelt of my wild turkey, and we bid each other "*Hasta luego*." Placing my trophy in my room, I went on a frantic quest to find store-bought souvenirs before my morning flight. I found something for my wife quickly, but it was more difficult for my (then) five-year-old. In a hardware-store window, though, I saw exactly what I was looking for. The edge was good, and the steel rang just like a chime.

Though not as large as the one Mito wielded, it was much too big for my son, so when I got home I put it away in its tooled leather sheath on a high shelf in the closet, where it rested beside a Zulu assegai and a Tibetan dagger. Maybe by the time he grew into it, my son would be ready to hunt Mexico with me, and perhaps with Don Pepé, too, to see what could be seen nowhere else on earth.

# Chapter 12

*The night before, he sat on the cot, rolling his riflescope in its rings.*

*"Is this supposed to do this?" he asked, genuinely curious.*

*The next morning he carried a borrowed rifle. We hiked some miles up a rocky canyon under a flat March sky before spotting a herd of javelina on a hillside. They stood in the open 150 yards from us, feeding.*

*"Yes," he said when I pointed to the javelina. He sat on the ground, wrapping the sling around his arm, locking his elbows over his knees, squinting through the 6x scope. I crouched behind, fingers in my ears, waiting for the shot. Thirty seconds passed, then a minute. He lifted his head and looked back me, smiling faintly.*

*"Where are they?"*

*"There." I pointed over his shoulder.*

*He nodded and looked through the scope for another minute.*

*"Where?" he asked once more.*

*"Right there."*

*"Funny, I just can't see them."*

*"See the big pink rock and the century plant below it? See the barrel cactus five feet to the right of the century? That barrel cactus is a javelina boar."*

*"Oh," he said. A minute later, "I don't see it."*

*The conversation went on like this for ten minutes. I maneuvered him around so the crosshairs of the scope were on the javelina. It made no difference. I asked him to unload the rifle and point the muzzle up. Sitting beside him, I bolted a round in my .220 Swift. I shot the boar that looked like a barrel cactus, the javelina flipping onto his back, dead. Now the rest of the herd ran across the rocky face of the desert hill.*

*"Ahh," he remarked. "You meant there."*

*My short, unofficial life as a big-game guide, and welcome to it.*

# THE FIRE IN THE BEAST

*When beasts went together in companies, there was said to be . . . a*
*singular of boars, a sounder of wild swine, and a dryft of tame swine.*
—Joseph Strutt,
*The Sports and Pastimes of the People of England, 1838*

**I hunted wild** pigs in California in the Year of the Boar, in the coldest April in
many people's memory. The mornings in the Diablo Range of Monterey County
brought the first hard freezes the ground had seen all season. As I worked down
the grassy ridges before light, the bent blades sloughed off frost, wetting my boots
through and leaving my feet aching. At night as I rode along the old dirt roads
in the open back of a pickup the black air numbed my hands, one gripping the
steel rim of the truck box, the other my empty rifle. A sign that it was spring,
and not the heart of winter, was the afternoon hail that fell hard as rock salt, and
the layers of white fat the boar were starting to put back on.

In such a cold time it seemed no more than the hand of destiny that the name
of the guide would be August. We had hunted with him for two days now on
some of the fifteen thousand acres of land his father both owned and leased the
hunting rights to. This land was rolling in parts and steep in others, with oak
groves in the draws and hillsides variously open or choked with black sage, the
hilltops peaked by stands of digger pines. And despite the upside-down weather,
the new barley had somehow managed to be already well up in the fields, as were
the volunteer barley and wild oats. On the ridges stood tall yellow wallflowers;
and more deer and quail than any law-abiding man should by rights be compelled to encounter out of season.

We had already killed a pig as well.

My father, the lifetime sum of whose big-game hunting resulted, somewhat
improbably, in his taking two mule deer, an alligator, and a *polar bear*, did list
among his passions—most of them sadly small—the hunting of wild pigs. So on
our first morning out he spotted for himself a reddish boar standing at the head
of a draw and made, offhand, a rather noteworthy dead-center shoulder shot of
something over 150 downhill yards—and it was some time before the end of *that*
was heard. That left us with one genuine trophy boar (a pig with tusks over two
inches long, measured from the gum line to the tip along the outside curve) to be

taken by my friend Vance—who had come from Boise to hunt with us, wild pigs rather thin on the ground in Idaho. Then a boar for me after Vance took his.

The wild boar of Eurasia and North Africa, *Sus scrofa*, the progenitor of modern domestic swine, is the most ancient and primitive of even-toed ungulates. He is decidedly nonruminant, an eater of everything—as is man—who—again like man—learned successfully to tolerate some of the most widely disparate circumstances nature had to throw at him. Yet his home is not here; and a question hovers: What, exactly, was I doing hunting him in this New World?

Much, of course, did connect me to him.

Forty thousand years prior to our coming to North America, one of us daubed the wild boar's image onto his cave wall at Altamira in what is now Spain, then stepped back to contemplate his work. He represented the pig leaping in attack, its bristles raised, and hoped the painting would in some way deliver him unharmed from any encounter with the boar's nearly mystical tusks, or at least make the task of finding the pig when he set out to hunt it just a little easier.

The Assyrians, Egyptians, Greeks, and Romans also left behind for us their own images of the boar and the hunt for him, affixing him to temple walls, glazed amphorae, in bas-relief on the sides of sarcophagi, on chalcedony scaraboids, and as the emblem worn by the Roman Twentieth Legion when it marched into Britain.

Wild boar, or beings who assumed their shape (in, it would seem, much the same manner as the "bear-men" of the North American Indians assumed the shape of grizzly), were forever—often literally forever—laying low the heroes, gods, demigods, and devils of ancient mythology. Vishnu became a boar to slay the demon Hiranyaksha and free the land from a flood. The dark twin Set, as a boar, killed his brother Osiris, the Egyptian god of the underworld. The Syrians' Tammuz, the Greeks' Adonis, Cretan Zeus, Carmanor the son of Dionysius, Apollo's son Idmon the Argive, all had their lives taken by wild boar.

Great Ancaeus, the helmsman for the Argonauts, survived the many perils of the voyage for the Golden Fleece only on the very day of his return to be killed in his own vineyard as he tried to drive a boar from it. Another Ancaeus, of ever-bucolic Arcadia, was castrated and disemboweled during the famous hunt for the huge rampaging boar of Calydon, in which the virgin Atalanta—who had been suckled by a she-bear and raised in a clan of hunters, and who began the day of the hunt by shooting dead a pair of centaurs who meant to take liberties with her—drew first blood from the boar with her arrow and was awarded its hide and tusks after it lay dead. Outside Greece, it was for the love of Grainne, the daughter of King Cormac of Ireland, that the legendary Celtic hunter and warrior Finn Mac-Coul made himself into a wild boar to kill his nephew Diarmait O Duibhne.

If there is a common root to all these tales of death by boar, it would seem to be that most grow out of the seasonal death of bright summer, or the reaping of the crop at summer's end, and the relentless onslaught of winter's dark. In many stories it is given to the wild boar to come, in the ancient lunar year's thirteenth and final month, bearing in his coat of bristles the solstice's fearful darkness.

Now darkness was almost upon us. Before the last of the shooting light on the hunt's second day, Vance, August, and I spent most of an hour sitting far up on one side of a canyon, silently watching two enormous boar stir in the thick black sage on the other. The pigs would show us only the tops of their black backs, or their rumps moving behind a bush, so we never had a shot. Smaller pigs had come out into the open draw below us to begin the feeding that would carry them from evening through the night and to barely past dawn, but Vance was set firmly on a trophy. When the big boar got into sage so thick we could no longer see any sign of them, we climbed out of the canyon and back up to the ridge to start our way in, leaving the boar for another time.

We were halfway down the ridge, with its oaks and pines, when we saw the sounder of wild pigs out in the open field below us. They stood in the cold shadow the ridge cast in the sunset, nearly a dozen animals, all large adults. The largest stood alone at the rear of the sounder, tall and lean, his thick mane of bristles caping his neck and shoulders. We worked our way quietly down the slope to where Vance could get a rest for his rifle.

When Vance's .30-caliber bullet tore a hole in his heart, the big boar, without a squeal or a grunt, swung away from the rest of the sounder as it made for cover, describing for himself a wide galloping arc through the field's tall green grass before collapsing. By the time we got down to him, the crescent moon had begun to rise. We could see that he was reddish black with most of the features of a pure wild boar and with two-and-a-half-inch lower tusks that gleamed in the curved moonlight, but no brighter than Vance's grin.

A boar's upper tusks are there only to sheath and sharpen his lower set, those honed bottom tusks being his means of coping with the world. Sir Robert Stephenson Smyth Baden-Powell (1857–1941), First Baron Baden-Powell, founder of the Boy Scout movement, and the then-colonel responsible for the 215-day British defense of Mafeking against the Boers during the South African War of 1899–1902, who was as well an ardent practitioner of the mounted sport of pig-sticking while quartered as a young officer in India, wrote that the mark of a perfect pair of boar's tusks was that when placed base to base and tip to tip they would form a perfect circle. It was this crescent shape of his tusks that made the boar sacred to the Moon for the Greeks.

In the matter of hunting the wild boar, Xenophon recommended that the Greek boar hunter use a spear with a fifteen-inch blade, "keen as a razor," with copper teeth projecting from the middle of the socket to stop the boar from running up the length of the shaft when struck and held by the hunter. He also advised the use of "Indian, Cretan, Locrian, and Laconian" hounds, "prepared to fight the beast," as hunting dogs. The boar was to be driven from its lair and caught in a purse net, but if it escaped before being killed and attacked a hunter who was without benefit of a spear, that hunter was to hurl himself to the ground and grasp the underbrush to prevent the boar from getting its tusks underneath him and leaving him looking like poor Ancaeus, a or b. It was the obligation of the other hunters to drive the boar off their companion at the earliest opportunity.

The nobility of Europe continued to hunt pigs in much this same manner for the next two thousand years, until the use of firearms became widespread. Certain ancient beliefs about the boar were carried over from Xenophon to the A.D. second-century *Omasticon* of Julius Pollux, even to *The Gentleman's Recreator* of 1686. It was believed, for instance, that "very fiery heat exists in the beast," so that just the touch of his tusks to the coat of a hound could send that animal up in flames, and that even a dead boar retained so much heat that if you placed a few dog hairs on a tusk, the hairs would shrivel up as if placed on a "hot iron." (And for all I know, this may be no fable; no one I know of has ever taken the time to lay a dog's hairs on the tusk of a dead boar to observe the result scientifically; as for there being a fire in the beast, this I do know to be unquestionably true.)

In India the pastime of pig-sticking grew out of bear-sticking when the eighteenth century saw a dip in the subcontinent's bear population that was inimical to the continuance of proper sport. Pig-sticking, however, proved an excellent substitute. It was done on horseback with only "tough, springy, seasoned, male bamboo" spears with triangular steel heads, preferably the products of Thornhill, Rogers, or Wilkinson, all reputable manufacturers of fine English steel. A pig was never to be shot.

From Baden-Powell's most illustrative descriptions of the hunts, they were apparently large-scale affairs conducted at five o'clock on spring mornings—following rousing nights in the cook tent that involved repeated "goes" of claret and choruses of boar-hunting songs gleaned from back numbers of the *Oriental Sporting Magazine*. A hundred "coolies" (who in unguarded moments might offhandedly be referred to as "niggers") would be assembled and sent off to beat the pig cover, and frequently be severely gored. Three or four mounted hunters would be stationed at the ready, weapons in hand, and when a boar was "reared" and its line of escape made clear, the word "Ride!" would be given and they would charge hellbent after the pig for the honor of "first spear." Often these hunts would be attended by large parties of spectators seated in howdahs on the backs of elephant.

As the lead hunter drew up on the boar, the pig was apt to "jink" off into some Indian dirt farmer's corn or millet crop, which of course necessitated the rider's trampling in after it with his horse. Sometimes the boar would go to ground in an area that was "unridable," and here the solution was to set the cover ablaze and burn the pig out. If in the process a coolie or two were "roasted alive," at least they had the satisfaction of knowing they died in the cause of the "king of sports." The slightest infraction of the strict rules of riding etiquette by any of the hunters could be most sternly penalized by the imposition of such fines as "one dozen of champagne," and no doubt the final spearing to death of the pig was greeted by the politest of applause from the gallery on elephant back.

The imperial British deigned to consider the wild pig an opponent worthy of them because of its intelligence, hardiness, and ferocity. A wild boar would gore and even knock down a horse during a hunt. It showed little or no fear of dogs, camels, or even elephant and was not only said to be indifferent to the presence of tiger about it in the jungle, but actually had been observed *killing* them on occasion in fights. It was these splendid qualities as a game animal—and maybe something else that I was trying to understand—that brought the wild pig to North America and California.

In the state domestic swine had been drifting loose and going feral since mission days. The pure wild blood in the California herds, though, can be traced to the Ural Mountains. The somewhat hazy line of its genealogy seems to begin there and runs to an Englishman, George Gordon Moore, who in 1912 had thirteen wild Russian pigs, via an agent in Berlin, shipped to Hoopers Bald in western North Carolina. There he is said to have kept the pigs penned in on six hundred acres until in the early 1920s a bona fide pig-sticking match could be organized on the by-then sixty to one hundred animals. During the commotion of the hunt, it is purported that many of the pigs quite rightly crashed through their split-rail enclosure and escaped into the surrounding hills, where they survive to this day. Enough remained after the hunt, though, for Moore in 1925 or '26 to arrange for three wild boar and nine wild sows to be transported to California from Hoopers Bald and turned loose on Monterey County's San Francisquito Ranch, now known as the San Carlos Ranch—and not on William Randolph Hearst's San Simeon Ranch, a common fallacy often given credence by any number of natterwits, myself, alas, formerly included.

Joining up with the feral hogs already in place, the wild pigs, being pigs, bred and then spread, deploying themselves into the grazing, rooting, scavenging, and acorn-collecting niche in California's ecology once occupied by the grizzly and the hunting-gathering North American Indian, both lately eradicated.

No foolproof method exists for determining a pure wild boar in California from one crossbred to a feral pig. A wild pig does have thirty-six chromosomes and a domestic one thirty-eight, and interbreeding them produces offspring with thirty-seven. Yet let the generation of offspring interbreed, and you can achieve piglets with thirty-six, thirty-seven, or thirty-eight chromosomes, whatever fancy strikes that molecule of pig DNA, $x$'s and $y$'s doled out in a mélange of genetic randomness. This is not to say, though, that a wild boar doesn't have a definite *look* to him.

He will stand taller than the ordinary chuffy lard hog from which most feral pigs derive. There will be an angularity and slimness to his hips, and his head will be long and slender-snouted, with the eyes set far back to protect them while he roots—although his vision is so shamefully poor this seems hardly worth the trouble. His ears will be erect and heavily haired, and his long, bristly pelage will range in color from reddish brown to gray-black, with gray hairs increasing over his belly and jowls in a grizzled pattern known as "agouti" after the color scheme of a tropical American rodent.

A wild boar will possess a mane, or "comb," of long, erect bristles along his neck and spine, and in a cold California winter he may even grow back a thick underfur of curly wool like that carried by those of his breed still at large in the forests and mountains of Europe and Asia. Under his hide, which if you have it tanned for leather after killing him you will find thoroughly crosshatched with the scars of old battles, he carries an inch-thick plate of keratin, the stuff of hooves and horns. It extends on either side of his body, back from his shoulders to his last ribs, and shields his vital organs from the tusks of other boar when he fights them during the breeding time. If you slap your hand on a boar's side when you find him lying dead in a green field at dusk, as Vance did, this keratin

shield will boom for you like a hollow log being drummed. Care should be taken in touching a hand to the tusks before they have cooled.

The next morning was the last of the hunt, and white fog filled the big river valley far below us. Up here in the hills it was clear and continuingly cold, and by the time August and I decided to try going down through a dense hillside of black sage where the pigs bedded during the day, I had already missed chances at two good boar. We were ready by then to try anything, and there were unquestionably pigs in this sage. We were assured of this because as August and I moved down through the chest-high brush we could smell them. We could smell them; we could hear them snuffling, grunting, and snorting all around us; we could see them shaking the brush as they moved; we could do everything but get a clear shot at one. The pigs knew this. We tried throwing rocks to kick them out; we stood talking loudly to kick them out; we even tried kicking them, or at least the brush they were lying behind, to kick them out. They abided yet.

At one point up on the ridgeline a sow and two piglets broke across the narrow trail in front of us, then a minute later came three yearling hogs, the perfect eating size, no more than five yards from me, getting airborne as they leapt the gap in the brush. It was like trying to hunt pigs as quail, and I began to consider the option of a 12-gauge with double-aught loads. Stalking them in the brush, though—even with the knowledge that a pig may turn dangerous only when he is crippled and angry (popping his jaws in fury), and then he may start stalking you—I almost longed for the reassurance of a stout boar spear, a purse net, and a Laconian hound at my side.

In hunting wild pigs in California you try every legal and fair-chase means at hand because you never know what will work next, or at what precise moment a pig will decide to do . . . God knows what. When it finally looked as if the pigs were going to do nothing, and nothing we could do was going to work, August and I started the long climb back up the ridge. The day seemed done, but I could still feel my heart fluttering happily from having been in that sage with wild pigs, and that said everything to me about what I was doing in this New World hunting them. Or nearly everything.

When August's people first came into the Diablo Range of California three generations past and only a little before the wild boar reached Hoopers Bald, it was in a spring wagon, the worldly goods they brought with them including one shotgun and four hundred dollars in gold in a sack to buy a ranch from a homesteader. When my people came to California three generations past, it was on a clipper that had rounded the Horn one jump ahead of potato blight.

Even after three generations, there are times when it is my secret suspicion that North America is not where I belong. There are subtleties to this land and its game, rules and rites for the hunting of it that were refined to a very high degree over the course of at least ten millennia by people far different from mine, and which at times I am sure I shall never be able to fathom. My links to North America's game seem on occasion tenuous and outside me, as if I were slated forever to be no more than a dabbler and a stranger on this continent. Maybe hunting wild pigs in California—and perhaps this is something the men who brought them here felt, too—ties me to what I sometimes see as my true past, my only tribal memory, which is from a place other than this, but is a place of wild boar.

And that is enough white man's blues for one day. Obviously, this North America is where I now am, am part of, and mean to stay. Are you kidding? I ain't getting on any boat for "home"; that is a "there" that no longer is. In a very real sense it's been gone since before the Greeks, before the Egyptians. I would probably have to go back to somewhere around the time the paint was still tacky in that Spanish cave to reclaim it. This is where the boar is now, too, and has learned, remarkably well, to fit in. The boar stops here and is no longer a stranger. Maybe, learning gracefully from him, I shouldn't think of myself as one, either. It may very well be that anyplace we hunt, if we do it honorably, becomes our real home. I can remember many far places in this world that became "mine" after I hunted them. It could be that it only takes the understanding of one thing about anyplace in the world (such as how to hunt a native species of game) to make us no longer strangers there.

That does seem a portentous load to try to make a poor wild pig lug around with him—though certainly no more burdensome than a solstice—yet hunting wild boar leads to such speculation. If you let him, the wild boar can root into your thoughts the way he roots into the soil of a hillside, turning it over to expose it to the sun. Or you can as you climb the ridge see a singular boar looking as big and black as an Angus bull break from the cover you were just rocking, cross the canyon, and be over the next ridge in an instant, and forget all else as you give chase. And that's what August and I did.

By the time we topped that next ridge the boar was three hundred yards away, running across an open field. The first shot from my .375 kicked up dirt at his heels. The next was too far ahead. A third heavy bullet missed him clean, and the wild boar made the cover of a ravine, gone to ground.

And in the moment of his disappearance, that big wild boar became what he never ceases to be: He was history.

# Chapter 13

*Once, I was a resident of the state of Oregon's permanently rained-out coast (what my Iowa-born, Colorado-bred grandmother despised for being a "green hell"). The town was your basic crab-and-salmon port (the lumber mill upriver in the neighboring town). And what that port's citizens did, when they weren't fishing or drinking, was hunt black-tailed deer on timber-company land.*

*I lived alone above crumbling sea cliffs in the bottom half of a crumbling duplex. The place had an oil burner and sheets of once-clear plastic tacked over the windowpanes, and even with the rent running at about two bucks per day, it was wildly overpriced, unless you couldn't get enough of mildew. In order to escape my private green hell, I would hike across town to the waterfront for a bowl of the best, bar none, clam chowder in the world. My route would carry me past a gas station on the coast highway. In the station's office, behind the giant glass window with a pyramid of silver motor-oil cans in it, hung a set of antlers on a plaque reading* WORLD'S RECORD CO-LUMBIA BLACKTAIL DEER. *I never failed to glance at those antlers, before moving on. When deer season would come, I would go out to the edge of a clear-cut and sit in the drizzle with my rifle laid across my knees, turning to rust. I never killed a blacktail when I lived in Oregon, but I can say I hunted them.*

# CROSS STRAWBERRY CREEK
# MULE DEER LIVER: A RECIPE

**It is for** most of us our first memory of venison's taste. It is the venison of deer camps, woodstoves, cold lucent October nights, a venison that is for any number of reasons—as many of sentiment as of perishability—best eaten while still in that high lonesome. It can, all by itself, make a trip worth it.

To begin with, cross Strawberry Creek, climb onto a tall ridge marked by scrub oaks, and kill one mule deer buck. After tagging and dressing him, and hanging him well off the ground in a tree, slip his heavy liver into a plastic sack and carry it down through new snow to a cabin of weathered logs. Put up your empty rifle, then blow the cobwebs out of a chipped enamel coffeepot and fill it with icy springwater. Add a fair amount of salt to make the water briny, then place the liver in it. Find a cold shadowed spot, maybe in a snowbank behind the cabin, and let the liver soak, without freezing, for a day. (Make sure the lid is tight on the pot and the pot kept well away from where a badger might wreak havoc on it.) Return with friends and drag out deer.

At night, remove the liver from the water and dry it with a clean paper towel. Peel the thin bluish membrane from the organ's surface and, with your sharp skinning knife, cut slices one-third-inch thick. In a heavy iron skillet with a blackened bottom, lightly brown slices of onion in bacon fat, then remove and set aside, keeping them warm. Mix white flour with salt and pepper, to taste, in a plastic bag that used to hold a loaf of sandwich bread, and shake the slices of liver in it, flouring each evenly. Spoon more bacon fat from the red Folger's can and add it to the skillet until the fat is a quarter inch deep and very hot, though not smoking. Place the slices in the hot fat and fry quickly. Turn the meat when beads of blood begin to appear on the white topside.

When the liver is done, the flour coating should be crisp and the meat slightly pink inside, not gray as an aged pronghorn's tongue. Put the meat on a platter of cracked blue china, place the warm onions on top, get the old men to turn the series game down on the radio, tell the gin-rummy players to clear their Bicycle cards off the table, and set the meat down. Serve with fried potatoes, a salad of fresh iceberg lettuce and wedges of tomatoes, hot garlic bread, cold milk, and a drop of whiskey. Cut a piece with the same knife you've been using for everything else so far this trip and lift the fork to your mouth. As you pause for the

liver to cool, smelling its warm dark aroma, look to the cabin window slicing and polishing the night as if it were the quarried face of an unlimited obsidian deposit butting up against the cabin. Wonder if it has begun to snow again out there in the black, and take your time with this meal. It's what you came for.

# Chapter 14

*When the days have dwindled to their shortest, and the nights seem never-ending, then all the great northern plains are changed into an abode of iron desolation. Sometimes furious gales blow down from the north, driving before them the clouds of blinding snow-dust, wrapping the mantle of death round every unsheltered being that faces their unshackled anger. They roar in a thunderous bass as they sweep across the prairie or whirl through the naked canyons; they shiver the great brittle cottonwoods, and beneath their rough touch the icy limbs of the pines that cluster in the gorges sing like the chords of an aeolian harp. Again, in the coldest mid-winter weather, not a breath of wind may stir; and then the still, merciless, terrible cold that broods over the earth like the shadow of silent death seems even more dreadful in its gloomy rigor than is the lawless madness of the storms. All the land is like granite; the great rivers stand still in their beds, as if turned to frosted steel. In the long nights there is no sound to break the lifeless silence. Under the ceaseless, shifting play of the Northern Lights, lighted only by the wintry brilliance of the stars, the snow-clad plains stretch out into dead and endless wastes of glimmering white.*

—Theodore Roosevelt, *"Winter Weather"*

# WINTER IS A GREATER HUNTER
# THAN MEN WILL EVER BE

**At least northwest** Colorado was prettier that fall than the hunter ever remembered seeing it. The hills were patched in lime, rust, khaki, red, and in yellows ranging from lemon to gold. The whitetail jackrabbits, already whitening for winter—while the hunter paraded in state-required clothing the color of a campfire—were big as Persian cats. Mountain bluebirds fluttered on the tips of twigs, and the dark silhouettes of eagles sailed beneath the blue sky.

At night the hunter stood outside the cabin with a puddle of sour mash in the bottom of his cup and looked up at Polaris, Draco, the Pleiades, the powdery smudge of the Milky Way, the Squaw and the Papoose blinking in the Big Dipper, and all the other stars whose names he had never learned. He heard coyotes near him at night, but could not see them in the day. When he set out hunting at dawn, he found the fresh snake-line tracks of voles, the splayed spoor ruffed grouse, the little-bear sign of badgers. Among the shimmering aspens the elk tracks were thick. An old Basque sheepherder wearing handmade Mexican-silver spurs told the hunter that he was seeing elk these days in places he had never seen them before. Last September his youngest boy, who was out herding with him before going back to college, had been drawn to a ridgetop by the sound of early-morning bugling and had counted thirty-five elk in the small meadow below. Lot of elk in the country, the shepherd concluded. What there were not a lot of in this country above Meeker, Colorado, were the mule deer the hunter had come seeking. For the first year in the five that he had been coming here, the hunter would not carry a buck home when he left.

The season before had been good. The seven of them in the camp had taken seven bucks off the twenty-five-hundred-acre lease and had passed up as many more. They had returned to Southern California and spent the winter with venison in their freezers, antlers on their walls, and expectations of even better things to come next year in their heads. And while rain fell on Southern California, snow fell on Colorado.

When word of the Colorado winter reached the hunter, his mind—refusing to acknowledge the fact that not only were humans, but Nature herself was capable of tearing down the hunting—chose to confine all the bad weather to the Gunnison area. That region was mentioned in all the reports as being hardest hit, and it was nowhere near Meeker.

The snow came down northwest of Meeker as well, though, came down heavy enough to bury all the sagebrush and make it impossible for the mule deer to paw through. As the deer starved they foundered in the drifts, too weak to move or to defend themselves. So the coyotes, usually wary of adult deer, came. Weighing no more than the weight of fur and teeth and hunger, they were able to run on top of the frozen crust. To deer already dying of starvation, such coyotes were a kindness, and by spring there was talk of two hundred thousand dead animals, nowhere in Colorado spared.

All through that winter, while it rained in Southern California and snowed in Colorado, the hunter had been telling his friend Tom about the place where they would hunt in the fall. Telling him? Regaling him. It would be Tom's first season in camp, and he wanted to know everything. The hunter obliged by first telling him that the town of Meeker was named for Nathan C. Meeker, who in 1869 left the editorial staff of Horace Greeley's *New York Tribune* and, following his former employer's famous advice, went west—albeit, at age fifty-two, hardly as a young man. His subsequent career in the Colorado Territory proved at best checkered, at worst fatal. A strict teetotaler, Meeker succeeded in founding the temperance colony of Greeley, while never succeeding at making one thin dime from anything he turned his hand to. In 1878 he was finally granted the boon of being named agent to the White River Ute Reservation and bungled that badly enough to start the Ute War of 1879, and to get himself and every one of the agency's male employees massacred at a site five miles outside the present town that bears his name. In later, less bellicose days, Theodore Roosevelt came to Meeker to follow the hounds and in 1901 killed a cougar that stood as the world's record for sixty-three years. As far as the hunter was concerned, the next exciting event to take place in Meeker occurred when a 350-pound Texan, dried blood still on his Lone Star hands, stamped back into the El Rancho Cocktail Lounge one deer season afternoon, wanting to know who, exactly, had stolen the five-by-five buck he'd left outside in his Jeep. (A friend of the Texan advised the culprit to come clean, because the angry hunter had already "gone away" once, "and it didn't take.")

This sort of information didn't entirely satisfy Tom's thirst for knowledge. He wanted to know the specifics of the place where he was going to hunt. What sort of terrain would it be? What kind of weather should he expect? What time did shooting light come? The hunter answered as best he could, telling Tom in the process about all the deer he had seen in all the years past, the long shots made across steep canyons, and the bucks he had lucked into, the gangs of elk crossing the meadows at first light, the sage grouse, seeming big as turkey, exploding from cover right under his feet, the dry days, the wet ones, the ones with snow. But that still left Tom to agonize all spring and summer over what rifle to carry, what weight bullets to load, what kind of shoes to wear. He settled at last on a Mag-na-ported .30-'06 BAR throwing 180-grain Nosler Partition bullets. On his feet he would lace Adidas in warm weather and insulated pacs in cold. He meant to be prepared.

By early October, though, when they were packing to leave, Tom and the hunter and Roy and Charley and Bob and Dave and Manuel—despite all their preparedness and faint hopes—could no longer ignore the persistent reports of massive die-off. This season could not be like the last. And yet, in the grand-scheme-of-things sense, what the hell difference did that make? The hunter was put in mind of the closing passage of E. Douglas Branch's classic *The Hunting of the Buffalo*:

> And it is only 30 years ago [1900] that a band of Indians . . . saddled their ponies and rode away—"as of old, but in silence and sadness."
> "Where are you bound?" some white man asks; and they answer, "For the buffalo."
> "But there are no more."
> "No, we know it."
> "Then why are you going on such a foolish chase?"
> "Oh, we always go at this time; maybe we shall find some."

While the mule deer (as cloudy as their future may be as the West relentlessly urbanizes) had not met with the bison's fate, the hunter could see that the odds that fall would not be with him and the others. Yet each fall there was still something—something in the blood, let's say—that compelled him and the men he hunted with always to go onto the Colorado Plateau at this time; and bad winter or no—perhaps, even, mule deer or no—that something would not leave the blood.

They reached the campsite the Friday morning before the season opened. That afternoon, after camp was made, Tom and the hunter kept beneath the ridgelines and crept through the groves of scrub oaks, glassing across the canyons and searching the ground for deer sign. They soon knew that winter had set its mind to it. For two hours they still-hunted without rifles. They did not see a living deer, found no more than one or two beds, heard almost no sound.

"Probably not even any of those sage grouse left," Tom ventured, just before a flock rose like an atomic mushroom cloud in front of them and whirred far out over the coppery sageland. Something, at least, had made it through.

As they walked, the bones lay around them like spilled dominoes in the yellow grass. The smooth tines of the antlers rose symmetrically above the polished caps of skulls, the herbivorous jaws set in permanent rictus. There wasn't enough meat on the skeletons for ants to bother with.

The hunter tried to show Tom the best place to hunt in the morning—knowing it wouldn't make one whit of difference, but knowing, too, that you always had to try. He showed Tom the canyon where their friend Charley had killed his first buck and then did not know how to dress him. After some searching, Charley found Roy, the man who had taught the hunter and almost everybody else the hunter knew how to dress a deer, and negotiated a contract with him whereby, in exchange for Roy's merely showing him how to clean his deer, Charley would clean Roy's when he shot it—providing, of course, that Charley was in the vicinity at the time. Roy agreed to the terms and followed Charley to his buck. Charley was stripping the alimentary canal from the carcass, per Roy's instructions, when Roy glanced cross-canyon, whispered to Charley not to bother wiping his knife, put down his pipe, lifted his .243, and killed one of the biggest bucks any of them had seen in years. Of the hundreds of deer Roy had shot since he was a boy, he could not recall killing one at a more opportune moment.

That was one story about the place that the hunter knew how to tell Tom, but there were others he did not know how to tell. As they slanted their way off a high ridge, the hunter did not know how to tell Tom about the way Old Mac had hunted this ridge his last time out when he was seventy-five and everybody was afraid he was going to die on them. But when those who had been on that hunt met again at Old Mac's funeral two years later, all they could talk about was how good he had done that last time. Old Mac had been a tough one, but now the hunter didn't know how to tell that to Tom, who had never known the man. Nor did the hunter know how to tell him about the way they had come here after the other place they had hunted for so many years had gone bad when the owner let anyone willing to pay onto it; and it became like hunting in a Boy Scout jamboree or trying to fish the bank of a stocked stream on opening morning—there had been enough blaze orange in sight to create a false dawn. Tom simply would have had to have been there to understand, and he hadn't been. Not even attempting to tell him these stories, the hunter told Tom they should head in from their scouting.

Four days later the hunter sat in the kitchen of the cabin, playing a game of muggins with Roy, the white dominoes spilled like bones on the tabletop. The light dropped through the holes that snow, winds, and pack rats had made in the ceiling, and the warm air in the kitchen hummed with flies and yellow jackets. As the hunter played, he was trying to guess where he should hunt next, having hunted every likely spot at least twice in the last four days. That was when the Basque sheepherder rode up and knocked on the door. Entering, he accepted a beer and sat down to tell Roy and the hunter about the elk and the mule deer and coyotes and "snow up to here" and the winter. The sheepherder did not hunt much these days, but he loved seeing the deer around him when he tended his flocks. He believed the state ought to close the deer hunting for at least three years to give the herds time to build back up, that the state should bring in proper feed for the deer in the bad winters, and that somebody had to do something about these coyotes.

The hunter nodded at it all. He felt inadequate to argue against the beliefs of this man who had lived out on the land more than the hunter ever would, who saw the mule deer every day—in migration, mating, birth, and in dying—when the hunter saw them only a few days out of the year. If he tried to explain, using scientific logic and statistical data, that men and coyotes probably killed no more mule deer than a few weeks in January would anyway, he knew it would ring false, not only to this sheepherder but to himself as well. So he nodded. When the sheepherder shook hands and jangled out in his spurs, the hunter thought: Yeah, maybe we don't have any business being out here, maybe it ought to be closed down; but where would I go, next fall?

The hunter finished his game of dominoes; then, realizing there was no sense to wasting what hunting time he had left, he slung his rifle over his shoulder and started out on his own "foolish chase." Tom was already out, having taken off at dawn and come in at dark every day of the hunt, intending to stay out until, like those Indians, he "found some." That was a good sign to the hunter; it meant that no matter how this year turned out, and no matter how grim the prospects looked for next year, as long as Tom could come back and hunt, he would; and the hunter would be assured of having someone to join him in the fall.

As the hunter walked, he believed he could nearly be content out here with just the sun-warmed ground to put his feet on and the clouds shaped like sage grouse wings to see. Heading up a far canyon, he found a good seat in a fragrant bed of sagebrush partway up a hill. The hunter had thus far tried stalking for game, glassing for it, and spooking it out of cover by charging like a tormented warlock through the scrub oak groves. Now he would put to the test the age-old technique of just plain sitting. He sat there till sunset. He stared at the hills and trees and brush until they began staring back at him. Then he stood and started in.

The hunter saw the mule deer as he was passing a side canyon running off the one he had been sitting in. The buck was five hundred yards away, moving toward the ridge. As soon as the hunter spotted him holding his rack-laden head high and walking with the easy grace only big bucks acquire, he sank to his hands and knees and began crawling through the sage toward the animal. When the hunter reached an old weathered fence post, he slowly rose and steadied his .300 on it. The buck had halted just beneath the ridgeline and seemed to be looking back at him. There was good light left, and the hunter had the

crosshairs anchored to the top of the deer's sleek-coated shoulder. As his finger lay on the trigger, he was able in his mind to see the entire progression: the exhale, the recoil, the buck coming down like a collapsing scaffold.

The hunter would climb up and, unable to resist, lift the head and hold the polished antlers in his hands a moment. Then he would swing the deer's tail downhill and roll him onto his back. When he opened the animal, he would marvel at the layer of pearly fat that would have carried this buck through the most determined winter. In the cold October evening, he would notice the heat rising off the flesh and have to remind himself again of the good taste of fresh liver at breakfast and how delicious the chops would be in a rainy Southern California February when the snow would be five feet deep in Colorado. And while the hunter saw all this in his mind, he watched the buck turn and let him continue on to the jagged ridge, climbing unhurriedly until he topped out and ambled into the approaching night.

As the hunter found his way back to camp, he met Tom in the darkness. Tom had not seen a buck all day, but was nonetheless delighted by sightings of numerous does and fawns—delighted, in fact, by the simple act of being out there. The hunter wondered if he knew how to tell Tom about what had just happened and that when men, unlike winter, hunted, their hearts could carry away more than their hands.

After turning it over for a minute, the hunter decided: Hell, Tom knew that before he ever got here.

# Chapter 15

*For success in still-hunting it is essential that the individual who engages in it, should be acquainted with the almost impenetrable depths of the forest, as well as the habits of the Deer. He must be expert in the use of the rifle, possess a large stock of patience, and be constitutionally adapted to endure great fatigue. Before the dawn of day, he treads the paths along which the animal strays in returning from its nightly rambles to the covert usually its resting place for the day. He ascends an elevation, to ascertain whether he may not observe the object of his search feeding in the vallies [sic]. If the patience and perseverance of the morning are not attended with success, he seeks for the Deer in its bed—if it should be startled by his stealthy tread and spring up, it stops for a moment before bounding away, and thus affords him the chance of a shot; even if the animal should keep on its course without a pause, he frequently takes a running, or what is called a chance shot, and is often successful.*

—John James Audubon
on the "Common American Deer,"
or the Whitetail, paintings by his son,
John Woodhouse Audubon,
*Viviparous Quadrupeds of North America*

# BUCKS OF SUMMER

The island, larger than Long Island or Hawai'i, big as Jamaica, lay south of Détroit de Jacques-Cartier (its discoverer in 1534) and before the coast of the Péninsule de la Gaspésie. Very much a part of French Canada, the island's name, "Anticosti," may have derived from the Spanish for "before the coast" (*ante costa*) or from a native word, *natiscouti*, meaning "the bear-hunting ground," although any bear on the island now existed almost certainly in mythology alone.

Not so the white-tailed deer. In 1895 the French chocolate magnate Henri Menier purchased the island for $125,000 and transplanted some forty deer from the Québec mainland onto it. Today, with a human population of just 250 and no verifiable wild predators larger than a fox, the deer herd averaged some 125,000 animals, season to season. Making Anticosti one of the finest places in North America for hunting free-ranging white-tailed deer. Which was why I went there early one September.

Most deer hunters who came to the island wanted to do so in November, during the rut, when the highest percentage of eight-, nine-, and ten-point bucks were taken. I had somewhat different priorities. I wanted to be on Anticosti when the Atlantic salmon still circled in finned vortices in the clear, limestone-bottomed pools, when the days would be long, the grass green, and the bucks of summer in velvet (and still gaining weight). Now that I no longer lived in California (having moved much nearer to where the buffalo roam), there was always enough winter at home; I didn't need to travel more than two thousand line-of-sight miles to find any additional.

Where I went to hunt was along the south-central coast of the island, in the exclusive hunting territory of *une pourvoirie du cerf et sau*, an outfitter for deer and salmon. Staying at the outfitter's lodge was more like being in Europe than North America, with cooking that could aptly be termed cuisine (and *haute* at that) and the other hunters sharing the camp speaking French, Flemish, and Italian far more fluently than English. The hunting, though, was thoroughly North American.

The primary European hunting method was from stands; but on Anticosti, in September, whitetail were found only one way, and that was on foot. In September when the bucks were still in velvet, their antlers were sensitive to touch; and so the bucks preferred not to be in thick cover but in more open terrain. In the outfitter's territory, that fact did little to make the bucks easily accessible.

Ringed by a main gravel road and crossed by only two others, with a handful of ATV trails scattered across it, much of the two-hundred-square-mile territory had been cleared by fire, stands of skeletal snags left behind, bare masts without ships. There were no croplands for the deer to be drawn to, but the "bush," especially in September, provided abundant natural feed almost anywhere the deer cared to be. So any buck wanting land, lots of land and a starry sky above, with little or no contact with people, had as much as he could ask for, some perfectly capable of living and dying without ever seeing a human. And because there was no rut under way in September, bucks didn't need to seek out the company of other deer.

To find summer bucks on Anticosti a hunter walked, following the ATV trails into the bush until they played out and then navigating cross-country by compass. If that somehow sounds like "downside," consider what was definitely "upside," that fat, velveted-antlered bucks, were to be found almost anywhere on Anticosti in September. And in September, although there had been a buck-only season since the beginning of August, the deer for all intents had been unhunted since December 1 of the preceding year.

I saw how unhunted the deer were the very first morning of the three-month either-sex season. At dawn on September 1, with the sun at my back and the wind in my face, I stepped off down the forest trail my guide Michel had shown me, a detailed map of the area and my compass in my pack. I would hunt the upper drainage of the Petite Rivière de la Chaloupe while Michel would hunt the lower portion with my friend Steve. When I came out of the spruce trees at 8 A.M. and crossed a meadow knee-high in grass, I walked right up to within thirty yards of a big six-point buck, head down, feeding. I stood until he moved off, the deer unaware that I had ever been there.

I hiked the dry bed of a creek, whose white stones erupted with fossils, then circled back out to one of the gravel roads where I found Michel's pickup, but not Steve and him. They finally appeared at midafternoon riding Michel's ATV, a seven-point buck tied to the back rack.

On the first day, the five hunters in the lodge brought in three bucks. By the second day, there were five. Each day the hunters rotated to a different drainage, and on September 3 I hiked above the Rivière Maccan. From the gravel road I followed an old track barricaded by deadfalls, walking a mile and a half to a stand of fully leafed poplar, then along another hot white riverbed and a skeleton forest of burned spruce. Coming out of one more stand of poplar, I pushed my way through a foot-tangling horror of low willows, berry bushes, and burned snags and stumps. At midday, coming to a grassy meadow ringed by tamaracks, I flopped down to eat lunch and, yes, nap.

After half an hour's rest, I got up to move north to my planned rendezvous with Michel and Steve. The heat by then was a wave that rolled without cresting, the hard light of the sun overhead turning meadow grass and the needles on the trees to a green blaze in the head. I was almost across the meadow, walking in the open, when two bucks appeared on the edge of it, running.

I had a second to decide before the bucks split up and decided for me. The smaller sprang back into the tamaracks, but the bigger remained in front of me. The first shot was too far back. The buck staggered, and I felt my jaw clench. The second shot dropped him, and he lay still.

He was a heavy buck with a solid, thick, absolutely symmetrical eight-point rack, the brown velvet unblemished. Tagging and dressing him—lifting him up to drain and wiping out as much blood as I could from the cavity—I dragged him to a berry bush and pulled him onto it, chest up, so air could circulate in and around the carcass. A blowfly big as the tip of my last finger landed on the meat. In the sun, the green-iridescent chitin of the fly's abdomen was shiny lacquered as dried blood, its wings like leaded panes of waved window glass. The fly's head was all eyes, reddish brown.

In a way there might be as much to recommend a fly, as a work of nature, as there was a white-tailed deer, or a man. For one, every winter all were killed, but their hidden larvae remained to resurrect the species every summer. When another one landed, though, I thought of yellow puffs of eggs on red meat I had come a long way to kill, and a deer who should not have died to feed maggots, whatever their relative value in the grand scheme of things.

I broke a branch from a tamarack and fanned the open carcass to keep the flies away until the buck's opened eyes had glazed over, with a sheen like chitin, and a hard dry pellicle that the flies could not penetrate had formed over the exposed meat. Then I hiked out to find Michel and Steve, flagging the way back to the deer so we could retrieve him at sunset.

Hunting summer whitetail on Anticosti, and in wild country anywhere, means bucks that have plenty of natural feed and so are likely to be ranging over wide areas, often in the open. And unless the weather is uncomfortably warm, those deer are also likely to be out feeding at almost any hour of the day. Hunting them means covering as much country as possible on foot, using wind and sun to advantage, watching all the time and glassing frequently, and being ready to jump deer, both unaware and wary, at sometimes close range.

That is the way all the bucks were taken during the first five days of that September in the territory of *une pourvoirie du cerf et sau*, because when I found Michel and Steve, they had another seven-point, two deer allowed on each license; and back in camp that night seven bucks hung in the cold room. A Belgian, who had held out for something exceptional, came in with an ancient, spectacular ten-point the next day, and on the last day killed a younger buck for his second deer.

For my second deer, and the tenth in camp, I had decided one eight-point buck was all I was entitled to on any hunt. Yet to be sure there would be enough good summer whitetail venison to last my family and me the winter, I took a doe near a road in the cool of the evening, not a fly touching it.

# Chapter 16

*As I look back over twenty years of hunting, my pursuit of these dwarf deer stands out pleasantly. I can remember sweet sunny October and November days alone on the very top of a rugged desert range, poking cautiously along through the chaparral, watching the wind, trying to be quiet, pausing now and then to admire the beauty of the desert below me. I can remember lunches eaten by some tiny mountain spring with the mystery of lofty wilderness all about. Then suddenly the chaparral spouts deer. A couple of bucks, deciding the jig is up, dash for safety. Then comes quick, hot action. The buck is down. For a moment I pause to admire his sleek beauty. I remember, too, long painful scrambles back to camp with a dead deer limp on my shoulder. But these are labors of love.*
*—Jack O'Connor, Game in the Desert*

# THE PERFECT DEER

**The best deer** is always a subject of lively debate. For its aficionados, a wide-antlered Texas whitetail in a prickly pear patch is the one. Big, bush-lurking Alberta bucks have their advocates; while according to its devotees, an old, wary Rocky Mountain mule deer is the buck of choice. Of them all, though, the perfect deer is the Coues'.

Bold words, and I thought so, too, when I first heard them, about a jillion miles north of Coues' deer country during a Dall's sheep hunt. We were bivouacked along the braided rocky channels of a blue meltwater river below a glacier in Alaska's Chugach Mountains. We two hunters and two guides were waiting, as is so often the case in Alaska, for an overdue Super Cub. To pass the time in the interminable postprandial daylight we played baseball with a driftwood bat and rounded river stones and talked about what hunters always talked about on hunts, other kinds of hunting.

It was mid-August, but the other hunter was already thinking about the winter and hunting Coues'. He had access to a county-sized southern New Mexico ranch where there were mild December evenings to stand in shirtsleeves beside a mesquite fire, and side hunts for blue quail. It was the deer, though, who made it perfect, those desert white-tailed deer who might weigh a hundred pounds,

stayed gray year-round, wore a rack that would fit into a woman's hat box, and who, he said, "live in mule deer country and think they're wild sheep." This was a deer I would have to look into.

For some time nobody could quite figure out what that deer was. Known as the Arizona whitetail, Sonora whitetail, dwarf whitetail, or, à la Jack O'Connor, "elf of the brush country," it was thought to be its own species, before it was identified as a subspecies of whitetail. The question has remained about how to say its name, whether *cows* or noticeably less decorously *cooze*. The man for whom the deer was named, Elliot Coues—as author of *Key to North American Birds*, late-nineteenth-century "America's best-known ornithologist"—believed the original Norman-French pronunciation of his surname to have been *coo-ays*, and that this was anglicized to *cows* when his ancestors migrated to the Isle of Wight. It was sometimes even spelled "Cowes" by the family on the isle, giving the nod to that as the proper way to say the deer's name—though it's doubtful hunters will ever get enough of the snickering amusement derived from calling it a "Cooze," which is in any case close to how the name sounded to begin with.

As late as the 1930s, one zoological expert could claim that the Coues' deer's "abundance" in the Southwest was like "that of jackrabbits." When I first hunted Coues's deer in the Chiricahua Mountains of southeast Arizona at the end of the 1980s, they were considerably more extraordinary than hares. Hunting them required, and still requires, intense scrutiny to locate good bucks. The young guide I hunted with had been glassing an eight-point buck for several days before I arrived (he glassed it, in fact, for years, in time collecting six seasons of its shed antlers). He had it spotted, feeding on a hillside across a deep canyon; and all we had to do was work our way around and drop down from the hilltop. It took us twenty minutes to reach the backside of that hill; but once we eased over the crest, the oblivious buck would be less than two hundred yards below. Which is when we stepped on the doe who had been lying motionless in the yellow grass in front of us, watching as we stalked. She bounded over the hill, and the guide and I sprinted behind her to the crest. By the time we looked over, the scrub oak at the bottom of the hill was swallowing the buck.

It took another decade, right up to the last December of the millennium, for me to hunt Coues' again. I traveled this time to the Sierra Madre in northern Sonora. There was a hacienda there, more than sixty-five thousand acres from desert floor to seven-thousand-foot cordillera, with a large whitewashed ranch house and a small chapel to the side. Four tall straight junipers were planted in front of the house that bent in a square U around an inner courtyard. Inside the house, the short *Indio*-looking cook patted out *masa* tortillas, and we ate supper in a long room with a ceiling of dark open beams and the dusty heads of Coues' deer, mule deer, pronghorn antelope, and, in the far end over the fireplace, a buffalo bull, all the heads having come off the hacienda, the buffalo from a trans-planted herd and the pronghorn having been taken long ago. There were also Gould's turkey in the country—the largest of the subspecies of *Meleagris* and named for King George IV's taxidermist—but this hunt was all about Coues'.

In Arizona where they are subjected to heavy hunting pressure on public lands, Coues' deer can be as wild as jackrabbits. Though there is usually an October and a December season for the deer, hunters all seem to want to hold out for a permit in December when the bucks will be rutting and will let all their defenses down. Except the bucks don't rut until January when there is no rifle season (though there is one for archery), and never completely let down their defenses. December is a good time to hunt in Mexico, on the haciendas where the deer are not killed for meat by vaqueros or shot out by outfitters who want to make a fast dollar off fee hunts. Unlike rutting bucks who roam widely in search of does, the bucks in December stay put; and hunting them is a matter of finding where they stay.

By dawn on a mid-December day on the east side of the hacienda, I made a long slow hike behind a vaquero named Oscar, who looked about fifty in cow-boy years, followed by Chris, a young Arizonan who had come to Sonora to hunt with me. (On the other side of the hacienda two other hunters, Colin and Mike, looked for Coues' deer, too.) We climbed up and around a rocky hill to be able to glass into and across draws, Oscar setting a pace that carried us uphill so imperceptibly that I was surprised at how far below us the desert floor was when there was light enough to see.

Through the morning we sat and glassed, then got up to move and sit and glass some more. The only cover on the rocky hillsides was the tall spiny stems of the ocotillo plants, which looked as if they wouldn't camouflage a vinegaroon, let alone a small deer. Late in the morning I was turned away, glassing a herd of buffalo on a far cedar ridge, when Chris with his 10x binocular and Oscar with his naked eye spotted a doe and fawn jogging through the ocotillo across the draw. It took me five minutes of hard glassing to spot them, and when I did I understood that another of the qualities that helped make the Coues' deer per-fect was its ability to hide behind a cactus needle.

By noon we had circled off the hillsides and were making our way back to the ranch house across the desert flats. I'd started a blister a few days before by wearing the wrong boots on a "nature" hike (hiking for hiking's sake nearly al-ways a bad idea), and now was limping rapidly to keep up with Oscar.

"*¿Cuantos años?*" I asked, hoping he'd stop or slow down to reply.

"*Setenta*," Oscar answered without breaking stride.

*¡Madre de Dios!* I thought. He was 70 and it was a fair guess that he'd been a vaquero for 60 of those years, which ought to have made him physically about 197. I walked even faster, trying to disguise my limp.

We spent the afternoon farther to the west, scouting and glassing, but seeing nothing. At sunset—and the only way to describe a sunset in the Sonora in December is a chill sky lighted from below, the clouds come in from the Sea of Cortez, over the western sierra boundary wall of the hacienda, turned to bales of gauze saturated with grenadine—we heard four aimed shots. When we returned to the ranch house that night, Colin had a story about a stalk being blown by two cow-hunting vaqueros riding through, and then at well over 350 yards seeing, and shooting at, and missing, a buck he could only bring himself to describe as "*El Rey*."

By first light the next frosty-morninged day, we were all back on the hill from which Colin and Mike had spotted the king the day before, a battery of 60x spotting scopes set up on tripods to scour the tall hills and benches in a 270-degree arc. As the sun found the tallest hill, we spotted two bucks near the summit, moving away, then a little later, below the other two, the buck Colin missed. He looked to be a 130-point deer (based on the Boone & Crockett Club trophy-scoring system), the equivalent of a 185 or 190 northern whitetail. While we watched, far out of range, he climbed easily on small hard deer hooves into daunting bighorn terrain, bedding with his rump against a sheer rock wall and dozing through the morning—it would have taken a rappelling squad of Army Rangers to get anywhere near him. After one more visual search for any *accessible* bucks on that hill, we stopped looking there.

The hill where Colin had his stalk blown was in the opposite direction, almost a lone pyramid rising from the foothills below the timbered mountain ridges. A deep arroyo ran between this hill and the one we spotted from, and at nine-thirty on the side directly across from us, six hundred yards out, a good many-tined buck appeared and ambled downhill into a quarter-acre patch of cedar and oak on the slope, disappearing.

We could see all the way around the sort of cedar-and-oak merkin on the hill and glassed from where we were for another half hour to make sure the buck didn't slip out. He would likely lie there now for the day, as was the Coues' deer's wont this time of year. Colin said he was mine if I wanted him, since he'd shot and missed the day before; and Chris and Oscar and I made a plan.

Oscar would stay on the ridge to watch for the deer while we were out of sight of it, and Chris and I would hike around the back of our hill, circling our way up to the ridge that ran down across from the slope where the buck was bedded, letting us draw up within two hundred yards of the deer. We established a set of hand signals with Oscar, then Chris and I set off, making our deliberate quiet way off the hilltop, then down and around to the backside of the ridge.

As we worked back uphill, we kept low, ready to crawl. The ridge topped out sooner than we expected, and we were standing when we came into sight again of the patch of cedars and oaks. We sat quickly, and I extended the bipod rest on my 7mm Weatherby Magnum. Chris signaled to Oscar, whom we could now see again at the top of the hill, and Oscar waved back with a gesture telling us that the buck was still lying in the cover. Now we waited.

Chris, who had hunted Coues' deer all his life in Arizona—though this was his first time hunting them in Mexico—leaned toward me and whispered that the buck would probably lie until around 2 P.M., when he would stand, stretch, piss, then lie back down. That's when you had to spot him, judge him, and decide—then shoot and kill him before he folded his legs again and tucked himself back up under the squat thick cedar until dark.

We sat flat on the stony ridge, glassing the cedar-and-oak patch through the morning, trying not to doze off the way the deer all around certainly were. About noon a long line of javelina came out on the buck's hillside, to the north, heading on a line to him. They crunched through the leaf litter and kicked loose rock as we listened and watched. The closer they got to the buck, the more we hoped they would push him out of his bed; but the peccary turned downhill before they got near enough to him, descending to the water running through the bottom of the arroyo. They stood by the stream, then wheeled back north in unison, running, our scent perhaps having drifted down to them, but not across to the buck.

My ass and legs were DOA by 1 P.M. when Chris lay back, stretched out, and was soon asleep. Nothing seemed to move in the December ocotillo silence as I went on glassing, and I could appreciate the profound cultural wisdom of Mexican society's having appointed this naturally somnolent hour for the siesta. At one-fifty I heard rocks rolling underneath and woke Chris. He crawled to the edge of the ridge and looked down into the arroyo but he saw nothing.

Now we both watched the cedar-and-oak patch. There was a bare spot, a circle of red dirt in the middle, right above where the buck had gone to ground four hours earlier. At two-oh-nine the patch contained only red. At two-ten there was gray in the red.

Chris and I glassed the buck, only then seeing how very, very good he was. He headed uphill, stopping every few feet to browse. I had him locked in the crosshairs, and Chris said to wait until he picked up his head so I didn't shoot through and hit antler. The buck raised his head and turned, quartering more, giving me a more solid target, and I told Chris I would take him.

At the shot there was a hard thump and the buck sprang downhill, vanishing into the cedars and oaks. We watched for him to run out, but he did not.

"If we were in Arizona," whispered Chris, "we'd head over there right now. You shoot at a buck up there and miss, and he's running. I'm pretty sure this one is dead, but I just don't know about these Mexican deer."

Nothing moved for several minutes. Then Chris and I decided that he would circle around the hill the buck was on and come up from behind, leaving me to keep an eye out in case the buck was not down and busted from cover. Chris dropped down our ridge into the arroyo, disappearing behind the hill. A few minutes later he reappeared in a saddle above the cedar-and-oak patch and walked down into it, going out of sight in the bushes that grew over his head. The silence, if anything, got deeper than the background December ocotillo silence.

I couldn't stand it anymore and shouted, "Well?"

"He's dead," came Chris's answer.

I hollered in relief.

"How's he look?"

And of course he answered, "Perfect."

Oscar came down, and after I got the blood back in my legs we made our way together off the ridge and into the arroyo, then climbed straight up to the buck. He lay in the shade on his back, caught on a heavy root where he slid and fell after being hit behind the right shoulder. He was fat and big for a Coues' deer, with antlers that were an exquisite jumble of twelve points. We gutted him and carried him down to the arroyo and out to where we could reach him with a pickup and carry him back through the sycamore canyons and cactus plains to the ranch house.

That night, lighted by lanterns and a fire, in our shirtsleeves, chilled cans of *cerveza* set on the ground near at hand, we skinned the buck as he hung head-down from the thick limb of an old oak. A half circle of vaqueros, young and old, watched, white straw hats set square on their heads, and their hands behind their backs out of politeness. With the gray hide off, we cut out the backstraps and gave them to the cook for tamales and to wrap in tortillas. The vaqueros would take the rest of the meat and the hide, and I would have the twelve-point head to carry back north, after some fine meals of venison. And perfect wasn't the word for it. The word was *perfecto*.

# CHAPTER 17

*For half an hour the land had been as dark as the ocean on a moonless night. The first light was at Spotted Horse, so we pulled off to have a drink. The bartender was alone. He stood behind the bar in a T-shirt and tractor cap, blinking as we walked in.*

*"Buy a drink?" I asked.*

*The question seemed to stump him. Then he bent down and set out the bar's entire stock: a fifth of Black Velvet, half a plastic fifth of generic vodka, the bottom of a half-pint of Jim Beam.*

*"Glasses?" I ventured.*

*The bartender thought. He found two Dixie cups under the counter, blowing the dust out of them.*

*"I'll have some Coke and Jim Beam," my friend Toby said.*

*The bartender walked back to the glass cooler and pulled out the single can of Coke standing on the steel rack.*

*"Cooler's broken. Coke's hot," he said, feeling the side of the can with the palm of his left hand.*

*"You mean 'warm'?"*

*"Hot."*

*"Ice?"*

*The bartender disappeared into a room behind the bar and came out with an aluminum tray holding four eroded cubes.*

*Toby and I each fixed a drink while the bartender ciphered what we owed.*

*"Don't get many people out this way, do you?" I said.*

*The bartender did not look up.*

*Toby and I raised our Dixie cups.*

*"To the antelope," I toasted.*

*"To the antelope."*

# PRESBYOPIA, PRONGHORN &
# BLOOD ON THE POET

**When I was** a suburbanite—born, raised, and aged on the outskirts of a great Pacific Rim metropolis—I saw things as a suburbanite. Hunting at that time was an extraordinary undertaking that only became credible after long, sometimes tortuous journeys to what seemed exotic locales, exotic if for no other reason than the thinness of their human populations, compared to home, and the visible presence of wild animals. Then I moved, rather late in life, to one of those exotic locales; and my hunting began to become, in the words of novelist Thomas McGuane, "less and less expeditionary"—not only unexpeditionary, but unexceptional, as well.

What I fell victim to in short order was the transplanted suburbanite's disease of instant redneckhood. The pose I adopted was one of taking hunting for granted. It was almost understandable, in a way, especially if you took pronghorn hunting as an example.

One of the first places I hunted antelope after leaving the city was not out on some classically unbroken prairie where the skies were not cloudy all day, but under scattered showers among scrapped farm implements, dismantled silos, and the toppled skeletons of windmills. Despite appearances, the area had, in fact, been painstakingly prepared as a landing site for UFOs, according to the eccentric hermit rancher who owned the place, and who was ultimately crushed beneath an avalanche of his own yard junk before he ever made contact with the extraterrestrials he was certain were en route. (Or maybe he did make contact.)

Despite entrenched fantasies of picturesque western vistas, game is where you see it, and one year a goatheard-cheesemaker-poet friend Dainis ( . . . —o . . . /the glory days are nearly/here/dear—&—done—the littlest/assembling on wind-raked limbs,/clack-twittering . . . ) showed me the antelope on his prime hunting grounds on public land in the semi-arid heart of the state of Wyoming, a place he found no less than beautiful. No UFOs here, just rumbling Terex earth haulers carting ore from the uranium mines. The terrain was cobbled with tailings, landfills, and fenced-off sections bearing signs warning of the irradiated consequences of trespass. Steel crickets bobbed monotonously, pumping crude, while gas wells started methane on its way to Chicago and cattle wandered among the greasewood. All in all, a sans-daffodil panorama likely to inspire little awe and fewer ballads. In most people.

Still, the tall mesas and Native petroglyphs, sage and sage grouse, mule deer and pronghorn, and Dainis's secret dry campsite tucked in a grassy gap between stony ridges and in a patch of ancient junipers and limber pines, where the northern lights were visible at night and where no one else had set foot since Dainis camped there the year before—all that should have shown me something of the grave beauty Dainis's eye managed to discern. Yet even though it was a couple of hundred miles from our homes, the locale seemed, at first, no more striking and no farther away to me than a backyard campout, compared with the interstate hunts of my past. And because the hunt's apparent homeliness made it seem somehow less serious, I had brought what I considered my somewhat less-serious rifle.

I have no-nonsense rifles I carry for their cold efficiency, and others because they happen to strike my aesthetic fancy. Now I had a Browning Model 1885 single-shot, "high-wall" .45–70 with a crescent steel buttplate and buckhorn sights. Over the years I'd used it to take whitetail, black bear, wild boar, even alligator and buffalo, but I still thought of it as a casual option, an adequate hundred-yard rifle for this local hunt. After all, I wouldn't be hunting for a head, but just a doe to stuff in the freezer. That's the way I saw it, anyway.

Two or three good hours of light remained in the day after we got the tent up, and Dainis and I headed out in his old Blazer to wander the two-track trails to acquaint me with the territory and to glass for pronghorn. Several times we spotted small bands off in the sage, too far to shoot and too problematic to stalk, at least on the first day.

In the late afternoon, a dozen antelope crossed in front of us and jogged out into a big flat. The band's alpha buck took it into his head to run off a potential usurper; and the two animals raised golden trails of dust like rocket cars on a

dry lakebed as they crossed nearly a mile of flatland, achieving velocities more usually seen in stooping raptors.

Back in camp that night, we ate elk-port-and-chestnut stew I'd brought from home, along with a salad made from the last lettuce and nasturtiums from Dainis's summer garden, his bona fide goat's-milk feta, and home-baked bread. Afterward in the lanternless dark, zipped inside my down bag and listening to the tent walls luff in the wind, I watched pronghorn, backlit by sunset, race across the backs of my eyelids until even that light was gone.

We were out at daybreak the next day, hunting from the moment we left camp. There were bands of antelope near the road, but we passed them by, until at midmorning we spotted a fair-sized bunch tucked into a little bowl, a place where it might be possible to stalk up on them from behind the cover of a ridge. Dainis, who had not even drawn a pronghorn tag this year (but who wanted to show me "his place" anyway), came with me on the stalk, and was just behind me when we peeked over the ridge and spotted the nearest pronghorn out a hundred yards. As soon as we looked over, the antelope looked back, the bedded ones getting to their feet. They hesitated, and I had only a moment.

I got a sitting rest with the .45–70, and that's when I saw something I hadn't seen before. When I'd sighted-in the rifle back in the summer, the buckhorn sights had looked fine; but now as I held them on the doe who was the closest pronghorn to me, they had been transformed into a bat-silhouette smudge. I blinked twice, wiping my trigger hand across my eyes. The doe was 20/20, but the sights got no better. I set the blurred blade into the even-more-blurred notch as best I could, and told myself I was on. Thumbing back the knurled hammer, I pressed my finger to the trigger.

The shot was more a dull thud than a sharp crack, and all the antelope were running. The doe ran widest, circumnavigating the inside of the bowl, until after two hundred yards her run changed to a jog, then a walk.

"Miss," said Dainis, glassing her. "Low."

I was glassing her, too, now, but wasn't so sure. Then I saw the stain of red, back of her brisket. She stopped, then lay down, head up. The rest of the pronghorn were trotting out of the bowl and out into the sage, and the last one to leave was the largest buck. He paused beside the doe, butting her with his muzzle. When she would not stand, he left her and followed the band.

She lay on the far side of the bowl, and I thought I saw a way of slipping around behind the ridge and coming out where I could get a close, finishing shot. I gave her almost half an hour, thinking she would stiffen up; but when I went around, then crossed over a saddle and edged along the base of a low hill, I ended up a longer way from her than I'd estimated, her looking right at me, as if expecting me. She sprang up and ran.

I watched her, trailing her long-gone band, as her run turned to a walk after a quarter mile. She wove slowly through the sage and greasewood, then dropped from sight. There must have been a wash there, because I did not see her reappear after several minutes of watching.

Now I really had to wait, and Dainis and I hiked back to the Blazer and sat, sat for a full hour in silence, watching white clouds drift across a blue September sky. As I sat, trying not to think about the antelope, I saw a number of things more clearly than I had before: That somehow, without quite knowing how, I had developed old man's eyes; that I'd have to get very close to finish the doe; that all hunting, no matter how near or seemingly mundane, whether for a head or not, was serious; that no rifle was ever less than serious, every one capable of perpetrating serious deeds. I saw all that, and saw even more the inescapable duty owed every animal we hunt: I had to see to it that that pronghorn doe did not end up lying out in the sand and brush.

After an hour, Dainis and I got out of the Blazer and began tracking. The blood had dried or soaked into the porous soil, so the trail was a broken one. I'd carefully marked the spot where the doe had dropped from sight, though, and we were able to walk directly to it. There was a wash there, and I moved cautiously to the edge and looked over.

She lay on the other side on a little shelf on the steeply cut bank, her head no longer up but tucked against her chest. She lifted it when she saw me and stood again, but this time slowly and unsteadily. She did not run, but staggered, and after no more than twenty yards she fell. In the end I was able to walk to within feet of her, coming from behind so she would not see. We dressed her and placed her in the back of Dainis's Blazer, using canteen water to rinse our hands.

Back in camp, Dainis and I lifted her into a gnarled juniper, and after skinning her we pulled a cotton game bag around her. That night we had mule deer, merlot, beet cake, and a couple of Nicaraguan cigars. Checking the ash on mine, I thought of the things I'd need to see to, now that I'd seen to the pronghorn: new reading glasses; ghost-ring sights for the .45–70 so I could hunt with it seriously; a new respect for the gamelands and the game at hand, those things close by not to be seen as less significant than those far away.

In the last of the evening light, I looked to the juniper at the edge of the beautiful camp. The pronghorn was still there, turning in the wind, almost cooled out. At this distance, she resembled something or someone white-robed, floating above the ground. Floating, or maybe ascending.

# Chapter 18

*What's in a name? Consider Roosevelt's elk.*

*Nineteenth-century naturalists tended to be "lumpers" or "splitters." Lumpers believed that a caribou, for example, was the same species wherever you found it. Splitters, on the other hand, seemed able to distinguish numerous subspecies and types for each animal, which granted them, perhaps a little too conveniently, the honor of naming those subspecies.*

*Theodore Roosevelt, an adamant lumper, very publicly ridiculed splitters, particularly the most prolific, C. Hart Merriam. Revenge, a dish best eaten in scientific journals, may have been Merriam's when in 1897 he named the oversized elk of the Pacific Northwest after the then–Assistant Secretary of the Navy, noting that it was "fitting that the noblest deer in America should perpetuate the name" of . . . Roosevelt. No record exists of Roosevelt's objecting, and one is permitted to envision Merriam's sly smile.*

# ELK IN THE HIGHWOOD

*Elk, what do you eat?*
*Sage I eat.*
*Elk, what dish do you use?*
*Stone dish I do use.*

　　　　　　　　*—Ancient Blackfoot children's song*


**In truth, elk** eat about whatever's set in front of them, stone dish or no. They draw their balanced diet from a catholic list of foods, from buttercups to clover, pines to mushrooms, with a bull eating his own shed antler velvet and a cow consuming her placenta to conceal all trace of her calf's birth. An elk will even eat sage.

This utter lack of finicalness always served the elk well, particularly during that time when he was the most far-flung of American deer—indeed, of American ungulates. He was once, outside of such extremities as Maine and Florida, a native of almost any habitat on the continent between the Atlantic and Pacific littorals, from the subarctic well down into Mexico. Ten million is the figure often quoted for the elk's peak population in this expanse of land, that peak able to be reached, more tragically than ironically, when elk were freed from the hunting pressure of Native Americans, who were mowed down by European disease and European powder and ball.

When the first English-speaking settlers encountered two new varieties of deer, they quickly named one, the whitetail, "deer" after the roe deer still common on their island home. Nothing in their past experience, though, prepared them for the sight of the other, the one the Shawnee called *wapiti*, meaning "white rump," who was so large and unfamiliar a beast that they resolved to call it "elk," concluding it must be quite similar to the Scandinavian moose of the same name—a beast with whom they also happened to be completely unfamiliar. No matter. In short order those settlers did learn that this elk was exceptional fare; and as they pushed farther into the depopulated Indian territories, that ten-million figure began to dwindle. By 1922 the number was more like ninety thousand for the continent as a whole. Only after long struggle and much good effort has the species been restored today to a million head or more in North America.

When in 1755, in the company of Crees, the fur trader Anthony Henday became the first white man to venture into the Blackfoot country of Alberta (then part of that vast stretch of Canadian soil known as Rupert's Land, comprising all the drainage of Hudson Bay and granted in 1670 to the Hudson's Bay Company by the English monarch), he observed elk roaming all across its southern plains, the animal (both Rocky Mountain and Manitoban subspecies) being distributed at that time throughout the province's present geographic area to within fifty miles of the Northwest Territories' southern boundary. Then during the nineteenth century the great extirpation, by many causes but mostly by the hand of man, got under way. Before it ended, Alberta could boast in 1913 of having three herds, totaling exactly as many elk as the days in a year. (Even at that the elk of Alberta were still doing far better than the Eastern and the Merriam's subspecies, which had already been handed their eternal hats.)

Prior to the 1917–1920 period when Rocky Mountain elk were transplanted from Yellowstone—the incubator and salvation of the species—to bring about the regeneration of Alberta's elk, one of the remnant herds retreated to the Highwood Range in the foothills of the Rockies southwest of Calgary. It may be that the herd had even retreated as far back as 9,126-foot Mount Head that I saw in the dark western sky, the mountain rising like a granite cake made of a dozen thin layers filled in between with white icing.

The mountain swallowed the western horizon. From the bare hill we had climbed before dawn on a cold Tuesday morning in late October, the Austrian-born Alberta Registered Class A Guide Joe, my friend Paul, and I took turns using Joe's Austrian spotting telescope to look north across the valley of Sullivan Creek at the herd of elk feeding distantly up a draw of yellow timothy grass. As the sun slid into the valley, we could distinguish the bulls' antlers at that far reach, not as solid acorn-colored branches, but as faint nimbi of ivory tips carried high above their heads. These elk were not going to remain in the open for long in the daylight, and as we watched, in single file they all moved into the spruce and poplars standing around the pasture's edge and were gone. Joe collapsed his telescope, and we headed off the hill. Elk season opened the next day.

The night before in Calgary, Paul and I ate hot moose sausages and potato salad with Joe and his wife in their home. Joe told us how he had come to Alberta from hotel and restaurant school in Austria with no funds and only a job in a hotel waiting for him. In his kitchen after dinner, he deftly butchered the antelope he had shot a few days before, summarily turning it into butterflied steaks, roasts, schnitzel, and stew meat. ("You must use meat with sinew for stews," he instructed, trimming an antelope shank down to the pale yellow bone. "A stew is never good the first time you cook it, but only after it has been reheated two or three times. Without sinew, you end up with a . . . a . . . *meat*

soup!") Joe told us how he had gone from kitchen worker to being a sommelier to managing restaurants to at last owning one of Calgary's finest French restaurants. In Alberta he had also found the kind of hunting he longed for when he lived as a boy in Europe and some of his greatest sport had been poaching the trout from the parish priest's private beat. He would confess his crime to the priest every Sunday morning before serving Mass, only to have to slink back into the confessional the next Sunday morning, the very same sin once more blighting his immortal soul and causing him to tremble with an almost lustful delight. Within days of his arrival in the New World he had gone out on his own and taken his first royal elk, this leading him inevitably into guiding.

It was the classic struggling immigrant's tale. Later, over delicate and finely made pewter tumblers of ten-year-old schnapps, Joe brought out the photo album and showed us the family castle.

The next morning, after coming down off that hill after scouting the elk, we drove into the creek valley on a gravel road and came to Joe's friend Laurie's ranch, out of which we would be hunting. Laurie, wearing his red rancher's cap and a beaded and fringed elk-hide jacket, greeted us in his low-talker's voice that made him sound as though he were forever sharing a confidence. He was skinny but strong and walked in the slightly creaky way of someone who in his younger days had climbed up on 'em and let 'em buck. In his way he was as much an immigrant to this land as Joe, his family having broken and settled it just a generation before. Besides being the edge of the elk's original range in Alberta, this Highwood country had not so long ago been the edge of the Blackfoot's home territory as well.

The Blackfoot was a Plains Indian, but his vision quests often bore him up to such high hazardous places as Mount Head back there, where he would build his tiny lodge of brush and leaves and for many days, through singing, prayer, fasting, and dreams, wait alone for his spirit helper to come to him to show him the way for his life to follow. Beside him would be his filled pipe, ready to offer to his secret helper when he came. And often he came as Elk.

Although nomads of the plains, which they burned down with some regularity—and in so doing maintained the grasslands and benefited the wild grazers—and people of the buffalo, which they ran down on the prairies or drove over cliffs at places such as Head-Smashed-In Buffalo Jump or Old Woman's Buffalo Jump near Cayley, just a little way east of the ranch, the Blackfoot were also chronic hunters of elk. Unlike other tribes who feared the big deer's turning and goring them and their riding stock, the Blackfoot insisted upon pursuing elk exclusively from horseback. In point of fact, the Blackfoot insisted upon pursuing everything from horseback, feeling—like the Northern Shoshone and the mountain men who learned their etiquette from them—demeaned if called upon to cover even the least distance on foot. (James Willard Schultz, another fur trader and a hunting guide of the late 1800s, wrote about his adopted Blackfoot tribe's "slender-legged men . . . who hunted on horseback or not at all.")

Perhaps the Blackfoot sat so resolutely astride his pony because he recalled with little nostalgia the time before the conquistador's beast's appearance on the scene, when he had been a dog Indian, his mobility limited by how heavy a packload his meat-eating dog could carry, or how big a travois it could drag. When at last he got the horse, the Blackfoot took a careful measure of it against the dog and asked himself how he had ever managed to live so long without his trusty steed. As for the dog, the Blackfoot's years of forced familiarity with it had probably bred such fierce contempt that this was the reason the tribe, unlike neighboring ones who found it quite the delicacy, steadfastly refused ever to dine upon the creature.

It was from horseback, and at any season, that the prideful Blackfoot overtook elk on the prairie or rode them over jumps or drove them into water where he could kill the animals with his bow, lance, or Winchester '73. He found a lone animal more difficult to catch, more prone to running on, while it was usually easier to cut one out of a herd as the animals bumped and ran into each other, tiring themselves out more rapidly. The Blackfoot's preference was for a large mature bull, who would yield the most meat. The effort required for taking a smaller animal was not that much less, while the reward could be considerably so. It was simple economics, yet the Blackfoot also taught his sons to view the bull elk as an exemplar of gallantry.

Though the buffalo—whose herds were more a broad phenomenon of the local climate, like average days of sunshine or annual rainfall, than a collection of individual organisms—were the main source of the Blackfoot's not inconsequential wealth, permitting him a life of some luxury marked by regular feasting and gambling, elk were also of great value to him. Curiously, he was not overly fond of the flavor of elk meat, finding it too "sweet," too much like the white man's prized beef; yet he would turn to it readily enough whenever he could not obtain bison. (All parts of the elk were eaten by the Blackfoot, noted George Bird Grinnell—the great hyphenate who in his lifetime was an anthropologist-conservationist-sportsman-explorer-author and member of any number of other chosen professions—"save only the lungs, gall, and one or two other organs.")

From the elk hide the Blackfoot made robes, shirts, dresses, dancing skirts, moccasins, leggings, war shields; tipis, lean-tos, and ground cloths; parfleches, ropes, and belts. He would use it also as an item of exchange in intertribal bartering. The antlers served him as bows, saddletrees, and fleshing tools, the points becoming wedges for splitting wood or for the knapping of his flint arrowheads before he turned to iron to tip his shafts. As many products and trophies as there were from the elk, the ones most esteemed were its tusks.

These two round upper canines, stained by plant juices, called bugler teeth, whistlers, or simply ivories, had been used as ornamentation by the Indian for almost fifty centuries. No other part of any animal, not bear teeth and claws, not the fangs and claws of cougar, not wolf teeth, bison teeth, or horse teeth, was so highly valued. Elk tusks were the Indian's "Star of Delhi."

It was the immense effort that went into gaining the ivories that gave them such worth. Years of hunting, and bargaining with other hunters, were needed to acquire the sometimes hundreds, or in one case over fifteen hundred, elk teeth required to sequin a woman's dress. A dying hunter would bequeath his ivories to his heirs as their legacy. The Crow, instead of having to quest for their visions and "medicine," might purchase them outright for the sum of five hundred ivories—though it cannot be said who the merchant for such a transaction might be. One tremendously wealthy Shoshone village in southern Montana, visited by a Chicago newspaper writer in 1901, was reported to have twenty thousand ivories in its possession. The Blackfoot came to value the elk's ivories only about the time he obtained firearms, but a woman's gown adorned with only a single horizontal row of teeth might fetch in trade two good horses, each "the best buffalo horse."

Before the 1870s a brave acquired elk ivories only to present to his wife, choosing for himself to wear no more than one or two on a pendant or a bracelet. (The only Indian men who wore elk ivories on their clothes were homosexual transvestites—who were held in high regard by their tribes—or "clowns" who impersonated women on ceremonial occasions.) But as the Indian encountered increasing numbers of white men—many of whom were members of a fraternal order associated with the elk, but who had in all likelihood never seen a live one, let alone hunted one—wearing with much self-satisfaction the ivories of elk on the fobs dangling out of the watch pockets of their vests, he, the Indian, began in sad mimicry to don his own ivoried vest.

At the conclusion of his epoch as a hunter of the elk—and with the elk devastated by market hunting for its meat, hides, and tusks—the Indian could be found outside his lodge, carving bone into simulacra of ivories to sell to white men. The workmanship was said to be first-rate, and to the untrained eye the final product was nearly indistinguishable from the genuine.

That was all some time ago, of course. And the amazing thing is not what the elk was subjected to, but that he survived it, and with the eventual aid of sounder laws and sounder management—in short, greater restrictions on men's hands—survived it so well; so well, in fact, that there are today more chances to hunt him than at any time in the last hundred years.

On opening morning of Alberta's elk season on Laurie's ranch, Joe and Paul were gone long before dawn, climbing on foot through the darkness up the backside of the ridge above the timothy grass draw, packing their rifles and binoculars and the spotting telescope. Laurie and I were going to ride—across a pasture, then into the timber and far back into the country we believed the elk would be passing through later as the sun rose.

The coffee was still warm in me as I came out of the old cabin where I slept in a bed with an white-painted iron bedstead, carrying across the ranch yard my beeswaxed rifle scabbard under one arm and my .375 slung on my shoulder. Beyond the log rails of the corral fence I saw the square block of light inside the stable where Laurie saddled our horses. Looking up, I saw in the night sky the bright fires of all the constellations whose names I still had not gotten around to learning.

The horse Laurie saddled for me was part thoroughbred and part quarter horse. He was a big gray gelding who in the daylight looked almost blue. His name was Joker, and this Joker was a tad wild.

As best I could gather from what Laurie whispered to me in the stable, up until the past moose season when he and Joe had used Joker as a pack animal, the horse had been solid as Gibraltar. Then came an unbalanced load, a smashed pannier, and about four hundred pounds of dead moose scattered to hell and gone again across a willow swamp, and Joker was left a mite on the touchy side. As we waited for some light to come into the eastern sky before setting out, I spent my time stroking Joker's head and neck and shamelessly trying to ingratiate myself into his good graces.

The weather, Laurie told me while we waited, was not good. Too dry and warm for this time of year. Too likely to keep the elk in the timber where stalking them would be difficult. This opening morning would give us the best chance for taking an elk until the snows finally came later in the season and pushed the herds down from Mount Head.

At last in gray light we saddled up. And Joker was off like a shot, shod hooves striking blue sparks on the cobbled floor of the stable. We sailed through the open corral gate and across Sullivan Creek, named for a family of dead pioneer children taken by disease. We galloped out of the creekbed and onto the edge of the pasture, and even with me hauling manfully on his reins, Joker snorted and flew directly into a pile of brush and dead timber, trying to scrape me off. We tacked and maneuvered awhile, and I managed to get him pulled around in time for a breathless Laurie to catch up and compliment me on my horsemanship. I smiled at him modestly—though I will admit that in the dim light somebody could easily have taken it for a paralyzed look of sheer terror—and didn't suggest that "good horsemanship" was another way of saying "knotheaded horse."

We rode silently through Herefords, heading for the timber at the far end, when Laurie pulled up his horse and stared across to a distant edge of the wide pasture.

"Elk," he whispered more softly, if possible.

There was still not enough light for me to recognize them clearly, but Laurie got down and used his binoculars, then swung back into the saddle. We swept around to the pasture's edge where it abutted the poplars and spruce growing down off a high east-facing ridge. We dismounted, tethering the horses to the trees, my heart exalted to be off Joker's back. Pulling my .375 from the scabbard, I followed Laurie.

"Hurry. Quiet. Hurry. Quiet," he alternately commanded as we moved through the trees. Then there was the herd in front of us, grazing on the pasture's edge fewer than two hundred yards away, behind them a lingering polyp of spruce timber extending into the pasture, with more empty pasture beyond it sloping back down to Sullivan Creek. Laurie pointed out the bull. It was hard to calculate tines, but from the length and volume of his rack, and for my first elk, he looked more than respectable.

One of the cows began to move up the slope into the trees, and I saw that the morning feeding was all but ended. This seemed sooner in the hunt to kill an elk than it should be—certainly sooner than I had anticipated—but as in hunting any big-game animal, it was the elk who set the agenda. As carefully and silently as I could, I worked the bolt on my Model 70 and chambered a 270-grain round. Taking a rest on a stump, I let all the cow elk drift out from behind the nearly snowy bull, his belly, neck, and raised head chocolaty in color, his antlers laid back. I let off the safety, drew in a breath and expelled one half, put the reticle behind his right shoulder, and sque-e-e-ezed the trigger. And missed. A classic clean All-American warning shot, known in every sporting country around the globe. No harm, though hardly no foul. As the elk wheeled and stampeded into the spruce peninsula behind them, I was tempted to shout after them, "Just kidding!" while dancing a merry little jig and waggling my hands like jackass ears at the sides of my head, the silver bells jingling from the many peaks of my fool's cap.

Laurie, on the other hand, knowing exactly where the elk were headed, took off at a dead run; I, behind him, at a dead trot. We wound along a game trail at the edge of the pasture, which carried us across the neck of the spruce stand. Then we saw the open pasture below, and there was the bull standing at the edge of it with two cows, the rest of the herd already gone into the trees and headed for the ridgecrest. The bull was a little over 320 paces away, and there was no place for me to take a rest. I sat, but the wild grass was too tall, so I had to kneel to see over it. I worked the action once more, and the bull stood broadside to me, and this time the sound of the bullet hitting his shoulder was louder than the shot itself.

The bull turned away from the cows as they bolted into the trees and walked slowly into the pasture. I ran down to a young broken poplar and took a rest on its greenish, smooth bark. The distance was now 265 paces when I worked the bolt and hit him again. He began to stagger, his head low to the ground, then he toppled. We hurried down to him.

He lay quietly, head up, the cows barking to him from the timbered ridge. Another bull up there somewhere whistled. The hardiness and defiance of elk are legend—actually they surpass legend—and when we got to within eighty paces of the bull he recognized us and clambered to his feet. Now he was a mass of energy, the $E$ in him equaling something far in excess of $mc^2$ as he tried to escape. My final shot broke his neck as he ran.

He lay within the perimeter of the stand of young poplars, the naked trees like a gray mist spreading down the ridge face. I jacked out my empty cartridge and set my open rifle against a tree. In honor of the Joe's Old World traditions, I cut a *Bruch* (branch) from the nearest tree and give the elk his "last bite." Clipping the metal license tag around the base of his antlers, I knelt and lifted them up.

The antlers were long-pointed and ivoried. One side had five points; the other, six. Each of the six points had a name. They were brow, bez (or bay tine or simply "dog killer," the tine the elk sighted along like a fencer along his foil when it was carried *en garde*, and which should be longer than the brow tine), trez, dagger, and the forked terminal. Even the raised beaded rim around the seal where the antler base joined the pedicel had its name, being called the coronet. An elk bull had to grow an entirely new set of antlers, from coronets to terminals, every year.

This is how he grew them: Triggered by testosterone and nerves, an antler buds out of the pedicel (part of the elk's forehead bone and the remnant of his ancient "dawn antler") by a buildup of cartilage, which under the blood-rich velvet covering creates a fibrous bone matrix that becomes impregnated with inorganic materials—mostly ash, calcium, and phosphorus—mineralizing, in its way, not unlike the petrifying of a tree. The result after the velvet is shed is dead bone stained dark by the elk's slashing and rubbing against plants and trees, with the tips polished white and the tines constructed along a six-point plane so bulls can grapple with each other but still be able to disengage easily.

Yet as I sat beside my dead elk—the first elk of my life—waiting for Laurie to bring the horses down so we could dress and pack out the bull, watching still another herd of Albertan wapiti move over the top of the ridge, followed in only a minute by the skulking black shape of a cow moose traversing the sun-warmed face of the ridge—the moose all long white-stockinged legs and lumbering trepidation—I much preferred not to consider science but to speculate about how many fine hunting bows the Blackfoot could have made from antlers such as these.

When I left Alberta some days later, I carried into Calgary's modern jet airport, built out on a stretch of prairie where the Blackfoot once ran their extravagant strings of hunting ponies, one fleshed elk skull and antlers, a fleshed and salted elk hide, a large quantity of cut, frozen, and wrapped elk meat (including meat with sinew for stews), and two elk ivories tucked into the top left pocket of my buffalo-plaid shirt. At customs they asked me what it was I had to declare, and the answer seemed obvious. Or not.

# Chapter 19

*Caribou are the deer of the North. Shaped by the snows of millennia, they are completely at home in the country of winter. Theirs are the lands so recently emerged from beneath the snow and glaciers of the great ice age: the windswept tundra, the "land of little sticks" where the stunted trees of the boreal forest cease their northward march, the ice-hung cordilleras. Over these meager lands they travel, obeying the commands of the seasons: the melting of snow, the budding of plants, the hatching of mosquitoes, the freeze-up of lakes and rivers. Like the wind that passes over the tundra wilderness and is gone, caribou are forever on the move. They appear on one distant horizon and vanish on the other. And it is their comings and goings that set the cadence of life on the barren-lands.*
                    —George Calef, *Caribou and the Barren-lands*

# TOUR DE CARIBOU

**Two-hundred years ago**, the capstone of any English gentleman's education was "The Grand Tour." Having completed his formal schooling, the proper young Georgian would embark, often in the company of a tutor, on a year or two of travel through the capitals and historic rubble of Europe and the Levant. It was felt that through his beholding such man-made marvels as the cathedral of Notre Dame, the Parthenon and Pyramids, the glory that was Rome (and no doubt some duskier carnal wonders, as well), he would come to a richer understanding of the world and humankind, and thereby be better prepared to assume, along with a wife named Penelope, his ancestral estate in some place like Twickenham where, garbed in fox-hunting pink, he could live out the life of an unspeakable in pursuit of the uneatable, his wanderlust sufficiently sated.

While such Grand Tours are pretty much a thing of the past, there may be another, more important kind to be taken today—particularly by hunters—in order to experience marvels not man-made in the least, but which can teach us a great deal about wildkind. By definition, such tours would have to be of something foreign, "otherworldly" in the sense of being not what we can experience in the places where we were raised or where we usually go to hunt. Besides showing us something foreign, the tours I have in mind would also have to show us something extraordinary: extraordinary animals, and also extraordinary states of animal existence. The high-mountain sheep, the argali, of Central Asia might be one stop on a Grand Tour of Game, as would the giant eland of Central Africa. A record-book whitetail buck—never less than foreign and extraordinary in any place at any time, even in the woodlot behind your house—would always qualify.

Then there are the great herds and flocks, the encountering of which never leaves the encounterer quite the same. In times still within the extreme limits of living human memory, bison and passenger pigeons in the tens of millions were to be seen. Today, the sight and sound of tens of thousands of snow geese all lifting up before dawn, or wildebeest by the hundreds of thousands crossing sunlighted African plains can yet be experienced. And across the north of this continent moves one the most extraordinary marvels of the hunter's Grand Tour, the caribou.

At the beginning of the twentieth century, naturalist-writer-illustrator Ernest Thompson Seton estimated the number of caribou at thirty million, and while that figure is probably a good deal more speculation than fact, caribou numbers are certainly far less than what they once were. Yet the condition of the caribou, bearing in mind the general expansion and bumbling of humans, remains considerably less changed than that of other wild animals, so that today, from Alaska to Newfoundland, they number somewhere between three and four million. And where, across six and a half time zones, is the best place for a hunter to include on the itinerary of his Grand Tour if he wishes to experience caribou?

One September, I went to see caribou at Helluva Lake in northern Québec. On Helluva (pronounced *Hell-oo-va* rather than the more colorful *Hell of a*), a Native-owned hunting and fishing club named Tuktu had set up one of its numerous caribou-hunting camps. *Tuktu* means "caribou" in Inuit (or the animal we recognize as "caribou"), while the Neskapi, native to the country around Helluva, use the word *atiukw* (*at-chook*). The word "caribou" goes back to the early Algonquins, who called the animal, graphically, *mekalixpowa*, the "snow shoveler," and to the Micmacs, who knew him to be *xalibu*, "the pawer," for its penchant for scraping through the snow with its hooves to feed. Whatever their name, the caribou of northern Québec and Labrador represent one out of about every three caribou in all of North America.

On this Tour de Caribou I even had a tutor. Denis, who'd left the city and city life to work for Tuktu as a guide, was a trim dark-haired and bearded Québecois with, by his own admission, three passions: "zhe hunt," and after the hunt, "zhe weemen" ("weeth teets like elephant ears!" he added with characteristic Gallic suavity), and "zhe dreenk." On the sunny and warm first morning of the hunt, Denis showed me the way out of camp, taking me along a caribou trail through black spruce, then across a boggy meadow and some rocky creeks, and at last up a tundra-covered hill to a place about halfway to the crest where we could look back toward the lake to the east and south across an open valley to another hillside. And at a young bull five hundred yards to the southwest, feeding our way.

"Phantom of zhe toondra," said Denis, glassing the young bull. I glassed to the south; and a small herd of caribou was coming out of low cover eight hundred yards away, moving toward us. Hours, even days can be spent on the tundra without a single sighting of caribou. Then, without warning, there will be a couple of dozen, short white tails raised, swimming a lake; fifteen in a tight herd, trotting over a ridge; or a lone cow, forty yards away, staring at you. Or like now, one young bull, having moved to within three hundred yards, still unaware of us while the two bulls and two cows in the small herd came steadily on, nearly on a straight line to where we sat.

As I glassed the animals, I tried to write the description of a caribou for my imagined tour guide. With a gray face and body and a white neck, covered in air-trapping hairs, the caribou has the look of a creature evolution has not yet gotten around to streamlining. Its hooves are outsized (and are said to make a clicking sound as the caribou walks atop the spongy ground), and its muzzle is completely fur-covered (unique among herbivores and suited to the caribou's life of nuzzling away snow to uncover feed). Then there are the art-nouveau antlers it brandishes on its head.

While elk antlers are constructed with an almost heraldic symmetry—even culminating in "royals"—and the horns of wild sheep grow in equiangular spirals derived from the "divine section," caribou antlers are simply rigid states of chaos. They begin with the oddity of "shovels" and progress upward to the curiosity of palmated bezes. Then, particularly on the Québec-Labrador subspecies, come long bare arcs of main beams, punctuated often by back points that can go from no more than nubs to nearly two feet in length, until the multi-rayed tops, also palmated, are reached. And yet even this description may leave an impression of caribou antlers being structures far more orderly than they actually are. They are always a riddle inside a puzzle wrapped, frequently, in velvet.

The question was whether the steadily moving small herd—which we saw held two good bulls, one with what looked to be a tremendous set of bezes above the shovels—would get to us before the lone young bull, nearly on top of us, realized we were here and spooked, alerting the other caribou by his flight. When the small herd went out of sight in the brush below us, Denis and I shed our packs and moved in a crouch to where the herd would climb our hillside if it stayed on the line it followed. As we moved, I looked down the hill to where the young bull, having gotten to within a hundred yards of us, now ran away in the loose-limbed clop caribou use, his scut lifted. But the other caribou remained not only out of sight of us, but also out of sight of him, and they continued up the hill.

Denis and I reached a clump of brush with a small spruce growing out of it. I bolted a round into the .257 Weatherby Magnum I carried and set the safety, finding a rest for the rifle in the branches of the spruce. The caribou came out of the brush and onto the open hillside, sixty yards away. First there was a cow, then the smaller of the two bulls, then a set of gray-and-white velveted antlers, with those big palms out over the muzzle, all backlit by the sun. The caribou traveled at a steady walk and were not going to stop. To be sure of halting the bigger bull, I centered the duplex crosshairs of the scope on the front part of his shoulder and let off the safety.

When the 120-grain bullet took him in the shoulder, the bull locked up and the other caribou wheeled toward the sound of the shot. I put a finishing shot behind his shoulder; and the bull ducked his head to his left, his entire body following, spinning downhill to the ground, dead, as the rest of the herd ran.

As we crossed to the bull, the other caribou headed over the ridge above us. I could see that the caribou's bezes were actually some bizarre amalgam of bezes and shovels, fused together into two enormous *things*. I had permits for two caribou, and this one would do for the first. Denis and I quartered him, and by the time we had the meat and antlers back in camp, it was just past noon and all the good weather was gone.

So for the next three days we had the other kind of caribou hunting, the kind with bad weather and no animals. We hiked out every day to sit in the rain and cold among rocks turned brown from the iron oxidizing out of them.

Caribou hunting always seemed to be either/or: either famine or feast. But the "or" was something else I was hoping to see on my tour. Because the caribou are not only extraordinary in and of themselves, but also capable of massive migratory movements, of becoming *La Foule* or "the throng" as they moved to wintering grounds in one season, or back to calving grounds in another.

It was actually inaccurate to think of migrating caribou moving in a single mass, like flocks of blackbirds or shoals of fish, distributed evenly over the land. When the caribou moved, it was in small herds—sort of quanta of caribou—following select routes and paths, making for traditional water crossings (although these routes are subject to change, often drastic, without notice). When *La Foule* came, it was in what seemed an endless stream of quanta, rather than one pulse wave.

By late morning of the third day of bad weather, the sky began to lift and the caribou began to move (three days of bad weather, Denis believed, was often a portent of caribou to come). Looking to the far end of Helluva Lake from where we sat, dripping, in the hills above it, Denis pointed to what looked like a naval flotilla at this distance, but what was some three dozen caribou swimming, their insulating hides buoying them high out of the water, as if they were walking on a shallow bottom.

In the afternoon the rain stopped, and we traveled by freighter canoe to that far end of the lake, where the meadows looked as if they'd been torn up by the tires of mud buggies, when in fact no vehicle had ever been across them, only caribou hooves. Denis and I pulled the canoe up on shore and walked a few hundred yards from it to a spruce in the meadow. We were there five minutes before the caribou arrived.

We saw the white capes and antlers—some with velvet, some freshly peeled and blood-tinted, some even clean and dark-polished—of a small band of bulls coming through the spruce along the lakeshore, past our canoe. They seemed to have to turn and dip their heads to maneuver their racks through the dense timber. At last they came out into a clearing only thirty yards from us.

The lead bull was white and probably very old. Part of the purpose of my tour was to make meat for the winter, and caribou killed in early September be-

fore the rut was some of the best of venison. The caribou was looking slightly away from me, toward the lake, when the .257 bullet put him down. As Denis and I headed back up the lake a little later, meat and antlers in the canoe, more quanta of caribou moved through dark trees along the shore, or swam the lake behind and ahead of us, scuts hoisted, breasting water, shaking like retrievers when they climbed out onto the rocks.

It was a sunny morning the next day when we returned to the end of Helluva Lake, this time to photograph caribou. Again we landed the canoe and again we found spruce to stand behind, and the caribou were there almost immediately.

In a way it was good not to be hunting them today, not to have to worry about killing and quartering and packing, but only about getting them in focus as they proceeded, one after another, past us.

A million caribou, give or take, were on the move across northern Québec and Labrador, a number that surprised even the biologists. Whether there would still be a million in Septembers to come was anybody's guess. But for the time being in this distant country, thankfully, that was a matter almost entirely out of human hands.

I don't know if a hunter's education is truly incomplete if he never goes to the North and sees *La Foule*, or even just one caribou, all by itself. But I do know how incomplete mine would have been if I had never made my tour there and seen the caribou, perhaps not in the millions or even thousands, but certainly in the hundreds upon hundreds, moving around and across Helluva Lake that day. I would have known less about wildkind and my kinship to it.

After a while in the meadow, I even began to wonder what I was doing with a camera when there were all these caribou to see. So I let it hang around my neck, wanting nothing between me and the caribou moving around me, not even a glass lens.

The caribou walked past with little noise, their own Grand Tour a part of my Grand Tour. I stood motionless, being—a tourist? a sightseer?

If anything I was, I hoped, a witness, and a student. I knew all those caribou did nothing to sate any wildlust I had. They only succeeded in whetting it, the way knowledge fanned the desire for greater knowledge. Especially when I, listening hard, heard for the first time the actual clicking of hooves as caribou walked—wild-made music as important to hear as the bells of any basilica—the passing sound only making me want to hear more.

# Chapter 20

*"Moose was whale once. Away down Merrimack way a whale came ashore in a shallow bay. Sea went out and left him, and he came up on land a moose. What made them know he was a whale was that, at first, before he began to run in bushes, he had no bowels inside, but just like jelly fish."*

—Neptune, leader of the Penobscot,
quoted by Henry David Thoreau
in *The Maine Woods*

# AN IMPROBABLE ANIMAL

As Jack O'Connor said, "The moose is a pretty improbable animal." Just hunt one and you'll see what he meant.

To begin with, there is his curious physique—hump, bulging nose, short-proportioned body, and legs up to *here*. In the myths of the Abnaki, this was attributed to his having been squeezed out of shape in the hand of the giant Gloosknap. There's never been a bigger deer, nor one more widespread, being found almost anywhere on the terrestrial portions of the globe between the Arctic Circle and the fiftieth parallel of northern latitude, with excursions far south of that line. Whether called *elg*, *élan*, or *granbesta*, something all moose have in common anywhere in world is the kind of country they inhabit, which is invariably bad.

Another place moose inhabit, to a degree maybe greater than any other animal, is hunters' imaginations. According to the 1637 *Jesuit Relations* (the Québec missionaries' reports to Paris), it was the belief of North American Indians that to dream of a bear was ill-omened, except on the eve of a bear hunt. The moose, though, was an animal of good omen, and "those who dream of them often may expect a long life." As much as I've dreamed about moose, I guess I can expect to live forever. In my hunting life, as it is in the hunting lives of most, moose have been far thicker in dreams than on the ground. I killed a bull thirty-five years ago. It was the first one, and the last, until . . .

When I hunted moose in the Talkeetna Mountains of Alaska in August 1968, I had yet to understand that moose hunts seldom go as planned. I remember the lush tall greenness of the grass and stalking through alders to catch the bull as he climbed out on the far side of a draw. I only had time to kneel and hold behind his hump as he headed into another brush thicket. I fired one shot from the .300 Weatherby I carried and broke his spine and hit his lungs and the bull went backward like a horse rearing, tumbling into the grass of the draw. I climbed down to him and found fifty-inch-plus antlers flocked in velvet. The real work, of dressing, quartering, and packing, began after that.

If that hunt went like clockwork, the next one, many years later, went like Clockwork Orange. I hunted on horseback in a gray central British Columbia November, the hunt costing exactly three hundred dollars. The morning it began, I brought out the rifle scabbard I had purchased for the hunt, and slung it on the saddle of the horse I'd be riding. The Indian who was guiding me glanced askance at the unblemished leather as I cinched on the scabbard.

"That no be new," he said with undisguised disdain, "when you get back." And twelve hours later, he was right.

On that hunt, I rode five hours out from a backwoods cattle ranch, squeezing between lodgepole pines growing thirty-six inches apart, my knees beaten blue, until I arrived at an essentially undisclosed location. The guide and I would look for moose for two hours, find none, then ride five hours back, returning to the ranch in the dark, repeating as necessary. The highlight of the hunt was when we bumped into some cattle on the trail and the veteran ranch horse I rode spooked at the sight of them, blowing up underneath me, bucking me ribs-first into one of those lodgepoles and down into the snow. The fundamental reality of moose hunting had begun to sink in.

I actually saw a moose the next time out, but it wasn't mine. Four of us pitched a wall tent on the tundra along the Noatak in Alaska's High Arctic. Toward the end of our second week there, two of us were in camp, fleshing caribou capes, while the other two had headed out to hunt. That's when we heard shots in the alders behind the tent.

The two of us in camp looked at each other wide-eyed and—having seen the fearsomely large, instantly recognizable tracks along the river after a snowfall a few days before—voicelessly said in unison, "Grizzly!" We heard our other friends' shouts and called to them; and they called back, "Moose!"

One of them had shot a smallish, but legal, bull within two hundred yards of the gravel beach where the bush plane would land to fly us out in three days. So no "short quartering" this bull: We skinned him down to the pasterns and lashed a whole front shoulder or hindquarter to a packboard. Three of us would hoist the packboard onto the back of the fourth; and he would stagger, shinbones feeling as if they were bowing, to the river to pile the meat on a tarp where the plane could get to it—and we hoped the grizzly would not.

After that came a moose hunt by canoe on the Bigstone River in Manitoba. The fall weather was flawless, tamaracks turned to flame and the river a glass ribbon rippled by V's of beaver and mink. We paddled the same routes the voyageurs had when they made their way back to Hudson Bay with their bundles of plews; and every quarter mile we slid into the bank to make plaintive cow calls. Late one evening, our call was answered by the echo of a bull pulling his hooves out of the muck behind a poplar dam on a side channel and stepping onto the bank. He was five hundred yards from the canoe, walking away along the river, heading for a stand of spruce. The guide pulled quietly with his paddle, and I got my rifle, the .375, out of its soft case. I had the bull in the crosshairs as the distance closed slowly, and seemingly more slowly, until the bull vanished into the trees before I even had the safety off.

The next moose hunt turned into such a bad-weather, bush pilot-in-training, sodden-hip-boot, stinking-Visqueen-covered-camp, incompetently-outfitted-and-guided fit of the fantods, I'd rather not talk about it.

Finally, one September I hunted waterfowl in central Alberta with my old guide friend Stan. I'd hunted black bear on the Peace River with Stan more than fifteen years before; but that day, between Canadas and greenheads setting into the spread, we talked about the whitetail and mule deer—and moose—he guided for in November.

Moose. I was like Pavlov's dog hearing a bell, the word standing out in bas-relief in my head. A shaggy beast of the northern interior, our own interior as much as the country's, the moose just won't go away. A hunter with the tiniest drop of moose virus in his blood is never completely happy unless he is hunting moose, plotting to do so, or dreaming about moose, again. Where I live is in fact moose country—one of its southern excursions—with record-book bulls on the mountain directly behind my home, and youngish, disoriented ones sometimes wandering into town, to be shooed back out. Drawing a hunting permit for one, though, can be tantamount to winning Powerball. And here was Stan saying the word to set me free. Adding to that pressure was the shocking fact of my wife's genuinely wanting a moosehead on the wall—what she wanted was one of the audioanimatronic ones from Country Bear Jamboree, and I was planning on only bringing back antlers and meat, but all the same—so I had the authorization to proceed. After close to two generations, it seemed high time to kill another moose.

Having pursued moose mentally and physically for years, I couldn't help approaching even this hunt phlegmatically, though. Stan promised that there was a large number of moose in his hunting territory, which included tamarack, spruce, and willow swamps but also a good deal of farmland, so much farmland that he did not need to use horses but could access it all by ATVs or four-wheel-drive pickup, able to spot moose and stalk them. He told me that if I got there for opening day, November 1, he could very nearly guarantee that I would take a legal moose in six days of hunting.

If you've chased them enough, you know that the time line for a moose can include dozens of six-day hunts, made up of long, cold, wet rides and hikes, without a shot being fired. So I managed to curb my enthusiasm as I packed the truck with my gear and .375, and hoped I wasn't jinxing myself by throwing in a box of ammunition and game sacks for the quarters. Driving north through heavy snow and a zero-degree night, then into a beautiful fall Alberta day, I tried not to ask myself if I were on some fool's errand.

I reached Stan's on Halloween, and settled into my small sleeping cabin, waiting for the Trick-or-Treat that would come in the morning. Stan's plan was for me to hunt the first morning out of a stand he had set up in one of the swamps. It would likely establish some kind of record if I killed a moose out of a stand; but Stan had been seeing so many moose in that area, he was confident about a bull's passing by sometime during the day. I said it sounded all right to me, but in my heart I was satisfied just to be hunting moose again, no matter the outcome.

As I saw it, I would spend opening day in that blind, not fire a shot, and then for the next five hunting days Stan and I would pound the bush, and with luck perhaps find something that made the regulation minimum by carrying a few inches of visible antler. And the truth was, that would make me entirely happy.

After breakfast the next morning, having gotten into Stan's truck with my rifle and ammunition and gear, I was thoroughly prepared for the long haul. Moose always seemed to be the long haul, whether you got one or not. The sky was just starting to go salmon in the east when we pulled out of Stan's camp for the several-mile drive to the blind. When we got up onto the road, we could see the big pasture encircled by poplars at the back end of Stan's property, and he pulled over to glass into its dimness, from force of habit as much as anything else. In the pasture, past a cricket oil pump working in the dark, were two moose, both bulls. Stan turned to me. We stared at each other.

This wasn't the way a dramatic script for a moose hunt was supposed to play out; but recalling the sheer bathos of most of my other hunts, maybe it was time for some light comedy. Considering the improbability of moose in any case, this did make every bit as much sense as any other moose hunt; and who was I to look a gift bull in the mouth?

Conventional wisdom holds that it ought to be physically impossible to drive up to a moose, and we didn't want to spoil all the illusions. So, turning back to Stan's camp, we left the truck and hurried on foot along the edge of a poplar belt following a creekbed, going into the wind. We moved through the darkness toward the moose, and legal shooting time, our steps muffled by the soft snow banked up in the shadow line of the poplars. After several hundred yards we came to a break in the poplars and went through, coming into the pasture encir-cled by the poplars.

A small rise lifted out of the pasture ahead, and first we walked, then ducked, then crawled to the top on hands and knees. As we looked over, the two bulls were ninety yards from us, broadside, heads turned our way. Stan checked the illuminated dial on his watch; it was two minutes into legal shooting time. I rose to my knees with my rifle.

This was unlike any moose hunt I'd ever known, yet it reminded me of some-thing. I remembered Theodore Roosevelt's account of his hunt for moose in the Bitterroots a century-and-more before. He saw a "mighty marsh beast, strange and uncouth in look as some monster surviving over the Pliocene." The "vast bulk" of these moose, like that of Roosevelt's, "loomed black and vague in the dim gray dawn; huge antlers stood out sharply; columns of steam rose . . . from nostrils; then [they] began to turn, slowly, as if [they] had . . . stiff neck[s]." They were going to run; and Stan judged their antlers virtually equal, high, wide, and with good front pans.

For an instant I wasn't sure I wanted a moose this serendipitously. Then I recalled those thirty-five years of hunting moose, and knew that answer was, yes, I did want a moose this serendipitously, at least today. I'm not sure I even had a say, the moose, if you believed in the Native American notion of the game presenting itself to the hunter, having made the call. I put the crosshairs on the rear bull, holding low behind his right shoulder, and saw blue flame from the muzzle as the bullet hit. Both moose started forward as I worked the bolt and held the crosshairs on the same spot on the same moose. With the second shot there was a heavy whump of a bullet striking, and the rear bull went down in the pasture as the first made the cover of the poplars.

We hurried to the black, humped form in the pasture, but the moose was dead. As the sun rose and filtered into the pasture through the surrounding poplars, the black on the bull changed to brown and chestnut and blond, swirled together, and his antlers, the color of deciduous leaves after turning, got bigger, ending up at forty-eight inches in width. There was still the real work to do, but it would be more than worth it.

By midmorning we had the dressed carcass, representing six hundred pounds of edible meat, hanging in the skinning shack at Stan's camp, the bull's hind

hooves touching the rafters of the fourteen-foot ceiling while his antlered head lay flat on the plank floor. As I looked at the moose, I acknowledged the fact that I had not only never seen a moose hunt like this before, I was likely never to see one like it again. My moose hunting would undoubtedly revert to being "improbable" in the way I had always understood that term. I had had my moose moment, and would go back to the dreams of them, now, while trying to dream about bear only on the eves of bear hunts.

# Chapter 21

*How infinitely small is the span of the written word as compared with the thousands of years in which man fought the bear.*
                    —Mikhail Prishvin, *Nature's Diary*

# A KODIAK MOMENT

**That journal I** kept each day of my first hunt for Kodiak bear, now many years ago, was a ledger of disappointment. Or so it seemed at the time. For fifteen fall days I sat on the black gravel beaches of Kodiak Island in snow, sleet, downpour, and gale, and glassed the white peaks above Uyak Bay—when they were visible—for sign of a good boar bear. Whenever I sighted one, he always seemed to be four thousand-feet above the beach, moving through deep snow to the mountaintop to cross over and den up beyond reach on the other side. One particularly memorable day I watched a big boar—an animal weighing half a ton— *swim* through soft snow coming up to his chin. Reaching a sheer face of naked rock, the bear reared and without pausing proceeded straight up like a fly on a windowpane. I lowered my binocular in amazement and frustration and that night in camp wrote something uncalled for about Kodiak bear in my journal.

On a typical day of that hunt I might record sighting as many as nine bear, sows with cubs; how one single-parent family plodded by me on the beach with that deceptive ponderousness of theirs; or how the Karluk man with the remarkable name of Bill Ambrosia and I spent three hours in the alders and snow giving chase to a boar whose nonstop track showed that he had not had the common decency to break stride even once. After my fifteen-day brown bear permit expired, and having sighted nearly fifty bear without firing a shot, I went out on the sixteenth day and used my deer permit to take, as I wrote in what appeared to be the only bright spot in an otherwise dark journal, "a beautiful little Sitka blacktail buck among wild roses." Sometime before that, before I even knew for a certainty that I was not going to take a bear on that hunt, I realized I would be coming back, coming back for the island and the bear of the same name.

*Ursus arctos middendorffi*, the Kodiak bear, the "great grass-eating bear," the "great fish-eating bear," is the world's largest land-going carnivore, easily capable of weighing between twelve and fourteen hundred pounds, depending on the season, with a hide that can square out at ten foot or better. His sense of smell is nonpareil, his hearing keen, and his eyesight far less dull than humans try to kid themselves it is. In moments of inspiration the Kodiak bear can cover ground like a track star or move all day at a walking pace no man could ever hope to match. And although the big brown bear (and that's the way he, the coastal brown bear, and his cousins, the grizzly of the interior, are identified) has in him more curiosity than fear—and rogue bear have not been unheard of—he will be far and away more likely to steer a path around men than into them when he knows they are about—unless he decides not to.

No big-game animal besides him is native to Kodiak Island, though various ones have been introduced. Every summer throughout the millennia the Kodiak bear has had spawning salmon to forage on, and this protein-rich food is what gave his race its enormous size, and will add two hundred pounds or more to a bear's body weight between spring and fall. The Kodiak's biological genus also includes the fabled cave bear of the Pleistocene, *U. spelaeus*; and he doesn't have to be looked at too hard to see him as one of the last representatives of the megafauna—American lion, dire wolf, saber-toothed cat, giant bison and ground sloth; *mammoth!*—who roamed the wide, snow-free plain of Beringia. His strength is certainly Pleistocene (Bill Ambrosia once saw a wounded boar bite through an alder branch big around as a baseball bat); and in the event of your wounding or cornering him, he would have no trouble making hash out of you in what is widely regarded as "a jiffy."

A Russian zoologist, Middendorf, was the first scientist to report the huge bear of Kodiak Island in a paper published in 1851; and in 1896 C. Hart Merriam, not surprisingly, presented the first complete scientific description of him. By then, a lively trade in bear robes had sprung up, and the big brown bear was liberally slaughtered along the Alaskan coast and on Kodiak Island in the enterprise. The robes taken from bear all over Alaska were shipped out through the port of Kodiak by the Alaska Commercial Company, so the name "Kodiak" was applied indiscriminately to all big brown bear, whether found on the mainland or on the island. Luckily for all big brown bear, the robe trade dried up with the amending in 1902 of the Alaska Civil Code to provide for the protection of *U. arctos*, if only rudimentarily at the time. The bear came back after that, but within living memory some outdoor writers could still describe the elemental thrill of dropping a sow and her three yearling cubs in their tracks, or of taking several big boar on a single hunt; and as late as 1922 a Juneau newspaper would denounce a political hopeful merely by declaring a vote for him equivalent to a vote for Alaskan brown bear, believed them to be worthy only of extinction because of their robust appetite for salmon—the coastal dwellers' primary cash crop.

Alaskan hunting guides were the first to see the financial potential in Kodiak bear—not in the selling of their hides, but in the selling of hunts for them. The list of guides who learned their craft on Kodiak includes the names of Hal Waugh, Alaska Master Guide No.1; Park Munsey, who started guiding under Waugh; along with Earl Stevens and the famous duo of Talifson and Pinnell. The very first of those guides, though, was Captain Charley Madsen. As early as the 1910s, this old-time trading-vessel skipper had taken up guiding for big

brown bear on the peninsula and all over the island, and it is possible to follow
his guiding lineage down through his son Alf Madsen and then to Emil Ambrosia,
who worked for both, and on to Emil's nephew, Bill.

When I came back to Kodiak the second spring after that dismal fall, it was
to a new bay—Spiridon—but again with Bill Ambrosia who was working for
Park Munsey. I landed in a small boat on the gravel beach at the camp; and Bill,
his hair still black as crow's wing, came out of the hunting shack to greet me. My
hunting luck had not been good for a while, and I hoped he could help change
that. I carried my gear across the grassy meadow above the beach and, as I was
about to shake his hand, sank to my knees in an unseen boggy spot. Bill, finishing a smoke, looked down at me and shrugged.

"Whenever they come back a second time," he announced to no one in his
low, husky voice, "I'm the one gets stuck with them."

Bill took my gear and helped me up, then brought the spotting scope out of
the shack and set it up in a sunny spot so I could dry while looking through it.
Adjusting the focus ring, Bill motioned me over to see my first bear of this hunt.
Their rumps dusted white, a sow and her three-year-old wrestled in powdery
snow on the ridge far above us, their distant exertions silent in the scope lens.
Mama bear grabbed baby by the ear with her teeth and toppled him, mauling
him affectionately for perhaps the last time in his life. In a matter of days she
would drive him off so she could mate again. In spring, the bear came out of hibernation and after dawdling sleepily around their dens for a few days, got real
itchy, ready to rub off their winter coats and run down the mountain for salmon
and sex. Ready, in short, to holler *hi-de-ho*.

I'd forgotten, or suppressed, how much the rock-hard beauty of Kodiak Island affected me the first time I was here, but in the next few days of hunting it
all came back. When I was not glassing for bear, I looked first at the bald eagles.
I tried in vain to decide what their screeing most reminded me of: laughing os-
cilloscopes, maybe. I was fascinated by them until the day Bill and I came wide
open in the Whaler around a stony point and found fifteen or twenty fighting
over the scraps of something dead on the dark beach. As we passed, the sky
filled suddenly with flapping raptors, a nation's symbols, so many behaving so
ignobly at one time that I was far on the way to losing interest in them alto-
gether. Give me honest vultures any day.

The foxes, though, with their orange miniature-wolf faces, black ears, and
gold rings of eyes, were more to my, and Bill's, liking. One morning we landed
the skiff on a small island accessible by foot at low tide, and surprised a fox on
the beach, come over earlier to dine on mussels. Seeing us, he bounded up the
cliff and hid. Bill, looking natty in a blue-and-white billed cap with a streamer
fly hooked through the crown, said that foxes hate to swim. When low tide

came, I found Bill staring out at the exposed shoals and saying urgently to him-self, "Go across now, fox. Go across."

Another time we saw a female, apparently in some heat, strolling along the shore and making little steam-whistle toots as she squatted frequently to mark her trail. Rising daintily, she screamed out like someone being murdered and strolled on: the story, and the glory, of love.

Besides foxes, lines of the introduced Sitka blacktail patrolled the shore; har-bor seals popped their heads out of the bay with snorts, then dived with loud splashes; beaver and otter glided sleekly in the Spiridon River's estuary where every manner of waterfowl paddled; gulls circled, white and crying, in the air; but our attention was always drawn back to bear.

One afternoon on the little island we glassed the bay's mountains from, we climbed under a sea cliff to eat our lunches out of the rain. Somehow the un-common occurrence of a boar's eating a sow's cubs came up in our mealtime conversation, and I suggested, trying to sound scientific without the least quali-fication for doing so, that perhaps by killing the sow's young the boar hoped to get her back into estrus *right now*.

Bill Ambrosia thought it over carefully before saying, "Maybe cubs are just good eating."

We chewed our Spam sandwiches meditatively, watching the Whaler bob below us on the end of its line, our rifles wrapped in a tarp in the bow as the rain pocked the bay.

We had seen hardly any tracks in the high snow yet, and those few we had seen all belonged to sows with cubs, leaving and entering dens near the moun-tain crests. Every day Bill awoke certain that we would have a boar by nightfall, but he also feared the bear were tardy this spring—perhaps because fall came later than usual and kept them out longer. He expected, he sighed, that any bear we saw would be way up there in the snow, in the worst places to have to climb to. This was not malingering, just Bill getting older and the climbs not getting any easier. He would go as high as he had to for a bear and only made the ascents more arduous in his head so when it came time really to make them they would not seem so hard on his legs.

One morning we ran out toward the mouth of the bay, looking with our binoculars for any tracks in the fresh snow at one of the bear's favored ridge crossings. Seeing none, and because the tides and wind are right for it, Bill played a hunch and ran the Whaler full-throttle up the Spiridon River, skim-ming it around sandbars, boulders, and submerged drift timber until we reached a set of rapids in a narrow canyon. Tying up the boat, we got our rifles and backpacks and headed upriver for a mile or two along the high bank and over palisades above the water, moving through the dead grass and among alders, cottonwoods, and wild rose bushes. We heard the rush of the river below us, and a great ball of sun burned through the mist above, clearing the sky for the first time in the hunt. The trail had been cut twelve inches deep in places by the passage of Kodiak bear.

Soon we came to the foot of a good hill from which to glass the two mountain ranges running back out along either side of the bay, and we headed for this hill's top. The river below us bent around sheer rock bluffs on one side; and on the other was a large meadow of dead grass. On the climb up the hill we found a bear track in the wet trail, too old to follow but as elegant in its way as the shape of a flower.

In the alders on top we sat all day, glassing the mountains. When I could stare at blank snow no longer, I watched a raven ride a thermal, tucking in his wings every so often and rolling over in the air, producing a soft, contented clucking. In cold wind under blue sky, I puzzled over how this obscure passion for Kodiak Island and its bear—a passion that had already taken up thousands of dollars and weeks of hunting—could possibly ever have gotten ahold of me. Yet I had only to recall that I had come here for nothing less than the largest and wildest animal to be hunted in the wildest, largest land to hunt, and my passion seemed not quite so obscure. My only wonder then was if my luck was about to change; but with the sun hot on my cap, I realized that at least I had had the luck of being on Kodiak and in the presence of Kodiak bear.

Then late in the afternoon of the 494th day since I had last fired a shot at a big-game animal (the Sitka blacktail), I heard Bill Ambrosia whistle. I stood and hurried over to where he sat pointing to the rocky bluffs across from us, a Kodiak bear boar—something I had not expected to see today, or maybe ever— having just crossed over into view and working his way down through the bare cottonwoods to the riverbank, not a thousand yards distant. Bill watched him for a few minutes through his binoculars, then nodded. As I hurriedly stripped off gloves and raincoat, pulling the lens covers off my .300's scope, checking my belt loops for my extra shells, Bill, in no hurry at all, went on watching the bear cross the river and begin working his way toward us on top of the high bank on our side.

"Doesn't do any good to chase a bear," Bill said mildly from behind his binoculars. "He either has to lie down and you go up to him, or he comes to you." The Kodiak bear's big head rocked easily side to side as he swayed forward. "And since he's coming our way," Bill concluded, slipping his binoculars inside his patched parka and reaching for his .350, "we better go meet him."

We stood and headed down the hill. Moving through the long bent grass along the bank, I slipped a round into the chamber and set the safety. Making it to a fallen cottonwood limb, I knelt behind it with Bill at my back and watched the bear come on. I was able to notice how cool and dry it had turned this after-noon, how pleasant the wind felt and the river sounded. In a moment I was going to kill a Kodiak bear. I slipped the safety off.

At thirty yards the bear climbed down into a tiny creekbed cutting into the bank and disappeared. I started a count, and at "four" he came into sight again, having crossed over, and paused above the creek to look off at the mountains.

"Behind the hump," Bill leaned in to whisper to me. "Now."

The bear roared as my first shot broke his shoulder and knocked him into the creekbed. I worked the bolt, and when he stood, as I was sure he would, and started running toward the open yellow meadow, I took him in the same spot. He staggered, kept moving, and my third shot entered his heart. He rolled over but rose one final time, and my last bullet into his chest pitched him forward where he lay still in the grass. It all took much less than ten seconds, and he trav-eled no more than twenty feet.

I reloaded fully before approaching him. Crossing the creek, I circled behind him. I found his eyes open and already beginning to cloud iridescent green. For an instant I felt what someone once called the "desolation of success": Here be-fore me, after so very long, was what I had come for. I unloaded my rifle and leaned it against a cottonwood, then knelt beside the bear. I took in his full length, the massiveness of his hump and head, the long curve of his claws. He was an animal to humble the most wildly arrogant. I pressed my face into the warm fur along his great neck and for the first time smelled the clean, sweet spring smell of Kodiak bear. Looking up, I saw Bill's gapped yellow smile bright as sunlight, and my apprehension was dispelled like the mist.

Another afternoon, only a few yards from where I was writing, pale spring light fell through the doorway of the salting shed on Bill Ambrosia pouring a fifty-pound bag of salt over a big brown bear hide and skull. Kneeling, Bill spread the white salt over the fleshed white skin with his twisted and broken hands—hands that were the sum total of a lifetime of fishing, hunting, and guid-ing on Kodiak. He stood, hissing at the pain in his back from packing out the hide the day before. Brushing the salt from those hands, he looked at the hide.

Shaking a smoke from the pack, Bill Ambrosia said to himself in his battered North Wind of a voice, "That should do it."

# Chapter 22

*Doubtless my face was pretty white, but the blue barrel was as steady as a rock as I glanced along it until I could see the top of the head fairly between his two sinister-looking eyes; as I pulled the trigger I jumped aside out of the smoke, to be ready if he charged; but it was needless, for the great brute was struggling in the death agony . . . the bullet hole in his skull as exactly between his eyes as if I had measured the distance with a carpenter's rule.*

—Theodore Roosevelt, from a letter on the killing of a nine-foot, "twelve-hundred-pound" grizzly at eight paces in the Big Horn Mountains in Wyoming Territory in 1884

# GRIZZLYLAND

**No man, the** Pomo Indians of California believed, had earned the right to hunt the grizzly before he reached the age of thirty. So in the spring of my thirtieth year I resolved to go north to hunt *Ursus arctos horribilis* for the first time.

I went to hunt grizzly in the spring because that was when the bear's hide, barring rubbed patches, would still be in the prime of deepest winter, thick and silver-tipped. The big boar emerged from the dens first in the spring, ahead of the sows and cubs, and commenced their roaming search for feed to replace all the body fat they'd lost to hibernation. Theodore Roosevelt estimated that fully half of the numerous grizzly he took during his long career as a huntsman in North America were simply happened onto while he was out after something else; and in the fall that is unquestionably how many grizzly were taken, a bear tag becoming a sort of lottery ticket that sheep and caribou hunters purchased on the chance that during their mixed-bag hunt they might top the rim of some open basin on a chill September afternoon and discover a bear ardently unearthing a chipmunk, turning over cubic yards of tundra with his long curved white claws in hopes of realizing one single ounce of meat. In the spring, though, there were only bear to hunt, and the only luck you would have would be the kind you made for yourself. Your sole reason for being in grizzlyland in the spring was grizzly.

The proper way to enter grizzlyland was on the back of a horse, and my horse's name was Shorty. Imagine a beer-wagon Clydesdale stunted out of his last six hands of rightful growth, and you will have a fair notion of Shorty. He was an employee of a young outfitter in Pink Mountain, 143 miles from Fort St. John up the dust-choked, windshield-busting Alaska Highway in northeastern British Columbia. The outfitter's hunting area spread east to the Alberta border, and south across the drainage of the Beatton River, which flowed grayly through densely timbered willow, poplar, and jack pine country down to the Peace. This green country was colored as well by the rusting metal around gas-well sites and by the yellow of seismic lines—trails scalped dead true across the hills in winter by the wide blades of Caterpillar tractors, providing geologists with the access their mechanized testing equipment needed to come in and search for more natural gas. There were signs of men almost anywhere you cared to look (though in over two weeks I saw not one stranger), so much so you would never think grizzly would inhabit such a place; but they did.

When Shorty and I rode into that country it was the middle of May and the snow was falling in heavy wet flakes among the jack pines. Ahead of me, leading a young packhorse, rode Ray, the outfitter's assistant guide and best friend since their days together as hot-rodding and hockey-playing teenagers on the wheat prairies of Saskatchewan. Riding silently in the dark timber, we came to a stringer with snow piled on its banks and jumped our horses across. When I cleared, I looked back and watched Mickey on the black gelding jump across with the other packhorse, an untried mare. The packhorse stumbled, her unshod rear hoof slipping into the icy water of the narrow feeder creek; and Mickey had to pull her out, the mare's eyes wide with momentary equine panic.

(Mickey was Ray's wife, a tall, slender Dutch girl whose love of the wild had led her first to the Camargue horse lands in France, then to live among Spanish Gypsies, then to the Colorado Rockies, and at last all the way to one of the wildest corners of the New World, where she met, fell in love with, and wed a trapper and hunting guide.)

We came out of the timber and rode onto a seismic line. The ground was wet and muddy, and the horses did not care for it. They tried to keep to the edges where the ground was less soft, and where you had to be forever reining them away from overhanging branches. (Give a horse a trail two miles wide and he'll still wind up trying to tightrope down the last twelve-inch ribbon of dry edge.)

Along with us trotted Ray and Mickey's black Lab pup, Tammy, trotting right under the horses' hooves until one of them had quite enough and I watched Tammy cartwheel, yowling, through the air—only to get up, shake herself off, and trot happy-go-luckily right back up to the horses. The worth of dogs and horses among grizzly could be infinite. As you rode down a trail, there was always the possibility of a bear standing around the next bend, munching on some tasty dead thing he had just discovered. Usually if one was there, you wouldn't know about it unless you found his tracks, because he would be more than pleased to clear out should he wind you or hear you coming. If he failed to, though, then your dog, suddenly halting and stiffening, his ears pricking up, or your horse pulling up short and snorting loudly, would tell you that while here there may not necessarily be dragons, it was a damned good bet there be bear!

A little before noon we turned off the seismic line and rode out a trail cut through windfallen poplars. The campsite stood in a clearing on the brow of a hill at the top of a long ridge snaking down to a creek with no name. The creek fed into the Beatton, and where they joined there was a large open meadow covered in moose-cropped willow bushes. It looked like any sort of north country meadow—unless you knew the kind of place a bear would come to, then you recognized it at once for what it could only be: a bear meadow. Our camp was at a natural lookout above it, and here we were to stay for fourteen days.

We built a fire before anything else. Some logs were already lashed between two jack pines and made a frame where we set up the Baker tent I would be sleeping in. While snow hissed into the yellow flames, we raised that slant-roofed cook tent, with the asbestos-shielded hole in the wall where a stovepipe was supposed to go—only there was no stove and during our time in camp all our cooking would be done over the fire's coals. After my tent was up, and the dirt floor covered, first with trimmed spruce boughs, then two thick saddle blankets and a tarp, with my sleeping pad and down bag rolled out on top of this, I helped Ray and Mickey put up their white wall tent.

The snow lifted. By the time we had camp made, it was late afternoon. All day I'd been hearing a sound like a vague but insistent heartbeat everywhere around me in the country. As we sat on the wooden panniers, eating steaming bowls of moose stew Mickey had canned from the bull Ray killed the preceding fall, I heard the sound once more, very near. Now it sounded to me like a multi-colored bowling ball being dribbled on a hardwood lane.

"Grouse," Mickey said, stirring the blackened skillet set on the blackened wire grill.

I walked to the edge of the clearing, spoon and orange plastic bowl in hand, and looked down into the timber to see the telltale ruffed grouse standing on a dead log. He was a dozen feet away, and as I watched him, eating my supper, he stood erect on the log, fanning his tail down and raising his ruff and topknot. He lifted his wings and, at first hesitantly, began to drum them against his chest. He picked up the tempo, the drumming becoming bolder, until his wings were a blur and the sound a constant thrum. Then the cock bird slowed and stopped and slumped back down.

Before all the light was gone I went out ten yards from camp, to where the ridge ran up from the nameless creek, and glassed the meadow below for bear. This far north, this time of year, you could with a good binocular very nearly find enough illumination to stay out all "night" glassing. But by ten or ten-thirty it was just obscure enough that with a relatively clear conscience you could draw the line.

As I walked back into camp, a hen grouse flew up into a poplar and began to pluck off the new buds. The cock grouse appeared then, his ruff like the black mane of a lion and his raised tail spread open. He strutted in front of me, not giving a damn, and posed under the tree while the hen, the slim branch bending precari-ously under her weight, went right on feeding, obviously not giving a damn either.

On my way to my tent I noticed that Ray had strategically picketed the horses around the camp, to prevent, as he put it, "surprises" during the night. I thought about this as I was climbing into my sleeping bag. I got my .375, and as Lewis and Clark's men had been ordered to do with their guns during their expedition's sojourn in bear country, lay down with it beside me and fell soundly asleep. That was my first day in grizzlyland. Others followed.

Hunting grizzly is a game requiring far more mental stamina—in the form of a vast, almost transcendental patience—than physical. (Maybe that's why the Pomos wanted their hunters to wait till thirty, when the coltish restlessness of youth, which made one crave only action and more action, had died out some, leaving them better prepared for the possible long haul of finding that one bear in all that big country.) The country bear live in can be rough, of course. But not that rough. Any reasonably fit individual, especially with horses, can get into the worst of it. What cannot be gotten into so easily is the grizzly's nature.

A century's worth of confrontational politics between him and high-powered repeating rifles has turned the bear from a reportedly daylight rambler into a midnight skulker. He has learned caution and circumspection (or rather reckless aggression and sheer foolhardiness have been selected out of the species), but most people who know him well agree that this in no way means he may have likewise learned cowardice. A boar on a kill or, most particularly, a sow with cubs will not at all costs flee from men. Any man rash enough to approach too near to these kinds of grizzly—or any kind of grizzly, for that matter—should account himself lucky if he somehow manages to live to regret it.

The bear's evolved reserve can make hunting him a long process of waiting for him to show. From our lookout less than ten yards out of camp, Ray and I each took a shift in the morning, glassing the meadow and surrounding woodland country. There was a well-worn bear trail that ran up from the Beatton and across the meadow, then entered a stand of leafless poplars on the hillside just below camp and crossed over the foot of the ridge and continued up the winding canyon of the nameless creek until canyon and trail and creek all played out in a willow marsh. Our firm belief was that if we could just make ourselves watch the trail long enough, morning and evening, a bear would appear on it. Almost as if, though not quite, by magic—the "magic" being no more than patience and single-minded determination. And showing up.

At four-thirty each morning I would be lying out on the hill, watching the frost build up on the tarp I had wrapped around me, seeing feeding moose gliding glacially across the meadow, their long legs hidden in the willows, hearing honkers flying along the river in mated pairs, noticing a beaver slicing a wake across the meadow pond's glassy surface. It was of signal importance both to make the watching a meditative end in itself—to keep from going utterly dipsy—and yet be fully prepared for the instantaneous apparition of a bear below. That's how a bear comes: One second only a wall of trees is visible, the next there is a bear outside that wall, shambling your way.

One morning while I was glassing, an animal trotted into view from out of nowhere, crossing the meadow. My heart began to beat like the grouse's drumming as I fumbled to get the animal focused in my binocular. It halted behind a willow bush with its head down, sniffing. Its fur was charcoal and the wind made it bristle.

Small black bear, I thought, dismissing it. Then it lifted its head and tail and my heart took off again. Wolf.

No matter what some folks may think of wolf—EAT MOOSE: 5,000 WOLVES CAN'T BE WRONG read a common bumper sticker in that small corner of British Columbia, where the wolf population was thought to be out of control—there is no animal more indicative of the wild. When you see wolf, you can be certain you've gotten about as far away from things as you're going to get.

I watched the wolf trot on and disappear into the poplars. For some reason I knew exactly where I could find him next. Without waking Ray, I slipped down the ridge toward the nameless creek. About a hundred yards from the bottom the slope of the ridge turned up and made a little knob before continuing down. Here the poplars ended on one side of the ridge, and on the other was open hillside. I slunk to this knob and on hands and knees crept over it. By the edge of the creek the wolf stood, pawing at the dirt and sniffing it. His weight looked all forward in his chest and shoulders, and behind them the ribs were beginning to show through his coat. I raised my binocular to see him better—forgetting that with binoculars, cameras, microscopes, and sometimes even through riflescopes, we might see more, but not always better. The wolf caught the glint of the lenses and looked up at me with his depthless lupine eyes, then stepped unhurriedly out of sight into the poplars. He had no idea what I might be, but he meant to find out. So I stood there, waiting for a wolf, as if it were something I did every day. When I saw him again he was halfway up from the river to me, having stalked up through the trees. By now, though, he knew what I was; and when I saw him he was coming out of the trees like a streak of black, his tail shot straight out behind him, heading up the canyon for parts unknown. He'd been hungry enough to make sure I was more or less inedible before giving up on me. The sight of him, though, had been more than sustaining for me.

After an hour or two of glassing in the morning, I would wake Ray, and while he glassed I would crawl back into my bed. Mickey would have breakfast ready around eight o'clock, then Ray and I, and sometimes Mickey and Tammy, too, would saddle up and ride off to hunt for sign of grizzly bear.

Our riding turned up precious little of it, though. For a while all we could find were some tracks of a moderate-sized bear around an old well site where he had been digging at the tuberous flowers.

"Coltsfoot," Mickey called them as she rode by, reminded of the yellow flora of her native Holland (though these plants were pink-flowered and something like spring beauties). Mickey caught up to Ray; and as I looked on in mute horror, that refined, polite, charming, European young woman, her hair neatly done up in a red bandanna, bummed a chaw of Beechnut off her husband and packed it into her mouth.

On our rides we found the shed antlers of moose, lying palmated and white, everywhere we went, though especially in boggy meadows; and we would put them up on bushes or in trees as signposts. Once we jumped a very much live moose out of a bog deep in some timber and heard him striding away over the wet land with a sound like an extremely large stationary diesel engine, its great flywheel whirling, tearing loose from the steel deck of a tramp freighter and sliding off into a storm-tossed green ocean. One afternoon a pair of coyotes, their fur long and silvery, made a halfhearted jogging hunt after us down a seismic line, but soon abandoned the undertaking when we kept turning around in our saddles and catching them in flagrante delicto—causing them to halt and start staring off into space, the picture of shammed innocence. Another day Ray glanced off the trail and saw a big lynx sitting tall on a downed log fifteen feet away, sunning himself where the light fell among the shadows of the trees. Ray pointed to him as we rode past; then we turned and rode back to look at him again, and he remained where he was, staring at us blankly with his tabby's face, never having seen a man on horseback before. In all, I saw four lynx, four coyotes, three wolf, mountain caribou, mule deer, innumerable moose, and three black bear on the hunt. There were, in addition, reliable reports of mountain goat, wood bison, and wild horses also running in that country, and there were times when the sight of mastodon passing by would have come as no surprise.

It was fast becoming apparent, though, that this spring was going to be a late arrival and that the bear had not yet broken away from the areas of deep cover around their dens. In the afternoons we rode back to camp, having seen many moose and wolf tracks, but no new sign of bear. You would sit hunched in the saddle at such times, your knees aching from all the riding, and listen to the wind in the tops of the tall jack pines. Everywhere in the dense timber, snags were blown over against standing trees; and where they crossed, the bark would be gone from each, and as they swayed together it would be like a wooden bow on a wooden string, producing notes of varied high keening pitches throughout the forest. In the cold air with the warm smell of the horse and saddle leather rising to you, you'd listen to that music and ask yourself why you were never going to be able to figure grizzly out.

Ray and I ate dinner—maybe bannock hot from the frying pan (the surest way to an Indian brave's heart), and chili with lots of fresh garlic—sitting at our lookout, glassing for bear. Ray would have his .358 Winchester, and I my .375. I'd talk about Africa and Alaska; he'd talk about Tuchodi and goat to the north; how he'd won the guides association's championship buckle for grizzly his very first year out; and how the only backup some old-time outfitters would deign to carry when they were leading a hunter after grizzly was an ax.

"'Just smack him real good between the eyes when he closes with you,'" Ray would quote these certifiable loons, all the while sweeping the country with his binocular, the river below us molten in the sunset.

On the tenth day of the hunt I crawled out of my tent on all fours and stood up to see that someone had hung a mirror on a tree. I approached with a certain trepidation. I had taken to wearing my coat of brown Pendleton wool constantly, and at night I was sleeping on spruce boughs like those that bear lined their dens with. I seemed to be walking with my back humped a great deal of the time. I'd pulled up a spring beauty one day just to sample the root, and the red kinnikinnick berries were beginning to look downright mouthwatering. More than once I found myself wondering which brand of beer went well with winter-killed moose, and if a snowslide wouldn't be a jolly thing to frolic in. Now I squinted at my reflection in the mirror and was not entirely surprised to note how grizzled my beard was becoming from the sun. It was obvious I was getting much too far into this business of bear.

That morning the Beatton was low enough for the first time for us to ford it—our feet on the horses' withers and our rifles drawn out of the scabbards—and hunt the other side. We rode up from the river to an old dirt road and there in the hardened mud was a track, not brand-spanking new, but of a huge bear, a nine-footer or better. We got down and looked at it, restraining ourselves from genuflection.

Riding into the timber, we found another track of a different bear, a little smaller paw, but at most only hours old, leading up into some impenetrable cover. Then down along another nameless creek we found more tracks wandering over the sandbars. The bear, at last, were breaking loose, and we waited on a hill above the creek throughout the afternoon, waiting to see if anything would go up or down it in front of us. Finally we had to saddle up and ride back down to the Beatton, where we dismounted and jumped the horses off a high bank into the river—nostrils flaring, mud splattering—and reforded the fast water. We rode on into what Ray called "First Camp," a well-used cabin in a yellow meadow by a beaver pond where a field guide's worth of waterfowl, including six long-necked swans, paddled. We pulled our rifles from the scabbards, loosened the main lines on the saddles, and turned the horses out to graze on the green grass sprouting through the dead yellow. As Ray and I sat among some beaver-felled poplars, eating peaches from a tin can, I thought of the bear on the other side of the river and tried to send word to them in my mind: Come across, you big-assed bear, come across. There is new fresh grass and tender roots over here. Come across.

And that night back at our camp above the Beatton, when in my sleep I thought I heard the horses nickering nervously, or maybe in the first real light before I went to the lookout to glass, or maybe while Ray and Mickey and I ate French toast and drank black coffee around the campfire at eight o'clock, one came across.

Ray turned the horses loose after breakfast to let them graze down the hill to the meadow. An hour and a half later he walked down, with his long loping stride, unconsciously checking around him for likely trees to shinny up should the need arise, to fetch them back up. The next time I saw Ray I was sitting on a log, trying one more time to read the *Iliad*, and he was galloping up the hill bareback on Shorty, the horse's black mane bunched in his white-knuckled fist. Ray was foaming. I got my rifle and followed him back down.

The bear had crossed somewhere upriver and come around the soft muddy bank, where the river made a bend, to the edge of the heavy timber walling off the far side of the meadow. Then he had gotten onto the wide bear trail and left his heavy, wide, long, fat-toed, big-assed, grizzly tracks for three hundred yards along it across the open meadow. He followed the trail on through the poplars before passing 150 yards below camp. If he scented us—and he had to down there where our tracks cut his trail, making him stare up our way—he never quickened his pace, but continued up the canyon of the nameless creek. The size of his track said he was an old bear with many years in this country, with probably many encounters with men. He must have always let them go their way, while he went his.

An outdoor writer of some note, and wide experience with bear, once put the odds on spotting a grizzly during a fifteen-day hunt in the north country at fifty-fifty, and it looked uncomfortably as if we'd just had our fifty. We did not follow the bear that day, fearful of running him out of the area, but let him go upstream and hoped he'd discover someplace to settle in and root to his heart's content. We rode after him the next day, trailing him until his track played out in a thicket of young willows. We spiraled around the country, seeking him, finding signs of more bear everywhere—but never the bear themselves—hearing the wind and wondering if it might be wolf. We stayed on past the fourteen days, till all our food and the horses' grain were gone. We broke camp and hung the panniers from the packsaddles with basket hitches, threw the diamonds over the soft loads on top, tightened the cinches on our riding stock, and headed out. Back along the trail, we rode down to the Beatton and saw our first strangers—workmen loading clean gravel into the backs of trucks with a skip loader. We had to cross a bridge to get to where we'd parked the stock truck; and leading the now well-tried pack mare and not pausing to think, I rode old Shorty—old, reliable, steadfast, plodding Shorty with his hooves the size of soup plates and a disposition cool as the marble in catacombs—directly onto the wooden planks of the open bridge forty feet above the river, let him take one look down, and brought my first grizzly bear hunt to a close (in literally its final hundred paces) by having the half ton of horse beneath me blow up as sky-high as the *Hindenburg* at Lakehurst.

After the rodeo concluded and we got the horses somehow across the bridge and loaded back onto the truck, I had time to think about grizzly and the Pomo again. They were correct to insist upon a certain degree of maturity in hunters of the grizzly. But merely because at thirty you might have a right to hunt the great bear, it did not necessarily follow that you had also earned the right to kill him, yet. That was something that might take even more years, or perhaps could never be earned—and more than twenty years later, it has yet to be.

In North America are some of the world's greatest big-game animals, and the bear are in the forefront of them. I had hunted the big brown bear of Kodiak, and black bear in California, Oregon, Alberta, British Columbia, Saskatchewan, and

Alaska, and one day I meant to find an Inuit with a dog team and cross the frozen white Arctic Sea to hunt polar bear. The greatest big-game animal in North America, though, remained downriver from here, somewhere, clawing at the earth, lifting his heavy head to catch a spring breeze bringing him smells of new grasses and berries and animal flesh before passing through his fur like wind in a ripe field of silvery grain.

# Chapter 23

*Then he saw the bear. It did not emerge, appear: it was just there, immobile, fixed in the green and windless noon's hot dappling, not as big as he had dreamed it but as big as he had expected, bigger, dimensionless against the dappled obscurity, looking at him. Then it moved. It crossed the glade without haste, walking for an instant into the sun's full glare and out of it, and stopped again and looked back at him across one shoulder. Then it was gone. It didn't walk into the woods. It faded, sank back into the wilderness without motion as he had watched a fish, a huge old bass, sink back into the dark depths of its pool and vanish without even any movement of its fins.*

—William Faulkner, *The Bear*

# THE LAST BLACK BEAR

**Captain Charley Madsen,** when he was one of the earliest guide-outfitters on Kodiak—in all of Alaska, for that matter—in the days before exclusive guide territories (now come and gone themselves), license applications, drawings, permits,
and quotas, knew the way to hunt bear. With his ninety-two-foot yacht, the *Kodiak Bear*, he coasted the island and explored its bays. When a bear was spotted,
Captain Charley or one of his assistant guides and a hunter would head for shore
in a jollyboat, land, and make a stalk. At the end of the day, hunters and guides
returned to berths on the *Bear*, and the vessel cruised to another bay. Nobody
much worried about restricting this kind of hunting because there were just so
many bear and so few hunters; and if it did any real harm to the bear population
on Kodiak, it can only be said that bear are still being hunted there today.

It is for the better that laissez-faire shoot-'em-and-move-on hunting is a
thing of the past and that genuine management is now the rule. On the other
hand, it is a baleful thought to think that the pursuit of bear in the stately manner of a Captain Charley—at its best—has gone with it. Bear and seawater are
an unique mixture in Alaska, and it could only make the world a smaller place
than it already is if there were no great bear-hunting boat left along its coast,
giving hunters both a place from which to look back onto the land—instead of
out from it to the sea—and a way back to how it used to be.

As it turned out, there was such a boat, in the waters of the Inside Passage.
An hour's flight in a Beaver floatplane could carry you to it. It was *The Alaskan
Grandeur*, a seventy-eight-foot transoceanic yacht launched in 2001. It had a
twenty-two-foot beam; and its six-foot prop, turned at two hundred rpm by a
geared-down Caterpillar 3407 diesel engine, let it make a steady ten and a half
knots. It had passenger suites; private baths and heads; a salon and galley.
Which was all well and good, but what mattered was what it was built for.

The captain, Jimmie, built the *Grandeur* to hunt bear. Jimmie came to Alaska
almost forty years before from Nevada, where he was a civil engineer building
tunnels for the interstate. He came as a hunter and stayed on as a licensed guide,
becoming Master Guide No. 61 in 1980. His whole family followed him into
guiding, with his wife, Mary Ann, assisting him for over twenty-five years, along
with his son Jimmie and his twenty-two-year-old, newlywed daughter Alisha.
They were all licensed guides, Alisha (who for some reason known only to herself and her family is nicknamed "Mutts") having become the state's 1,080th in

2001. Together they guided for Sitka blacktail and mountain goat; it was bear, though, that had been at the heart of their guiding—big brown bear, yes, but especially preternaturally big salmon-fed coastal black bear.

Big black bear were what I was thinking about as I stood on the wide swim step at the stern of the *Grandeur* one spring evening. I had made the hour's flight in the Beaver and was now smoking an after-dinner cigar in the perma-twilight that domed the calm bay, watching the Q-tip-headed bald eagles perched in the tops of the spruce, hearing the Canadas honking north (how much *farther* north did they intend to go?), and seeing the snow pushed back to the tops of the surrounding peaks—meaning the dens on the slopes had been uncovered and their occupants were out, looking for food and mates. I had made a small pact with myself about black bear: I had killed eight, and nine would be my last. No real reason, except that nine was a definite, square number and probably as many black bear as anyone needed in a lifetime. If I were to take my last bear here, though, it would have to be the biggest black bear of my life, pure black, and one I would not hesitate to preserve in a full-body mount.

It was greed, pure and simple, with a splash of hubris. I wanted a bear as spectacular as this land and ocean where I was hunting, and equal to the grand style of the hunt. If this was the last time for me, I wanted to go out with a bang, everything happening the way I had always thought it would. If there was any chance of that, here looked to be the best place for it. I finished the cigar and went to my cabin to sleep and wait for the next day, not appreciating the folly of expecting the expected.

The next day dawned about, oh, 2:30 A.M., but I didn't know that, asleep in my cabin. In fact, I didn't bother getting out of bed until almost 9 A.M. A hunter on the *Grandeur*, in the spring, who wants to be looking for bear during the entire duration of shooting light should budget at least twenty-one to twenty-two hours per day. And while he may be out there 24/7, the black bear won't. Nearly nocturnal, the bear can wait till almost dusk before stepping out of the impenetrable jungle that is the forest. They will come out onto the flats to feed on the sedge at the water's margin, preferring the salad to the meat course in the first weeks after hibernation. The only things that keep the big boar out in the open this time of year are the tender grasses and tender . . . well, the urge to breed. And the only thing that lets Jimmie and his guides and hunters reach those flats, even in the small aluminum boats they hunt out of off the *Grandeur*, is the tide. Waterborne hunters live and die by the tides, timing their trips into the bays and estuaries so they won't be stranded by low tide when it is time to come out and head back. Today, this meant we wouldn't begin hunting before 3 P.M.

In the interlude after breakfast, I talked to Jimmie about the bear and the country. Jimmie had concerns about both. After nearly two generations among them, he had his opinions. He worried—and not just because he was a licensed guide who was, by law, restricted in the number of hunters he could guide each year—about the impact of "transporters" who were essentially unlimited in the number of hunters, resident and nonresident, they could bring into an area. Because they were not licensed guides, transporters could not "directly" contribute to the taking of game by their clients, but they could fly them into the country, provide them with a camp (though not supplies or hunting equipment such as boats), and haul them out with their gear, meat, hides, and heads, before bringing in the next fresh batch of hunters. Nonresidents hunting in Alaska were not required to have a guide to hunt species such as black bear, moose, or caribou (and it ought to be remembered that this was public game on public land and ought to be accessible to everyone equally, within the regulations). Nonetheless, there was strong evidence for holding flocks of "transported" hunters responsible for the necessity of closing many areas to all moose and caribou hunting, eliminating some black bear fall seasons and shortening others, and raising the possibility of even-tighter restrictions for everyone, not just licensed guides and their clients.

As for the land, it was clear-cutting and roads that Jimmie had seen enough of here. Temperate Alaska rain forest was one of the most rare and, in its natural state, most productive wild environments on earth; and as Jimmie saw it, clear-cutting wiped out the work of centuries that went into creating "old growth." Yes, clear-cutting did open up the forest, and for maybe a decade it produced a flush of berries and edible new growth that game did enjoy. But sooner rather than later a nearly uniform monoculture of conifers would grow back up to shade out everything (unlike the uneven and broken mosaic of old growth) and in so many words, annihilate "all that's made / To a green thought in a green shade." Before that, clear-cuts would also be catch basins for deep snow, blocking winter migration routes for wildlife, while sitting—caused by runoff from clear-cutting and road building—and elevated water temperatures—due to the loss of canopy along the streams—didn't make life any easier for spawning salmon.

In my perhaps limited experience, many, if not an outright majority of, hunting guides viewed environmentalism as an "us versus them" threat to their livelihoods. This tended to lead them (perhaps in false bravado) into espousing opinions about the environment that would not have been entirely foreign to the proprietors of McKinley-era strip mines. That made Jimmie's opinions somewhat unexpected, and something to mull over.

The next unexpected occurrence was my finding myself in an aluminum boat with pigtailed Mutts (definitely a *girl!*) and her husband, Zach, a former rodeo bullrider, setting off from the *Grandeur*. In the early afternoon we'd sighted in the rifles in a secluded cove (so the shots would be muffled from bear). I was shooting a .338 Winchester Magnum, thinking it represented a sound compromise between power and range—which proved a mistake. Not that the rifle didn't shoot straight; carried to the cove, it shot right where it had at home from the rifle-range bench. It was just that . . . well, what I found out, I found out later.

Now it was past three o'clock when I sat in the boat with the .338 in a waterproof and floatable soft case, glassing for black bear as Mutts ran the outboard with one hand and glassed with the other, while Zach glassed, too. Every so often they exchanged some comment I could not hear, probably about bear, but possibly about the things newlyweds commented on, though I'm afraid I had likely forgotten what most of those might be.

Within half an hour, Mutts had spotted a bear some impossible distance away on a hilltop, and I didn't doubt her. Then a little later, we saw our first bear on the beach.

He was a boar that Mutts estimated at near seven and a half foot. From a distance he was both glossy obsidian sheen and the absence of light, like some ursine black hole. He was also the biggest black bear I'd ever seen in person in my life. And he was with a sow. And I immediately turned him down. This wasn't the right way, yet.

Still, I asked Mutts if we could stalk him anyway, without the guns, for both fun and profit (practice for the real thing). She angled the boat into shore, out of his line of sight, then climbed out in her hip waders and walked it in. I'd been told, and knew, to step only where she stepped as we stalked, the sole of my rubber wader filling her track before it could fill with water. We stalked up to about 150 yards from the two bear, and I watched them through my 8x42 binocular. The boar to my eye was magnificent, though with a rubbed spot on one hip, and my only rationalization for turning him down was that the sow and he were entitled to *some* privacy.

We went on up the bay, passing over solid reefs of clams in the clear water.

In a channel, water poured out with the tide, the outboard at full throttle barely able to make headway. Then we were into a tidal inlet and landed on a grassy spit where we could glass the surrounding shore for almost 360 degrees. There was the smell of fresh grass and new flowers; and as we sat, glassing for black bear, we might have been taken for picnickers in camouflage who'd mislaid their basket, maybe because it was in camouflage, too.

It was past five o'clock when we saw the first bear, across the inlet. He was a touch smaller than the boar with the sow (though bigger, again, than most any other bear I'd ever seen) and badly rubbed. We watched him, on and off, for thirty minutes, primarily out of the general human fascination with bear. Then the bear I wanted stepped out.

Mutts, with eyes that had been judging bear since age seven, called him at near to eight foot, and we needed to take a close look. Back in the boat, Mutts used an electric trolling motor to take us silently across the inlet. On the other side, we got out as quietly as we could in the ankle-deep water, even though the boar was over four hundred yards upwind, and now hidden from us (and we from him) by a creekbank and a stand of spruce. Mutts and I uncased our rifles and loaded them, set the safeties, and began to stalk.

It was like some very curious, very precise, slow-motion dance we performed. It seemed to take hours to close the distance on the bear across a mudflat and up the bank, footprints laid noiselessly on footprints. Finally we were on hands and knees in tall grass, crawling around the edge of the spruce. The boar was across the creek, about 110 yards away, grazing. He was also starting to jerk his head around, seeming to sense something he could not yet smell. Mutts whispered, yeah, right at eight with some slight rubs on the face and shoulder, and what did I want to do?

It was not even four hours into the hunt, but there he was, a bear as big as the Ritz.

I looked around for a place to prone out and get a solid rest and clear shot at the bear's heart and lungs, knowing that "dead" bear—whose slow metabolisms take

a long time to register the fact of death—can run a long way, and that the rain forest was just yards from him. If he could get there, even mortally wounded, and go
to ground, he could be lost. My last bear shouldn't be a lost bear.

I crawled flat to a spot out from the spruce and got the scope on the increasingly jittery bear. I waited until he stepped out broadside and I had a shot without any grass in the way before making the final decision. I let off the safety, and
held just behind his left shoulder, above the point of the elbow. I was expecting
one shot, clean and quick, but that's not the way it always is with bear.

The truth is that "anchoring" a bear with one shot can be like expecting to
anchor the *Grandeur* with a cinder block. Bear will drop with the first shot, but
will be up and running in seconds, unless a hunter actually shoots wrong and ac-
cidentally breaks the spine (tell me, please, where you intentionally aim to hit
the spine of a broadside bear?). Hoping to "break down" a bear by aiming for
the shoulder won't do much to stop one from getting away, either. The way to
kill bear, black as much as brown, is to use a big-enough gun and shoot for the
heart and lungs, and then be prepared to keep shooting with every bullet in your
rifle until the bear stops moving where you can see him. Anyone who says that
this is not so is simply suffering from a severe deficiency of experience in hunting bear, or is the beneficiary of a phenomenal string of lucky shots.

Still, what happened next should have been better.

Broadside, his head lowered nervously to feed, the bear had come to a
momentary stop when I pulled the trigger. The 215-grain H-frame bullet went
through, shattering his right shoulder on the off side. He was running, then.

A wall of trees was only a few yards to his right, but he ran in a wide left-
handed semicircle across the grassy flat, heading for us. I worked the rifle's bolt
and fired again, and again. I hit him and he went down then got up. I missed,
then shot again and hit him again, but he barely stumbled. And that was four
and the bear was now fifty yards from us, closing ground.

"I'm out," I said, as clear and calmly as I could, getting to my feet.

Mutts was already up, off to my right. Maybe I was just hearing things, but
I'm almost certain that this rather beautiful, modest, sunny young woman said,
quite distinctly, "Damn!" though maybe it was only "Darn!"

I pulled a cartridge from the pouch on my belt, pushed it down into the magazine, pulled another, dropped it, pulled a third and got it fed into the chamber.
Mutts had her .375 raised and was firing, trying to pick up her lead on the bear.

The bear came off the opposite bank of the creek and splashed into the water,
a plume of blood trailing in the current. His face remained that wary, stoic mask
that doesn't change until the instant a bear decides to bite or maul something. I
don't know whether he was coming for us or just trying to come through us, but
if he got to us the results would be the same, whatever his intention. I set the

crosshairs behind his injured right shoulder and fired. He went down in the middle of the shallow creek in a shower of water and tried to stand once more. I fired again, and he was done, twenty yards from us. From the first shot to the last had taken twenty seconds. Instead of going out with a bang, it had been *bang, bang, bang* . . .

Damn the .338, I thought in a daze (reminded of Master Guide Hal Waugh's saying it was "Heap Big Smoke & No Fire"). Damn all compromise calibers and compromise bullets. Next time I would carry a .375 or .416 and shoot big round-nosed, jacketed lead bullets; and it would be one clean shot. But how could there be a next time, I asked myself, remembering my vow. There had to be a next time.

After we had recovered from a stunned, and just slightly awed, silence, it took the three of us to roll the bear out of the creek and back onto the bank. His hide would square out at seven-foot, ten inches and his skull would measure nineteen and a half inches. He was big enough and black enough for my last bear; but did I want him to be that, after all? This wasn't how I'd expected it to be, and I didn't know whether that made it easier or harder to call time on my black bear hunting.

We tagged the bear and Mutts skinned and quartered so we could pack out all the meat (for sausages and hams and loin roasts) and the hide and skull. I thought about Captain Charley Madsen and how it used to be in the good old days, and how *The Alaskan Grandeur* and bear such as this made these days pretty good ones themselves. In my head I furiously recalculated all the black bear—then recalculated again—and realized I'd been in error. This was only the eighth. I could take one more one day without breaking my pact with my-self. (Maybe even a tenth, if it came to that.)

In the overcast light of 9 P.M., no-see-ums pocking my flesh, I felt relieved and indebted—relieved that I could honorably hunt black bear again after this, and indebted to this black bear for showing me the foolishness of believing that life could be (or even wanting it to be) as one expected. It was the unexpected life that was worth living; and if you ever thought you had it in your power to declare which bear hunt would be your last, you had another think coming.

# Chapter 24

*It was warm in the darkness, the air heavy as wet worsted, filled with the din of crickets and bullfrogs. The dog climbed out of his nest of burlap sacks beneath the doublewide. He was a Doberman, eighty pounds of pinscher, all muscle, pointed alert ears, and a mouthful of white teeth. He bowed his sleek back, stretched lithely, then turned and watched through the chain link the traffic go by on Highway 90. The dog turned back and smelled the canal. He padded down to the water's edge a few yards behind the mobile home. He stood, ears sharp, erect, then warily lowered his muzzle to drink. A ripple in the water lilies made him snap his head up, the metal tags on his choke-chain jangling. He stood poised, listening. A minute passed. When no more sound came from the canal, the dog went back to drinking.*

*The eleven-foot bull alligator broke the water; and before the dog could leap away, the many round conical teeth of this reptile, who once shared the world with the dinosaur, closed on the Doberman's neck. The 'gator pulled the struggling dog back into the canal and began to spin his own heavy long body along its vertical axis, churning gray mud up from the shallow bottom, sulfur rising into the damp night. When he stopped, the dog in his jaws no longer struggled. The mud began to settle as the cars went on by on Highway 90.*

# GOIN' 'GATORIN'

**Alligator in the** millions at one time swam and slithered and floated and rolled and roared and lay absolutely motionless, basking on the dry ridges, or cheniers, in the swamps of Louisiana and the rest of the South, and nobody quite knew what to make of them all. The Spaniard named the alligator he encountered during his explorations of subtropical North America *el lagarto*, "the lizard," but the alligator is of an order much different from the lizard, belonging to that group of reptiles known as the Archosauria, or "ruling reptiles" (which included the dinosaur). They appeared on earth some 180 to 160 million years ago, during the Triassic. Today they are the closest living relative of the bird.

In the mid-1770s, the artist, traveler, and naturalist William Bartram—son of John Bartram, who was called the world's greatest natural botanist by none other than Linnaeus, and the "father of American botany" by any number of others—made an extended exploratory expedition through Florida and up the St. Johns River. At one point in his travels, his Indian companion abandoned him in a "fine orange grove," but he pressed on alone. Traveling in his small boat, he encountered the then-ubiquitous and aggressive reptile in a most vivid fashion as he beheld an alligator "rushing forth from the flags and reeds. His enormous body swells. His plaited tail brandished high, floats upon the lake. The waters like a cataract descend from his opening jaws. Clouds of smoke issue from his nostrils. The earth trembles with his thunder." (Not surprisingly, Bartram's *Travels* were greatly admired by the English Romantic poets, Coleridge in particular. In all likelihood, the alligator Bartram described was performing a mating dance, rather than preparing to attack.)

Farther on Bartram was forced to cudgel his way past bold 'gator as he paddled out to fish in a lagoon, the reptiles trying to capsize his tiny barque. Back on the islet where he was making a camp, he was nearly caught like a dog in one of the "subtle attacks" of an alligator as he was cleaning his catch, and had the beast sweep a number of the fish into the water with his tail. Another 'gator who persisted in crawling up onto the shore and threatening him Bartram had to dispatch "by lodging the contents of my gun into his head." Later that day he saw the river blocked from bank to bank by shoals of migrating fish, and the alligator feeding on them were in "such incredible numbers" and packed so tightly together that one might have stepped across the wide river on their heads, "had the animals been harmless." The 'gator consumed hundreds of thousands of fish into the night, the noise of their eating frenzy keeping Bartram awake.

Bartram is said to have reported seeing alligator twenty feet long, and John James Audubon to have killed a seventeen-footer. A figure that is reported in several reputable locales lists nineteen feet, two inches as the official mark set by one Louisiana 'gator. Maybe so. Maybe such an alligator could have been disproportionately long and serpentine, or if he was of characteristic build he must have weighed a ton. And where would such a brute abide, and upon what would he feed? (Thirteen or fourteen feet is widely regarded as a kind of reasonable maximum to expect any 'gator in the wild to reach nowadays—though who's to say what could be lurking up some bayou somewhere?)

The alligator continued relatively unmolested well into the nineteenth century. His mild firm meat supported many of the settlements of the waterlogged South through their lean and formative years, and that was about all the pressure he had to contend with. He was even transformed into part of the frontier's mythology as the Kentucky keelboatmen who steered their cargoes of tobacco and livestock down the mighty Mississip' to New Orleans blustered about being "alligator-horses"—half-horse, half-alligator centaurs—whose raison d'être seemed to be, after unloading their vessels, to do as much gambling, drinking, wenching, brawling, and general all-around roaring as was humanly—or inhumanly—possible.

Then in 1855 the fashion designers of Paris decreed alligator leather to be the latest trend, and a market for the hides opened. To this was soon coupled the Civil War's need for additional sources of durable leather. Pressure on the reptiles grew. E. A. McIlhenny of Avery Island, Louisiana (and Tabasco brand pepper sauce), estimated that 3 million alligator were killed in the state between 1880 and 1933, and state tax records indicate another 314,404 were taken legally between 1939 and 1955. Wetlands drainage, depriving the 'gator of both room and board, had also been added along the way to the soup the reptiles were finding themselves increasingly in, and by the late 1950s their numbers had reached such a low point in Louisiana that it seemed no one would care to venture a guess as to how few there might be left.

Then in 1958 the state initiated an alligator research program. It followed this in 1960 by passing laws to establish a closed season and size limit on 'gator. In 1963 the entire state was closed to all alligator hunting. On Rockefeller Refuge near Grand Chenier in Louisiana a radio-collaring program was begun on alligator in 1969. In that same year the Lacey Act was amended to control the interstate commerce in reptile hides. The alligator was later included in the Endangered Species Act and the CITES treaty, but was already making his return.

By the mid-1960s that return was such that it had become obvious that live capture and transplanting of 'gator to new areas was not keeping pace with the population rise. According to the late epicurean writer Waverly Root, in a piece on the reptile as table fare, alligator had taken to showing up on golf courses, and at lawn parties and church services, to the consternation of everyone concerned, human and reptile both. The 'gator population of greater New Orleans alone was said to stand at one per every thirty citizens. Hunting was considered the most legitimate way of dealing with the surplus, and 1972 saw the first legal alligator hunt in Louisiana in almost ten years. In 1982 when the Louisiana 'gator population stood at some six hundred thousand, and the species had demonstrated the potential for an average annual increase of 55.5 percent, sixteen thousand alligator tags were issued.* I had one of them.

The late afternoon near Lac des Allemands, Louisiana, was hot and the sweat had spread in a blotch of cool darkness across the back of my shirt. We were in an aluminum boat on a canal in a place known as the Pleasure Ponds, near where Dobermans and other dogs, as well as ducks and chickens and who knows what else, got eaten on a regular basis. It was early September, the day before Louisiana's alligator season was scheduled to open, and we were setting baits.

Bait for an alligator consists of a two-pound mullet—which attains superior quality after it has hung out for two or three days and has had the smell of human hands supplanted by something a bit more robust—on a No. 3 shark hook, dangling a foot or so above the murky water (to prevent turtles and undersized 'gator from reaching it). The hook is attached to a goodly length of No. 96 rot-resistant tarred 100 percent nylon seine twine, with a tensile strength of 911 pounds, set in the notched end of an ash pole, called a picket, with the other end tied off to a real strong tree firmly rooted in a canal bank.

I was pushing the sharpened end of a picket into the muddy canal bottom while the guide, Pete, tied the twine's end off around the base of the tree. My father, making one of his rare hunts with me, was placing the hook in the body of a dead mullet so the fish was bent like the letter "U." Hooking dead mullet for 'gator bait was a newly acquired talent for him, but one that after only a few fish he had learned to perform with some expertise. He examined his work and was justly satisfied. Pete set the line in the picket's notch and adjusted the bait's

---

*Since 1982 the Louisiana alligator population has grown to an estimated million and a half animals, the state issuing between thirty-two thousand and thirty-five thousand wild alligator harvest permits annually.

height. Leaning back, he appraised the display, deciding how it would appeal to an alligator.

"*Bon*," he said finally. He fired up the hundredfold-horsepower motor of his flat-bottomed fishing boat, and we went skimming out of the canal into the smooth, sunstruck open water of the ponds, heading to place another of the thirty or forty baits we would need for the next day. Pete drove the boat from the stern, standing. He wore blue denims and a white T-shirt over his round belly, a tall, tall straw hat set squarely on his head of thick, black hair, the white rubber boots on his feet lending him the air of a lunar explorer. Pete was a fisherman, an alligator guide, and above all a Cajun; and clearly, like trees, only God can make one of those.

Parsing out the noun "Cajun" can be no mean feat. To begin with, you have to go back to Arcadia, a mountainous, backwoods sort of district of southern Greece's Peloponnesus. Probably because they didn't know a thing about it except its lyric name, classical Greek and Latin poets selected Arcadia to be, in the words of the *Oxford English Dictionary*, "the ideal region of rural contentment." Now jump forward from B.C. to the middle of A.D. the second millennium, and as William Faulkner Rushton outlines in his book *The Cajuns*, you have the explorer Verrazano, mindful of his classics, slapping the name on a landfall in southern North America. The name heads north with succeeding maps until it comes to rest in Nova Scotia, where the local Indians have a similar-sounding word, *Akade*, for a similar concept of heaven on earth. Thus we arrive at the word "Acadia."

The French, primarily Celts from Brittany who have been fishing on the Grand Banks off Newfoundland since the beginning of the sixteenth century, settle Acadia, in time making it a crown colony of France. But the English gain control over most of that colony in 1713; then in 1755, following many years of political unrest, they expel five thousand Acadians from Nova Scotia. The Acadian diaspora, complicated by the Seven Years' War, goes on for some time, until a number of them reach Louisiana. Here English-speaking Americans mangle their name into "Cajuns"—the same way Indians became "Injuns," and with a show of about as much respect. And all of the above cannot even begin to explain Cajuns.

A Cajun is proud unto death of his name, and he even seems to enjoy his other, looser cognomen of "coon-ass." There appears to be no connection between this name and those hardy members of the Procyonidae, the raccoons. The name is believed by eminent linguists to be from an archaic French profanation (the French having a word for everything), *conasse*, which to my understanding means, more or less, that is to say . . . a poxy whore. It would seem good policy, à la Owen Wister's *The Virginian*, to smile when you call someone a Cajun. It is downright essential when you call him a coon-ass.

We began hunting 'gator at first light of opening morning. In the olden days you almost always hunted 'gator at night, and in many ways night hunting was a more exciting venture. You would idle over the water in the soft buzzing darkness, wearing a miner's headlamp and carrying a six-volt battery in your back pocket. When you picked out a pair of eyes burning bright as brake lights in a nighttime rush hour, you could, with sufficient skill, use a .22 short and, taking aim along an angle thirty degrees off the midline of the reptile's head, fire a bullet through the eye and down a septum leading through the casemate of his skull and directly into the brain—a brain the size of the final joint on the tip of your little finger. That, apparently, is all the cerebral matter needed to command up to a dozen feet and a quarter ton of something that was the next best thing to a dinosaur, to make that something lay his stubby legs back along his body and torpedo through the water with powerful, lateral, wavelike motions of his tail. But if you managed to hit that bit of brain, you could make an alligator come to a screeching halt.

Another unique aspect of night hunting was the opportunity it afforded for gliding up from behind on foot-long yearlings and snatching them up just in back of their necks and lifting them out of the water. 'Gator of this age and size were as cute as a minute, cool and green and yelping like puppies. A hunter could hold one up in the light and coo at him and burble until the hunter would bring him too close and the little sucker'd clamp ahold of his upper lip for dear life.

The 'gator-hunting season in Louisiana was set well after the alligator's time of breeding, to help protect the population even further. This reasoning also lay behind the outlawing of another colorful hunting technique known as poling. A female would be tracked to her den by the wide trail she left across a chenier. A long pole would then be shoved into the den and swizzled around until mama 'gator came roaring out, gnawing on the pole's end. While she was engaged in reducing the pole to matchsticks, somebody'd smack her real good on the head with the back of a hatchet and then lug her out to the bayou, leaving the eggs or hatchlings to fend for themselves.

The opening morning of the '82 season, the first baited line we checked had a 'gator on it, lying unmoving back up on a weedy bank, glaring out at us with cat eyes. We looked at it, decided it was not big enough, and cut it free, Pete climbing out onto the bank to cut the twine, and having to leap back into the boat as the 'gator charged toward him to get back into the water. We moved on to check the other baits.

Anyone with hopes of shooting an alligator swimming on the water, or lying sunning on a bank, I soon saw, should quickly disabuse himself of them. I assure you, any basking 'gator worth his salt will hit the water with great swiftness at the first sight or sound of an approaching boat. And the best target a swimming 'gator is likely to present is just his eyes and nostrils showing above the waterline at absolutely no less than 150 yards. This means you would get to attempt a shot, from a bobbing boat, at the flat surface of a bayou, at a kill spot the size of your fist, underneath the surface, on a prehistoric animal, and if your bullet didn't ricochet off to God knows where, or didn't merely wound the reptile (and a couple of inches either way is all it takes to turn a good shot into a bad one on a 'gator)—if it actually did succeed in killing him outright—would be apt to send the alligator straight to the bottom, however deep it might be.

After the day's first 'gator had been turned loose, we went up the long canal leading from the Pleasure Ponds to Lac des Allemands itself. The open water was choppy as we went banging over it at planing speed. Most of the baits were still hanging along the shore where the big cypresses grew, though some had been pulled down by the drifting banks of water lilies or by the efforts of herons. Then we saw a 'gator lying blackly on the shore, the heavy brown line running from his closed jaws. Seeing us, he slid with great swiftness into the water. We pulled him up again, but a foot or so of his tail had been lost to history or experience, and we let him go.

Our round of bait checking sent us back to the Pleasure Ponds, where we pulled up one downed line and found it had a blue cat of no less than fifty pounds attached to it. We killed the fish and brought him aboard for the camp's dinner. Then we went off to check our last bait, this one near where dogs kept getting gobbled by something very large.

'Gator "hunting" is really an amalgam of the three disciplines of hunting, trapping, and fishing. What it vaguely resembles is the running of an extended trotline, over an area of many, many square miles, for scute-backed wet things with big teeth. Yet it can be best understood only for what it uniquely is: 'gatorin', an undertaking not exactly like anything else. The techniques of 'gatorin' for sport are pretty much the same long-used techniques of commercial alligator hunting (the sport permit even came stamped on a trapper's license). At its least interesting, 'gatorin' is about like shooting a rather large, exquisitely crafted Louis Vuitton leather suitcase. At its most interesting it can remind its warm-blooded participants of nothing so much as all the mobilized defense forces of Japan battling to halt some rubber-suit monster in its tracks as it slouches toward a scale model of the Ginza, bursting high-tension wires and flattening streetcars en route.

When we came to that last bait that morning, it was the turn of a bowhunter to see what Pete would find at the end of the line, if anything. When Pete nosed the boat up to the bank, the line was slanting tautly down into a hole under it. Pete grabbed the line and tugged. The line slammed back, and the fight was on. When Pete finally got the 'gator's head up, the mightiest set of toothed jaws I had ever seen appeared above the surface, swamp water cascading out of them. I shuddered involuntarily. The bowman was ready, leaning over the gunwale, his sixty-five-pound compound drawn back and the broadhead aimed for the tiny kill spot just behind the thick boiler plate of the alligator's skull and in front of the broad shield of bony buckles mailing his back. And when the bowman fired, he almost hit it The arrow, instead of penetrating, bounced off the 'gator's head, and the big bull went simply berserk, rolling and thrashing until he threw the shark hook.

He took off up the canal like leviathan from the Book of Job—for whom, as it was spoken out of the whirlwind, "darts are counted as stubble"—making a "path to shine after him" as he marked his progress along the soft bottom with a trail of silvery sulfurous bubbles. Then the bubbles stopped, the 'gator lying on the bottom, waiting for us to go away. He had no gills, only lungs, and he was holding his breath. We floated over him, waiting silently. The heat was windless. An immense bank of water lilies, green flecked with purple, drifted slowly by us on the current.

One hour and fifteen minutes after the alligator went down, he surfaced. The bowman now fired a pistol shot at him, grazing his head. The alligator swam out of the canal and into the shallow open water of the Pleasure Ponds, Pete and the bowman following in one boat, and the rest of us in another. Pete overtook the 'gator in the pond, and this time when the reptile raised his head, the hunter put a bullet into it. Pete grabbed the animal's tail and one webbed, clawed foot and hollered for us to get over to him before the 'gator sank. We came aboard Pete's boat like a party of privateers seizing His Majesty's flagship, and each of us grabbed a section of alligator. I had the tail, black as a truncheon and big around as a man's waist.

What if this billion-year-old bastard's undead? I wondered. What if he's merely stunned or playing possum and should come to with a start, slamming his two hundred pounds of tail muscle around inside this aluminum boat? Do I abandon ship and hope he stays on board, or do I try to stay on board and hope he somehow flails himself out without me clamped in his jaws? I couldn't figure what the answer was, so I just kept pulling. We got all of him in, and while the hunter was attaching his yellow plastic tag to the tail, Pete methodically bound the jaws shut with seine twine, just to be on the safe side.

Back at camp we hung this monster-of-the-day up before skinning him. He was an eleven-and-a-half-foot bull—females seldom get above nine foot—and an honest four hundred pounds in weight. After we skinned and filleted him, one of our party, a physician, had an idea. The good doctor was an inveterate prober and examiner, and he was curious to know what might be on the inside of this alligator. I, for some reason I have yet to understand, volunteered to assist him in the operation; but when we opened up the 'gator's stomach, the smell was beyond my dizziest imaginings. The doc, though, was in his element. When he could not ascertain to his satisfaction visually what the 'gator had been dining on, he thought nothing of plunging his ungloved hand inside the cavity. He proceeded to remove bunches of water lily leaves. Large chunks of stomach-acid-etched driftwood. Turtle shells. Whitened alligator tails. Unspeakable muck. Plastic shotgun hulls. And, finally, as the pièce de résistance, two empty two-liter, clear plastic soft-drink bottles. There was no such thing as foreign matter to an alligator's alimentary canal; but even as I was trying to keep from retching, I was somewhat disappointed that no partially digested choke-chains had been found along with everything else.

I killed a good 'gator of nearly eight feet a few mornings later. The kill was one shot and clean, a 405-grain bullet from my .45–70 doing the job. I spent the afternoon helping to skin him out. The belly and flank leather was supple and strong, pebbly-grained and pleasant to look at. I would have the hide tanned and handmade into boots that the Hispanic cobbler in Mercedes, Texas, promised would fit me like a glove and that would always remind me of Louisiana September days.

We filleted off all the good meat, careful to remove and discard as much of the fat from it as we possibly could. (The fat is rumored to figure in voudou potions, but more explicably, also to give you a raging case of the runs.) That evening in the air-conditioned hunting shack, with my father and the other hunters gathered there pleased as well with the 'gator they had all taken, Dub, Pete's fishing partner, 'gator guide, and camp cook par excellence, prepared a genuine Cajun alligator sauce picante for us from the meat of my kill. When served, it proved delicious, somewhere between veal and pork in flavor. Through the shack window as I ate I saw, framed by Spanish moss hanging from Spanish oaks, great blue herons sailing across a cinnabar sunset. 'Gator and birds, huh?

In the end, I couldn't say if I would be back to go 'gatorin' again. All I knew was that I was proud to have done it once.

# Chapter 25

*In 1914, Theodore Roosevelt, fifty-five and the Bull Moose Party's unsuccessful presidential candidate in 1912, spent New Year's Day giving chase to a jaguar in Brazil. Returning to the paddlewheeler Nyoac on the Rio Cuiabá, his skin torn by thorns and bitten by wasps and fire ants after eleven sweltering hours of running through jungle and swamp in the course of the fruitless hunt, he was asked how he felt.*

*"I'm bully," Roosevelt replied, as of course, he would.*

*By the end of his expedition into the Amazon wilderness he had lost fifty-five pounds and, malarial and suffering infections, had to be borne on a stretcher, the ordeal undoubtedly contributing to his early death in 1919 and preventing his likely run for the presidency again in 1920. It is not known that he ever said the trip was a mistake.*

# HAVE *GEVAER*,* WILL TRAVEL

**The camouflage jacket** in the crowded airport must have been the giveaway.

"Going hunting?" The substantial woman of a certain age rested her elbows on the newsstand counter.

"Coming back."

"Where from?"

"Norway."

"What did you get?"

How to explain?

"I got," I said, "a shot at a red deer."

"Where do you live?" It was suddenly an interrogator's question.

I hesitated.

"Wyoming."

The large woman placed two large hands—that looked as if they'd dressed their share of deer and elk—on the counter and pushed herself upright.

"Why," she demanded with indignation I took (or hoped) to be mock, "would you go to Norway to hunt deer when you *live in Wyoming?*"

*How* to explain?

Hunting isn't only about animals, especially hunting where you have never been before. It can be as much about people you would have never met had you not gone, and other things as well. Had I not, for example, ever gone to Norway to hunt red deer in the far western region called Bremanger—my friend John and I trudging with our duffels and rifles off the express catamaran from Bergen and into the rainy September gloaming in Florø, the farthest western place in Norway that is still recognizably a town—I conceivably would never have met tall, slightly ungainly Rune Indrehus, identifiable by his thoroughly goofy red *jegers* cap, who was waiting for us on the quay.

Rune raised undocked sheep on a farm a thousand years old beside the Nordgulen Fjord, where the gray Precambrian granite of the Fennoscandian Shield breached like whaleback from the usually quiet water and where the grass his sheep grazed was as green as any on earth. A proud son of Bremanger, Rune (who represented one of the final links in a long chain of contacts I had made when I decided—why?—that I wanted to see what the hunting in Nor-

---

*Norwegian for "rifle."

way might be like) felt compelled to indicate to us the area's every point of even remotest interest. So on the winding, water-glistening road to our hotel in Svelgen at the head of the Nordgulen, Rune, hunched over the wheel of his compact sedan, would gesture toward the new, wider section of wet asphalt and, relying on Norsk rather than his broken English, decree it "*spesiell*," as opposed to older, narrower stretches of "*normal*" road. Rune would go on to point out during the course of our sojourn "*spesiell*" foundries, soccer fields, churches, pine trees, Volkswagen Beetles that turned in front of us (Rune not wishing us to miss a thing), and in one memorable instance of seemingly autonomic boosterism run amuck, even a "handicapped person" being escorted by two attendants down the street.

Rune, wanting to make certain we absorbed as much local color and hunting lore as we could stand, delivered us into the homes of various of the area's sportsmen. One was Åge Tansøy ("hunting veteran" in one of Rune's perilous forays into English) who invited us into his paneled basement with old rifles, fox skins, objects of carved wood, taxidermied grouse, and antlers on the walls and showed us fading photographs of dead stag, moose, and reindeer, before producing waffles, jam, and a plastic jug of musty-smelling homebrew he proclaimed "hunter's drink." Another hunter was a woman whose first name was Reidun, and whose surname was also Indrehus. She was not at home when we called, leaving us to stroll around her farmyard and look at her shooting range with its reindeer silhouette target, the sets of red–deer antlers scattered around her woodshed and lit by rain-washed light through ancient wavy glass, and the pellicle-covered quarters of venison dangling from the rafters of her shadowy barn. And there was Arild Sande, son of Alfred, grandnephew of Erik, and great-grandson of Augustine Sande, in whose house we heard the *soga* of the *trollhjort* (the "monster deer") of Bremanger.

Affixed to his paneled wall, Arild had the *trollhjort's* antlers, with forty-inch main beams, an array of seven points a side, seven-inch bases, and a spread of nearly three feet, the once-white bone blackened with tar to replicate the stain left by rubbing. It was claimed that Erik, Arild's granduncle, had shot the red–deer stag 140 years before. The animal had weighed a quarter of a long ton; years later, an old man who had labored on the Sande farm in those days recalled staggering beneath the load of a single leg as he packed it out of the woods for his employer.

Two days after he killed the biggest red deer anyone had ever known of in Bremanger, Erik drowned in the dark sea off Kalvåg. His father, Augustine, knew at once, as surely as he knew the changings of the moon and the seasons of his flocks, that had his son not put his rifleball into the heart of such a stag, the cold deep waters would not have taken him. So Augustine gathered all that remained of the deer, the meat and hide and antlers more massive than any existing even in memory, and at a bay called Straumen flung them all into the sea, to dissuade the soul of that animal from claiming any more of Augustine's own in retribution for his dead son's heedless vainglory in presuming to kill so great a deer.

Seventy-five years later a storm blew into Straumen where an English coal carrier was overwintering, having left her cargo at the ironworks that now stood on the shore. In the high seas the anchor slipped and the ship nearly ran aground. The captain, his crew returned to England while he waited for the spring and another cargo to sail home with, had to take the ship out to where the anchor flukes could find hard bottom. To help him navigate the fjord, the captain asked Alfred, grandson of Augustine and a complete stranger to the captain, to pilot for him.

Alfred had no idea why the captain wanted him when there were many other pilots the captain knew on the Nordgulen; but he came aboard at the appointed time, nonetheless. They began to crank the windlass to raise the anchor from where it lay in the deep, soft mud of the ocean floor; and as the shank of the anchor broke the surface, they saw the points of a red–deer's antlers rising from the water with it.

They stopped the windlass, and Alfred climbed down into the jollyboat tied to the ship and rowed to the bow, where he lifted a set of antlers, hooked by the anchor, into the boat. The antlers were whole and bone white and too big to be anything other than those Augustine had cast away a lifetime before.

Alfred possessed no superstition, but as he held the antlers he knew why the English captain had felt compelled to ask for no one but him. Because the antlers had somehow called, bidding Alfred to come so he could witness that the curse had been washed away by the years and the sea; and that it was time for the antlers to return to the air and light and be carried back to the house of Sande, where to this day they remained.

It was as good a Norwegian hunting story as I'd ever heard, and worth the time spent in the home of Arild Sande. I had come for the hunting, though, along with the stories. On our first afternoon in Svelgen, John and I joined up with one of the hunting teams of Bremanger. The large factory that was the main employer in Svelgen gave several organized groups of employees permission to hunt on the company land in the steep rocky hills above town. The hunters identified themselves with round cloisonné pins showing a stag in a bull's-eye. When a hunter took a deer, a red dot would be added to the pin, signifying the kill.

When we met the mostly young men of the hunting team, few of them had red dots on their pins. Still, they were imbued with a slightly melancholic Scandinavian sense of optimism. As they shrugged into their military surplus coats and rucksacks and slung their rifles (everything from Model 700s to Olympic free rifles) onto their shoulders, one of them, named Per (a disconcerting number of Norwegians are named "Per"), asked, "Do you have gun? Yes? You'll need it today."

In the drizzly September weather, just past the equinox, we began to climb. Our half of the team was to be standers, while the other half would be drivers. That half was on the other side of the hill and would start to push when the standers called on their cell phones, telling the drivers that we were in position. Most of the drivers didn't even carry rifles, but demonstrated their team spirit nonetheless by striding over the hills, any red deer that might be taken to be shared by one and all.

We standers moved up through moss, willows, grass, ferns, and *troll* mushrooms the size and color of raspberry berets. We climbed along tumbling creeks and shale ledges under dripping rock faces. As we moved through yellow-turning birches and alders and stands of blue spruce and Norway pine, I could not, try as I might, keep myself from thinking, Isn't it good, Norwegian wood?

The first afternoon I sat on a stand in the tall wet grass while John, in much better physical condition than I, went on far higher with the team. I was supposed to be in a good spot where one of the team had killed a deer earlier in the season; so I, adopting the Nordic optimism of my hosts, held out semi-high hopes. What else could I do, now that I was all the way over in Norway? In the end, though, all I saw was one of the drivers, who passed across the hillside like a steeplechaser, pausing for a moment to ask, in English, if I'd seen anything, before bounding off once again when I answered, "No."

The second afternoon, with sun falling through sparse clouds, I ended up hunting near one of the older hunters, one not named Per. This was Svein Erik. He wore a vinyl Elmer Fudd hat and was the last of the great Caucasian chainsmokers. With red hair and goatee gone to gray, he would have been the character in the '30s movie they called "Whitey." One look also told you that he was a deer slayer. You didn't need to see the red dots already on his pin to know that.

So I was not disappointed when the team put me in a grassy meadow between bare rock cliffs; and Svein Erik climbed a few hundred feet farther into the rocks and took his own stand, automatically lighting a cigarette as he did. John, meanwhile, climbed on with the rest of the team into the rocks and cliffs no red deer on earth ever contemplated climbing into, although after only two days of hunting with them, I realized that this mattered far less to hunters in Norway than it did to the ones I knew in America.

At home, hunters could claim that they hunted only to be out, to walk the woods and smell the air; but in Norway they actually seemed to mean it. Norwegians (despite preconceptions about gloom and isolation) seemed to crave fel-

lowship no less than lemmings do, and the primary function of their hunting did indeed seem to be to join with their friends to hike and climb up to somewhere high and difficult, then take out bread and sausage and drinks from their rucksacks and enjoy the view. It gave every impression of being a hunt for art's sake, with game a rare and definitely added attraction.

From where I sat in a pass above the end of the lake called Svelgsvatnet, a pass through which the drivers meant to push the red deer, I could look out to the east, to where the sun at the end of the day brought the heather and the bare ancient rock of those hills to a red glow. I could look around at the rain from earlier in the day spangling the needles and leaves of the trees and the blades of the grass. I could contemplate the tranquility and even begin to believe that this was what Norwegian hunting was all about. Until I heard the slam of a rifle shot and looked up to see a red deer hind bearing down on me at ramming speed.

No, hunting isn't only about animals, but it is not *not* about them, either. Nor is it *not* about killing, or at least trying to kill, not even for Norwegians, I thought, as I heard Svein Erik fire once again, leaning into his rifle as a gauze of tobacco smoke rose around him.

This shot, like his first, missed. The hind's hooves dug into the heather, kicking up clods like a thoroughbred on a muddy track, driving for the finish line. With her elk's head held high, the hind saw me and cut hard to her left, diving into a stand of spruce.

So much for navel gazing, and as much out of conditioned reflex as from a realization that there were a lot of folks working hard to put this deer in front of me, and that none of them would mind having his efforts rewarded with a cut of red–deer meat, I got to my knees and swung on the running deer and, like my host, missed. The hind was gone; and though I was certain of the miss, I got up anyway and checked for any sign of wounding where the hind had been when I fired. And found none.

On the third day I went hunting with yet another Per and ended up on another grass-and-moss-covered slope in a heavy mist, waiting for a red deer to run by. Alone with my thoughts, I reckoned that for all its punctilio and festivity, Norwegian hunting, like our hunting, was still about a fundamental effort at obtaining meat, about earning from nature to subjugate hunger. Even at its most ritualized, this remained the primal fact of hunting, even this far around the world from home. As the day, the last of the red–deer season, darkened, and my hunting in Norway ended, I knew that this was something else I had learned by coming here.

Besides the hunting, there was also fishing—but this is about hunting—and food, which is at the heart of hunting, especially when that food included perfectly aged *rype*, willow grouse, tasting just slightly livery, followed by cloudberries and cream. Or *urtegravet elg med ripsgelé*, moose marinated in gin, basil, tarragon, and sage, served with red currant jelly and a pear-and-mustard sauce. Or on my last night in Norway in a restaurant on the Bryggen, the Hanseatic League wharf in Bergen (not a level or plumb line left to be found in any wall or ceiling in any building), *hvalbiff* grilled with onions, which was not bad, for whale steak. (Secretly I have to believe that if Greenpeace holds a lease on a district of Hell, I am surely bound to burn.)

None of this seemed quite explanatory enough, though. So, over a year later, I phoned a hunter I had met on the flight home from Norway. He had been hunting moose, *elg*, the same time John and I had been hunting red deer. Rather than traveling from Wyoming to hunt in Norway, he'd traveled from western Montana.

What did he tell people who asked him why he'd gone to Norway, I asked.

It had, he said, been an "impeccable experience," one of sitting on "posts," or stands, over a hundred years old, while drivers and elkhounds pushed the woods; of dipping water from clear mountain brooks with hand-carved wooden cups; of coming from a place (Montana) where a hunting tradition was splitting a Snickers on opening morning, only to tap into traditions as old as the Vikings; of, eventually, not getting a shot at a moose, but of having the opportunity of turning several down.

He could, in other words, not explain it, either, at least not to anyone else's satisfaction.

I hadn't known that, of course, when I stood in the crowded airport, just returned from Norway, so maybe the explanation I came up with for the woman behind the newsstand wasn't so bad after all.

Maybe it said enough about wanting to look over the next mountain, or across the next ocean. About wanting to meet different people, hear different stories, and learn different customs, but still discover, despite the differences, the likenesses. And how hunting remained the best way I knew of doing just that.

Maybe it did, or maybe it didn't; but it was the only explanation I had, or still do.

"You had to," I said, turning to catch my flight home, "be there."

And for reasons I would probably never entirely understand, or entirely need to, so had I.

# Chapter 26

*Make haste, my beloved, and be thou like to a roe . . . upon the mountains of spices.*

—The Song of Solomon 8:14

# CZECHS AND BALANCES

**In the late-September** morning after the fog lifted, the woodcutters came in the heavy wagon pulled by draft horses. The forester Dan Lindenberg and I climbed from the stand where we had been since long before light and from which we had been able to look out across the rolling Bohemian farm fields and over the tops of the trees to the two tall bell towers of the twelfth-century abbey. On the ground, we still-hunted roebuck, moving into the trees and finding scrapes the size of saucers from a child's toy tea set. As we walked, I would notice Dan taking a sheet of folded typing paper from the inner pocket of his long, woolen Hubertus greatcoat, opening it, and studying what was on it. Just when it appeared that he was about to say something, he would fold the paper back up and return it to his pocket, and we would go on, each of us depending on awkward pantomime to cross the almost total language gulf that separated us.

A few mornings later, sitting in a pole-and-limb ladder stand—the wood so old that what was not covered in moss was weathered to dull silver—twenty feet above an uncut field of clover around the edge of which were planted peas, Dan pulled out his sheet of paper again. Before he could put it away, I gestured to him to let me see it.

Three columns of words in different languages ran down the paper. The first I took to be Czech, the third German. I could not recognize the second. Pointing to it, I looked at Dan and shrugged.

"Eengleesh," Dan smiled.

"That's not English," I assured him, shaking my head as I tried to read the words.

"*Ano*," Dan insisted, still smiling, pointing to the words himself, "Eengleesh."

"*Rajfl?*" I asked, reading from the middle column. "*Binokjulrs? Kongratjulejsns?*"

"*Ano*," Dan nodded, giving the spellings their pronunciation in Czech. "*Rifle, binoculars, congratulations.*"

"Ah," I said. "Yes, *ano*, I see." Reading down the middle column, I could even see now how to write the essential European hunting story in Czechered English: *Vajld pig. Vilju sut? Bladyhel, ju misd. Lets gou houm. Van bír?* The real story of European hunting, on the other hand, may not be so concisely told.

Here in North America, where our hunting tradition is vastly different from Europe's, we have a distinctly divided view of what Old World hunting may have to teach us, both about the chase and wildlife. Some hunters like to point to the intense course of instruction that many hunters in Europe must undergo before they can be issued a hunting license (one textbook German hunters study during the year of classes they attend in order to earn their hunting licenses is over seven hundred pages long and covers everything from game identification, dog care, firearms, hunting laws, tracking, field dressing, diseases of wildlife, and ecology, to the various traditional bugle calls used during a hunt). These hunters contend that American hunters and hunting could benefit from such extensive preparation, as opposed to the one- or two-week "hunter education" course that most hunters must take before they can obtain their first hunting license.

There is another view of European hunting, though. This is the view that in Europe all hunting is merely an extension of property rights. It is the view that the tradition of European hunting we know today grew out of the ancient Roman *latifundia*, the great landed estates to which the nobility retreated and where, protected behind high walls as various Vandals, Visigoths, Ostrogoths, Huns, and just the plain-old mob rampaged through the cities and countryside without, they went about defining the culture of the aristocracy, based on dancing, feasting, racing, the hunting of estate-reared game, and the occasional gibbeting of a poacher, that has come down to us more or less intact to this day. The contention of some, such as author Matt Cartmill in his book *A View to a Death in the Morning*, is that within this tradition hunting is nothing more than ritualized warfare, or even metaphorical rape, committed upon wild animals. Once again, Western Man in all his horrifying viciousness and despoliation.

As far as Western men went, Dan and I didn't seem to be committing a great deal of despoliation as we sat in the stands. As a government forester, in fact, Dan's job—from which he earned two hundred dollars per month—was to oversee particular tracts of government timberland, keeping tabs on both plants and animals. (One afternoon, driving in his compact Skoda sedan, we came around the bend on a paved forest road and discovered two men bucking up a downed tree and loading the logs into a trailer. Dan pulled up and began questioning them. One in wire-rimmed glasses looked like a bulked-up Warren Zevon while the other, still cradling a log in his arms, resembled a slightly more upscale version of those long-haired "Will Work for Food" guys who frequent freeway off-ramps. And though I did not understand a word, I caught the gist. Dan was asking them where their permit was for taking wood. Warren did all the talking—which in tone and rhythm sounded like the scam all grifters try to run—but no documents appeared and Dan soon had a spiral notepad out and was taking names. Dan said something to the other guy, who seemed to notice for the first time that he was holding a log in his arms, and that the long-sleeved undershirt he was wearing was covered in sawdust, and he tossed the log back onto the hillside beside the other logs they had not yet loaded. When he turned to throw the log, I saw the hilt of a large combat knife showing above the belt of his pants at the small of his back. Dan said a few more words to them, apparently about whom they should appear before to tell their story to in a day or two, and we drove off. Upshifting, Dan turned to me and said, without smiling, "Gangsters." Which is when I realized that his job here in the forests of Bohemia might not be quite so arcadian as one might imagine, and that Dan couldn't be in it just for the money.)

One thing that did seem very clear to me about hunting in Europe was the fact that the plants and animals you saw in the woods were the ones considered economically valuable to humans. It was understood, for instance, that I was to kill any fox I saw—I didn't kill any, though I'll admit to missing one. It was necessary to look back to the nineteenth century and before to find when the last bear (1898) or wolf (1756) or lynx (1708)—unloved by herdsmen—had been around in this part of what was now the Czech Republic. Besides an occasional rabbit or hare, and the odd mouse, the only other small wild mammal I saw was a squirrel (*veverka*) that Dan pointed to one morning, saying, "Shippundell." ("'Chip 'n' Dale'?" I asked. "*Ano*," said Dan, grinning broadly.) In the dawns there was a stunning lack of birdsong. It was obvious that this had not happened overnight, but was way things had been for decades, perhaps even centuries.

Yet there were still dense stands of timber—nominal forests even if they were almost exclusively plantations of commercial softwoods. And the variety and number of big-game animals probably surpassed almost anything to be seen in North America: Besides roebuck, the area I hunted around Mariánské Lázne (formerly known as Marienbad) also contained red deer and wild boar, as well as mouflon sheep, sika deer, and fallow deer, the last three introduced species. Although these animals were all free-ranging, they were also carefully accounted and cared for, being fed through the winter and sold off to hunters in the spring, summer, and fall (roebuck hunting commencing in early May), the price based on sex and trophy class, quotas strictly adhered to. Hunting *is* about property in Europe, but it is certainly well-tended property.

On another morning, we heard three shots in rapid succession, and Dan, knowing the country and who would be out hunting in it, was able to identify the shots, based solely on where the sound came from, as being the shots of a mouflon hunter.

Holding up three fingers and saying, "Bang, bang, bang," I tried to tell Dan the old saying about one shot, meat (wishing I knew the Czech word *maso*, then, but getting the point across anyway); two shots, maybe (a hand held out palm-down and wobbled slightly seemed to convey that all right); three shots . . . (I asked Dan for the piece of paper, and there it was) *hovno!* Yes, Dan agreed, no sheep this morning. No last bite to be given.

As I say, many American hunters have mixed emotions about European hunting traditions. Some place great store in all the elaborate ritual and homage paid to the fallen animal—never shaking hands while on stand, even after the animal is down (you must wait until you are standing beside it); never stepping over the carcass; the giving of the "last bite" in the form of a *Brüche,* or "branch," to the dead animal; all the business about *"Weidmannsheil"* and *"Weidmannsdank."* All of this they see as only in keeping with the true seriousness of the hunt and a refreshing antidote to the impudence too many hunting Bubbas exhibit.

Meanwhile others see it all as merely the gloss that has been applied to just one more in a long line of examples of our (Westerners') arrogant efforts to ride roughshod over nature. They see European hunting as a travesty of true hunting, and the wilds and wildlife of Europe as being shaped by the forces of the market rather than the forces of nature. So instead they look to hunting traditions, such as those of Native Americans, that are based on worlds supposedly still in balance, on natural orders that are proclaimed to be still both natural and orderly. But is the wild of Europe so out of balance, and if so, are hunters at fault?

Sometimes during our still-hunts Dan and I walked along a paved road, looking down into a ravine with pines, green undergrowth, the sound of a creek, and the barking of a hidden roebuck. It was peculiar to be hunting on asphalt, and it did accentuate the fact that what seemed to be missing most from European hunting was the truly rustic, both in the hunt and hunter. The hunting tradition of our own North American continent is still closely tied to the rustic; and so, I think, the attachment to *Brüche* and all the other observances of European hunting to our own would be an awful lot like playacting, like those silly people who want to dress up in tweed breeks and Barbour jackets and then go shooting on some pheasant farm, desperately trying to re-create Devonshire in northern New Jersey. I think we are all capable of discovering our own ways of paying due respect and homage to the hunt and the hunted without having to appropriate the rites unique to somebody else's culture, East or West.

Yet what was the real difference between this and hunting grouse along some old logging road, glassing for whitetail at the edge of a food plot, or shooting doves over a stock pond in North America? We are exceedingly fortunate in North America still to have wilderness in which to hunt, but much of our hunting country is not that dissimilar from the hunting country of Europe: Not city or town, neither is it pure wild country. Call it "rough country"; but whatever you call it, it fulfills a need in humans, the need to hunt wherever they are.

One misting morning on our way back to the pension where I was staying in Mariánské Lázne, after our dawn stand hunting, Dan stopped the Skoda beside a muddy trail disappearing into a dark wood. Through gesture, Dan asked if I would like to still-hunt down into the woods, and if he could bring his rifle and hunt with me. Yes, of course, I answered, secretly thrilled that Dan would, in essence, ask me if we could hunt together, rather than our being just hunter and guide.

In the soft mud of the trail there were, almost immediately, the sharp-pointed tracks of roebuck and the round ones of a large sika stag. Dan showed me the rubbing and bedding areas the sika *jelen* was using; the places where the roebuck rubbed, the biggest using the smallest saplings, small enough to fit between the narrow spread of their eight-inch antlers; the fresh rootings made by the wild boar and at the bottom of the woods the big pig wallow, empty.

That warm evening, sitting on a stand, I missed a fine roebuck out at two hundred yards, shooting low, then missing again and again as he ran to cover. Damn, damn, damn, I said, but Dan gestured that it was all right, don't worry. Then a minute later, smiling with a raised eyebrow, Dan lifted his index finger and began to repeat, in Czech, one shot, *maso*; two shots, *jemozno*; three shots, *hovno!*

"*Van bír?*" Dan asked on the way in that night; and in a small, smoky tavern he bought each of us a cold lager and slid pictures of his family across the table to me, while I slid pictures of mine across to him. When we got up to leave, I stopped to look at a cluster of black-and-white photos taped to a bare wall, showing in all their official, airbrushed glory members of the late pantheon: Lenin, Stalin, Brezhnev, and such local lights as the former Communist president Husák and General Secretary Jakes. Only now they looked more like potential targets in a shooting gallery than Heroes of Socialism.

Noting my curiosity, a young Czech, cigarette burned down between yellowed fingers, lifted his glass in mock salute, explaining, "Very popular pipple!"

I really did want a roebuck during my hunt in the Czech Republic, because the roebuck came to me to represent perhaps the most European of Europe's big game—mainly, I think, because the roebuck (with fairly limited commercial potential) has shown the greatest tenacity for survival, which seems perhaps the most fundamental European trait. After all, in almost every generation for as far back as they can remember Europeans have been surviving revolution, totalitarianism, or tanks in the streets. And they keep finding a way to go on, which may also be the ultimate lesson European hunting has to teach: The European hunter did not create the kind of country in which he now hunts (that was created millennia ago, and not by hunters but by farmers); but he has found a way to hunt in it, nonetheless. Because of that, European hunting isn't, finally, about either ritual or rape; it's simply about hunting and humans' overwhelming desire to find a way to go on hunting, to locate some small patch of wildness (or just roughness) even between the paved roads, the way the roebuck finds his.

And in North America, the land of the free and the home of the brave? I have a sense that those who immigrated here three hundred, two hundred, even one hundred years ago—many because they wanted to escape the kinds of laws and governments that barred them from hunting, among other things—probably wouldn't recognize the place today, or they might find it all too familiar to the places they left. Our tradition of hunting may be one based on a literally outlandish sense of freedom, but our reality becomes daily more restrictively European. I doubt we will ever see a total privatization of hunting and the cultivation of select hunting species here, but because of the growing pressures of habitat loss, human-population increase, and the foolishness in legislatures and in public opinion that these can engender, we will find a hunting that is increasingly less free, perhaps even necessarily so. But like the roe deer (and the European hunter), we will probably find a way to survive (survival the most fundamental human trait), always able to discover some wildness, somewhere, if only within ourselves.

I didn't get a roebuck. I did get a sika stag, one we spotted in the fog at dawn (ivory antler tips above a near-black body) the day after I missed the roebuck. Dan insisted that I take him, that he was too good to pass up, the 130-grain bullet from the .270 dropping him in the heavily dewed field a hundred yards from the stand. Dan offered *kongratjulejsns*, but would not shake my hand. While he went to get the Skoda so we could retrieve the stag, I spotted a roebuck (*srnec*, I now knew) with long, heavy tri-tined antlers on a foggy rise six hundred yards away and just watched him feed his way over the ridge. Then Dan appeared, driving over the hill in the Skoda, and I climbed down to meet him at the sika. Now we shook hands, and Dan gave the stag his *Brüche*, and one for me, dipped in the blood of the deer's wound, to be placed in the band of my hat. From his coat Dan produced a small bottle of vodka and we toasted the sika, each taking the bottle only in our left hands. Then there was the dressing of the deer and carrying him from the field, the things that were the same about hunting wherever you went and reminded you of what somebody had once written, that "all the country in the world is the same country and all hunters are the same people." Which is why you could hunt anywhere, why you could come to Europe and feel as if you had always been there, and why you would come back, hoping to find the roebuck still there. And know you would.

# Chapter 27

*My heart's in the Highlands, my heart is not here,*
*My heart's in the Highlands a-chasing the deer;*
*A-chasing the wild deer, and following the roe,*
*My heart's in the Highlands wherever I go.*

—Robert Burns

# AROUND THE WORLD IN 7MM:
# A TALE OF TWO CALEDONIAS

*Part I, Rusa Stag on the Island of New Caledonia*

**The question is,** *How best to measure the world? In frequent-flier miles or with coffee spoons? By time zones or projections of Mercator? Some years ago, I went out to see if it could be measured in seven millimeters and deer, in a season stretching across the hemispheres—north, east, south, and west—and seemingly running backward from winter into fall.*

If there are two more separated tracts of solid land on the globe, it would be hard to envision them. Eighty degrees of latitude, 170 of longitude, and some ten thousand miles of curved planet lie between. And while one represents Franco-Melanesian culture, the other is distinctly Anglo-Celtic. What they most definitely have in common, though, is a certain insularity, an ancient tradition of clans and men in skirts, wild fish, and stag. And a name, "Caledonia."

Caledonia was what the Romans called Scotland, and New Caledonia is what Captain James Cook—in an outbreak of delusional nostalgia for the British Isles—named the ancient group of nonvolcanic South Pacific islands of clouds, mountains, and a staggering assortment of flowers that he discovered a thousand miles east of Australia in 1774. When Cook landed and met the indigenous Kanak people, the island's native fauna consisted of lizards, birds (including the world's largest pigeon), and bats. He left dogs and pigs; and then the French came, annexing the island in 1853, calling it Nouvelle Calédonie, and planning to transport convicts there the way England had transported hers to Botany Bay. But a monumental deposit of nickel ore was found, and the plans for a new Devil's Island were scrapped in favor of colonization. Since then New Caledonia has been famous, or notorious, as the place where McHale's Navy went for liberty and for a liberation movement among the Kanaks, met with violence by the *caldoches*, descendants of the original French settlers. One other claim to fame began on the fourth of February, 1870, when a steam sloop, the *Guichen*, arrived from Java with a cargo of twelve deer—four stags and eight hinds—of the species *Cervus timorensis russa*, the rusa stag. For the colonists, the deer were at least a reminder of the big game of home. With no wild predators to contend with, and much wooded, mountainous terrain in which to hide, the rusa became something more than a reminder, to the extent that today there is nearly one for each and every of New Caledonia's two hundred thousand inhabitants, and more than fifteen per square mile of island.

Indigenous to the Indonesian archipelago, described by naturalists as a "primitive" subgenus of deer, the rusa is the size of a big mule deer; and on New Caledonia, wild and free-ranging, they grow bigger in both body and antler than they now do in their native habitat. In the roar (at the end of July and throughout August), the stags' guard hairs turn slate gray, making them look almost blue as they throw back their three-pronged antlers and bellow on the sides of the open coastal hills, come down from the steep mountains to find hinds. By the middle of the roar, the stags will have torn away their long manes in fighting with other stags. Strongly nocturnal and smart enough to come in out of the rain, rusa deer need, ideally, to be hunted in the earliest part of a dry day, at the start of the roar.

At the beginning of the roar at the end of one July, midwinter there, I left the capital, Noumea—a slightly low-rent Nice of red flame trees, topless beaches, and an open-air harborside Marches Municipaux stocked with *pâtisseries*, *café au lait*, and fresh tropical fruit—and went northwest up the western littoral of the main island, Grand Terre, with Dr. Daniel Marhic, a local veterinarian and outfitter. (Marhic, though he had lived in New Caledonia for years, was a *zoreille*, a recent French immigrant, via Tahiti, and a passionate hunter, his modest Noumea home packed with mounted heads from around the world, from walrus to Marco Polo sheep.) Marhic had made sure to pack his four-wheel drive with the essentials of Gallic hunting—baguettes, cheese, versicolor lobsters, wine, and thoroughly rancid rock 'n' roll on the stereo: French food must be taken seriously; French popular music, like French military strategy, must never be. Barely beyond the city limits, the good doctor cracked a beer and had his young assistant guide, "Dou Dou," pass one to me from the cooler in the backseat. *Ooh la la* and *zut alors*, this sure wasn't Kansas anymore.

We traveled the dry-savannah coast, trailed by Marhic's wife, Monique, and his grown son, Nicola, in another, smaller four-wheel drive. The sky above the light blue sea was washed by wind and rain, white clouds scudding through it, building as we went. Tall, stark, practically Triassic columnar pines loomed on the ridges, and among them were an absurdly abundant number of wild turkey, not to mention wild boar and wild goat. Three hundred klicks from Noumea, at a village called Poya, the coast highway swung inland toward the high cordillera to the east, and we left it to follow a dirt road down to the sea and the sunset lying under a bank of clouds, stags standing out in the gray. On a hill above the water were the cabins and headquarters buildings of Ston de Quanéko, a five-thousand-hectare ranch, or "station," spread over rolling land and draws patched with stands of eucalyptus and low ironwood pines, flowers everywhere.

This was camp, and from here I could listen to the rain when it came in the night and hear above the pelting on the cabin roof the roaring of three separate stags, like the bugling of elk with the croup.

At five o'clock the next morning I was awakened, and after bread and coffee we were out by six. The rain was blowing through and only a few drops still fell. Marhic, Dou Dou, and I hiked just below the ridges, glassing for the blue-gray stags before they slipped back into cover with the morning sun. On one of the ridges we came to a place where three draws ran down, and to the east we heard a roar.

Staying above the draws, we moved out on the ridge toward the sound. The walking was not hard, but the worry was the lack of cover. Coming to a wide canyon, we spotted the stag on the other side. He was with hinds.

We fell back, hoping the hinds had not seen us—the stag was too busy with other concerns to notice us, but all too apt to notice the hinds if they scattered. We decided to backtrail and drop down to a dry watercourse that ran between the two slopes. We skidded down the slick wet grass and mud and around exposed rocks to the wash. The sky was still gray, but the edge of the clouds was showing out over the ocean.

In the wash a heavy curtain of eucalyptus ran upslope between the rusa and us, and we worked our way to its end to look around it for the stag. Before we got there, though, we saw hinds already running out over the slope. All that seemed to be left to do was to get around the eucalyptus and confirm that the stag was gone, too. As we were about to do that, the stag roared again.

On hands and knees we scuttled through brush in the wash to where we could see the stag. He was alone now on the open hillside, furiously hooking brush. Sitting, I set up crossed-sticks and laid my 7mm Weatherby Magnum in the crotch, trying to get the stag in the scope. I couldn't see him clearly around the eucalyptus because Marhic was crowding me out as he glassed, judging the trophy. I tried to tell him to move so I could get a clean shot. After an exchange of confused and excited Anglo-Gallic whispers, he got the point and scooted over. He told me it was a good stag, and I had the reticle on the point of the rusa's left shoulder, the deer quartering toward me. It was 250 uphill yards. When the hammer fell on the cartridge primer, the 160-grain bullet crossed those 250 yards and sent the stag leaping, plunging forward and disappearing behind the curtain of eucalyptus.

We were up and jogging out to see where he went. He had gone ten yards, shot through both lungs and the aorta. It was fast walking uphill to where he lay on his side, his thick antlers stretching long and dark over the ground, tattered velvet hanging from them like shedding snakeskin. The hairs of the cape were long and perfect. Looking around, I saw from where I stood rusa hinds, wild turkey, and wild boar—making it one of the better places in the world to be standing that day, especially with a wild rusa stag at my feet, the morning sun breaking out. That night, Monique prepared rusa fillets, heavy with garlic, for dinner, and tarts for dessert; and as I lay in bed later, I would hear wild boar rooting outside my cabin, and stags roaring, still, on the hillsides . . . but that's only the half of it . . .

*Part II, Red Stag in the Highlands of Old Caledonia*

**Old Caledonia lies** farther north than New Caledonia lies south, so the northern fall I found there in October seemed to fit like a template over the subtropical July winter I'd hunted in half a world away. But while there had been palm trees at the airport in Noumea, they appeared decidedly thin on the ground in Inverness, Scotland, when I arrived with my wife and son.

In certain airports in the world, at certain times of year, if you hunt, you will invariably bump into people you know or recognize. Nairobi used to be like that in the dry safari months; Johannesburg still is. Anchorage in August; Laredo in December; Denver from September on. In Inverness it's the first three weeks of October, when the stags are roaring. It is then possible to see any number of the world's most prominent big-game hunters, come for the stalking. When I saw three or four such recognizably famous personages collecting their luggage and rifle cases from the baggage carousel, I immediately wanted to walk right up, get my own bags and rifle, and flee. I wanted my heart to be in the Highlands, a-chasing the deer, not schmoozing with noted sportsmen. Luckily, that's when our driver, whom our outfitter had sent to fetch us, appeared and drove us far away from all that.

Subarctic daylight still filled the late-afternoon sky and made the green land ache in the eye. Around here somewhere was Culloden moor, where in the last (and perhaps most bloodthirsty) battle in the British Isles "Colonel Belford's cannon blew away the clans," obliterating the Jacobite rebellion of 1745 and Bonnie Prince Charlie's foppish hopes of overthrowing the House of Hanover and reclaiming the crown. Up the road, we passed through Tain where the "16 men" made their glorious whisky in one of a legion of noble distilleries in the country. We could have kept on up the coast, in the direction of John o' Groats at the far northeastern tip of Scotland itself, passing the monument to the Duke of Sutherland, tall and ominous as a columnar pine just below a mountain ridge—and a favorite target of the local Scots for sighting-in their stalking rifles. We went northwest, though, and at last, in the dark and, by then, rain, came to Lairg Lodge at the end of Loch Shin. It was a large old warren of a house with paneled hallways and sharp turns, claw-footed bathtubs and, for some inexplicable reason, a mounted striped marlin over one of the staircases. The cook, Anne (widowed, as perhaps only a Scotswoman might be, by her husband's being struck by lightning while fly fishing for salmon), had dinner for us in the long dining room with a mounted blackcock on a table by the curtained window, and shortly after that it was time to go to sleep in the tall pillowy beds, thinking of stags.

I began my stalking the next morning, but not at dawn, and not before breakfast. It was not, in fact, before 8:30 A.M., the sun fresh after the night's rain, that I reached the estate where I would hunt and met my "stalker"—that is the name of the chief guide, while his assistant is the "gillie," making me, of course, the "rifle" or, in a nod to former times, the "gentleman." As the English cervid maven G. K. Whitehead notes, "stalking the Scottish Red deer differs considerably from its [early-starting] pursuit on the continent or in the woods of England . . . due to the fact that the deer are on the open mountain and therefore easier to locate with telescope or binoculars." This is a good thing, not solely for the slugabeds among us, but for the manner in which it lets a stalk be successfully planned and carried out when the deer have been spotted at rest, often at midday.

It was midmorning when I went onto the "hill" above Strathcarron (the "River Carron," where salmon still leapt), being jostled in the back of an all-terrain Argo with the stalker, Jim Gilmore, and the gillie, Ronny Ross, up front. Jim was tall and young, Ronny short and old. It would be a misnomer to describe Ronny as a "gillie" because we were actually hunting on his estate, where he was the keeper. We were here to give Ronny a hand by taking a stag from his quota. The notion of "quota" is an inverted one in the Highlands, where the free-roaming hill deer are considered a nuisance by the government, threatening the greenie-inspired reforestation of Scotland, the return of the ancient Caledonian forest. It was not a matter of how many deer you were allowed to kill, but how many you were *required* to: By himself, Ronny had for many years taken thirty to forty stags, and 150 hinds, off the estate each season with only "garrons" (ponies) to pack out the carcasses, all to fulfill the quota. Under such pressure, any hill stag carrying as few as ten points (as opposed to the cosseted and spoon-fed park stags kept in enclosures and let to grow unholy twelve-, fourteen-, eighteen-, sky's-the-limit-point "heads") was a trophy of outstanding quality, and anything with branch antlers was a shooter.

The dirt road we followed was meant for the horses and carts of the stalkers and grouse shooters of Victoria Regina's day. Over a succession of summers back then, one man with a spade, living in a canvas tent and feeding himself on porridge, hand-cut the road through the heather and peat, making it four foot wide and with proper banks and bridges, earning one pence a yard and completing nine thousand yards each season. In a way it seemed somehow sacrilegious just to be rolling over it; we ought to get out every so often and bow in honor to the solitary builder. At the top of the hill we did stop and got out to glass.

Jim took a quick hike to look into a canyon behind us, while Ronny and I lay down in the thick cushion of the heather and scanned for deer, Ronny with his spyglass and me with my Japanese-made binoculars. Ronny, of course, wore a deerstalker cap and smoked a pipe, and in between pulls of tobacco as he peered through the spyglass resting on his knee, he reminisced about growing up when his father had made two pounds a week and his mother stitched all their clothes, and they'd even had to resole their own shoes. He'd joined the army and gone to Aden, but came back to where his heart, too, was a-chasing the wild deer. And when he thought about how he'd grown up, he remembered how they'd made their own entertainment and never been hungry.

"Sure, there was no harm in it," he said with finality, clamping onto the stem of his pipe and staring harder through his spyglass.

It had never been easy country, and the fleecy white sheep (who had scalloped out breaks here in the heather, tasseling them with wind-strips of wool where they'd rubbed) made things only harder, no matter how picturesque they appeared on postcards. After Culloden and the disintegration of the clans (as much a moral failing of the chieftains as an economic and political one), and after the sheep came, the likes of the Duke of Sutherland—aided by factors and sheriffs, some even named McIntyre—evicted all the tenants and torched their huts. Scores of families crowded into the churches and churchyards for shelter (at Croick Church, upstream from here on Strath Cuileannach—"black water"— they had scratched their names like some last disconsolate mementos into the glass of the windows and left the date, "1845"), before being driven to the coast to harvest seaweed, and ultimately to emigrate to Canada and the United States. The "clearances" left the Highlands one of the most depopulated parts of the British Isles, and actually preserved some of its remnant wilderness. I was glad, though, that the sheep were off the hill by this time of year, leaving only deer, and wondered, idly, why no one had gotten around to disintegrating the duke's monument, rather than merely plinking at it. Jim returned, and he and I worked our way around to the south side of the hill, leaving Ronny with the Argo, a golden eagle shadowing us.

Below in a glen ran a burn—and being able to say something like that is just one of the reasons to hunt stags in the Highlands—and on our side was a stag with hinds beside a fallen-down sheep fence. Looking around, we spotted three other small red–deer herds on either side of the burn. Across was a stag in the rocks above a bright green Scots pine, and Jim said we should work toward him, but then decided we should not waste a chance at the stag on this side, by the fence.

The rolling terrain gave us cover as we walked through ling and cross-leafed heather, the purple flowers dying and the leaves going brown. A brace of grouse flushed ahead of us, pushing a sika stag out of the bed where he was hiding, hoping we wouldn't notice—we hadn't, till he ran. Then a red–deer hind and calf showed, and we lay down until they moved off. We started to crest the first of many rises, and fifty yards before we topped out we began to crawl. From there we crawled through heather, bogs, rivulets, relatively fresh sheep dung, and extremely fresh dung of deer, going on all fours from one rise to the next, covering at least a quarter mile this way. It worked, though, because when another hind and calf spotted us, the hind just barked and stood her ground.

At the last rise we went from crawling to worming to see the "beasts" spread out on a large flat below. I had to belly-crawl another few feet to get a clean shot at the stag; but even pressed into the heather, this was too much movement for the deer. A hind just beneath the rise bolted through the herd, taking them all, including the heavy rust-colored stag, with her.

As the deer vanished, we got up and slogged after them across the muddy flat. The deer went out of sight around a large heathered knob, and that's where we headed. It was some distance to the knob, and by the time we crawled out onto it, the sun at our backs concealing us, the stag we had seen by the fence had come to rest on the other side of the glen, bedded on the steep slope beneath an outcrop of white rock, two hundred yards away. An elk in North America might have gone a dozen miles if spooked like that, but there were so many other deer in these Highlands, there weren't two, let alone a dozen, unoccupied miles to go. While his hind fed up the glen from him, he lay in the long heather, alternately roaring and dozing.

I set up the same 7mm Weatherby Magnum rifle I'd killed the rusa stag with in the same crotch of the same crossed-sticks and waited for my breathing and heart to slow. Then I had to go on waiting, Jim saying that I needed to have the stag stand. As the minutes passed and my legs went to sleep, I adjusted and readjusted my shooting position. All around there were the roars of other, unseen, stags, coming closer, coming to take the stag-below's hinds. I had visualized the shot about a thousand times, seeing the stag falling cleanly with each imagined one, when he finally stood, ready to answer the challenges of the other stags.

The crosshairs were on him as he stretched after standing, and I let off the safety. I squeezed the trigger and the shot was a clean miss. I held too high, not compensating for the down angle. I fired again as he ran and missed again. He headed up the glen, trying to gather his hinds, stopping above another rock outcrop. Jim whispered loudly to put the crosshairs low on his shoulder; and I tried to make the shot feel like one at the rifle range, breathing, releasing, aiming, squeezing, and shooting. In the echo of the shot the stag ran forward, then pitched headlong. He rolled once, then again, then was falling. Piling up near the bottom of the slope after turning end over end, he lay dead in the heather.

Leaving the bolt on the empty cartridge, I made my way slipping and falling down the steep slope of rocks and bracken, crossed the stony bed of the burn, and forded the water in the channel to reach the stag, Jim already there. The bullet had gone where Jim said to put it, but it should have been the first, not the third. He was a good branch-antlered stag, though, and the right one to take out of the herd. As Jim was "gralloching" the stag, Ronny, having heard the shots, drove the Argo over to us. In a little while we were bouncing back over the rises, past a cenotaph erected to a stalker killed in the 1800s in a shooting accident involving deerhounds and a gentleman, and in the last light I looked out at the heather and the Highlands, looking for the real measure of a place like this, or one like New Caledonia, where it was already spring.

When I was home from the hill, or at least back at the lodge with my wife and son, I told them that it was true: It was a small world, after all. Sometimes it was only seven millimeters across.

# Chapter 28

*People ask you why you live in Cuba and you say it is because*
*you like it. It is too complicated to explain about the early morning*
*in the hills above Havana where every morning is cool and fresh on*
*the hottest day in summer. . . . You do not tell them about the*
*strange and lovely birds that are on the farm the year around, nor*
*about all the migratory birds that come through, nor that quail*
*come in the early morning to drink. . . . You do not tell them about*
*the shooting club just down the road, where we used to shoot the big*
*live-pigeon matches for the large money. . . . You could tell them*
*that you live in Cuba because you only have to put shoes on when*
*you come into town, and that you can plug the bell in the party-line*
*telephone with paper so that you won't have to answer. . . . But*
*those are professional secrets.*
    —Ernest Hemingway, *"The Great Blue River"*

# THE CUBAN FLU

**Twenty-two years ago**, because I could, I went to Cuba to hunt, my reasons for going there no more distinct than that. Certainly it was not so I could assist in the cane harvest or to be better able to understand the "Revolution" or any of the other more seemingly usual explanations for why someone headed there in those days. For me, wildfowl seemed sufficient.

I flew to Cuba out of Fort Lauderdale early on a winter Sunday morning on board a well-loaded, well-maintained DC-3—a sort of tableau vivant from the pages of American aviation history. After gaining altitude the plane swung out over the Gulf Stream and turned south. En route we passed above the islands of Bimini and Andros, and the very turquoise, very shallow-looking Great Bahama Bank. The first sight of Cuba was the outer mangrove cays where the Old Bahama Channel ran, then the north shore. We came in over the Laguna de Leche, "lagoon of milk"—a large saltwater lagoon looking more mustardy than lacteal—turning east to fly on another hundred miles to the airport at Camagüey, landing three hours after takeoff.

Much of Cuba, I learned, was mountainous, but the adjoining central provinces of Camagüey and Ciego de Ávila (the "forest clearing of Ávila") were flat agricultural and ranch country. The roads ran straight, and from the air you could see an occasional truck, but more often bicycles, moving along the packed red dirt or asphalt. As you came in above Camagüey the city, you passed over postrevolutionary housing constructions, some run-down, others (even more postrevolutionary) shiny and new; all, however, built in the same grand roofless plain proletarian ghastly deadening tradition of Bauhaus. Most of the housing you saw in the provinces, though, looked distinctly "*antes la revolucíon*," expressing a predilection for shotgun houses with adobe-tile or thatched-palm roofs, *postigo* doors and *portales* to shade you from the sun, clean-swept floors, lighted TV sets, and sometimes a wall patched with rusting Coca-Cola signs.

Photography was frowned upon in the airport at Camagüey—Soviet MiGs still touched down on the field outside the small, aged, low pink terminal. There were no problems, though, with the gawking, jabbering, touristical use of cameras away from the airport. Clearing customs in Cuba was much like the process anywhere else in the world: public humiliation in the name of secure borders. (Why, the question would be asked in that abstruse Spanish accent Cubans possess, do you have in your suitcase eleven billed caps with adjustable plastic tabs on the backs and the name of an Indiana coal company printed on the crowns? It is not permitted to bring gifts to Cuban people without declaring them. Well, the answer would come in midwestern American spoken at full volume to shatter the language barrier, this cap was for duck hunting; this one for dove; this one for bass fishing; this one for luncheon. . . . ) Yet to bring in a shotgun, all that was required was to give the trip's organizer the gun's serial number a week or two ahead of time; no restrictions were made on the number of shotgun shells you could import; and I can recall no one waving an AK-47 at me and demanding to see my papers and wanting to know what I was doing bringing a weapon and ammunition into Cuba as I would carry my shotgun and shells away from customs, past the framed photograph of Comrade Brezhnev, and outside to the big air-conditioned Spanish-made tourist bus parked on the tarmacadam under the hot sun.

The long afternoon ride from Camagüey to the town of Morón, via the city of Ciego de Ávila, took me past many of the things that came to seem "Cuban" to me: green pastures with solitary ceiba trees bulking leaflessly against the horizon; clusters of tall royal palms, their bark the color of newly poured concrete, standing up to spanking breezes coming in off the Atlantic; goats methodically cropping the long grass along the road's shoulder; barefoot boys riding gaunt horses; old whitewashed haciendas set back in cool groves; vultures sailing noiselessly overhead; a black woman smoking a pipe, shooing chickens into her dusty yard; dewlapped Brahma cattle grazing behind a three-wire fence; a bleached pig skull lying on a rusting tin roof; towering smokestacks billowing clouds of sulfurous black smoke into the tropic sky; fields of cane and rows of citrus trees; and every so often a political slogan strung out along the highway on a series of billboards like a Marxist-Leninist model of the Burma Shave sign.

In Cuba I would hunt out of the Hotel Morón, which resembled every large men's dormitory built on the campus of every major U.S. university in the mid-1960s. It was an unquestionably weird sensation to know I was in Cuba, with all that it had stood for during the preceding twenty years in my mind, and the minds of my countrymen—the Bay of Pigs, Missile Crisis, Che, Angola, Ethiopia, Mariel Harbor—as I promenaded across the crowded hotel lobby, the afternoon sun slanting in across the polished stone floor, wearing camouflage fatigues, with Winchester-Western SuperX 12-gauge shells rattling in the bellows pockets of my fatigue jacket, and with a camouflage-painted 870 Wingmaster pump laid with studied insouciance across my shoulder, without drawing a glance. The Cuban government had an obvious interest in seeing that American sportsmen visited the island, left behind hard American currency, and were not tampered with in the process; but this seemed a case of taking politesse to the realm of the ridiculous.

While I was drinking one night with an official of the hotel in the Hotel Morón's lightless disco ("drinking with" a major Cuban social obligation for resident and visitor alike), a white-jacketed waiter materialized at my shoulder and presented me with some baffling document to sign regarding, I believe, my exchange of U.S. dollars, several rounds of drinks, and a peroxide blonde. When I examined the thing by matchlight and still could not fathom its purpose, the official leaned across the table and shouted the explanation into my ear, above the music, "It so nobody fuck with your!" As he sat back, grinning proudly at his command of that most essential English, I saw no choice but to stroke the pen across *la cuenta* with a magnanimous flourish. And fuck with mine absolutely no one did while I was in Cuba, anti-Americanism being confined for the most part to official displays on posters, in government publications, and in massive red-flagged parades around the Plaza de la Revolución back in Havana.

(If the average Cuban had one complaint against the United States—in those pre-Elián, pre-Soviet-collapse, pre-Grenada days—it would have been for what he perceived to be the arbitrary, capricious, and purely punitive trade embargo—*plus ça change, plus c'est la même chose*—that had created the most spectacular collection of vintage-1950s Detroit autos to be seen on the streets of any nation. Grandly finned Dodge Furies, De Sotos held together by three hundred coats of paint and Crusonian ingenuity, '57 Chevies that could still break the heart of Saturday night, all passed in stately navigation around Morón's plaza square. New cars, government-issued Russian makes and Fiats, were said to be quite reasonably priced, but were rarities that tended to find their ways into the garages of doctors, professors, and politicos. For an everyday Cuban, a '54 Buick sedan purchased from the original owner might represent an investment in the neighborhood of ten thousand pesos, with the official exchange rate in Cuba running then at $1.30USD to the peso.)

In the People's Republic, we were free to spend our afternoons hunting ducks without fear of protest. We traveled by bus with our guns and shells out to the Base Náutica on the Laguna where we boarded a sixty-two-foot diesel cruiser and with our guides crossed the choppy water. With us was a representative of the tour organizer, a robust and bearded Texan who spent much of his year in Cuba with his knockout Cuban wife, looking after American hunters and fishermen who came south. And with us also was Mariño.

Mariño was tall and thin, eternally smiling, the retired personnel manager of a sugar mill, and what he did not know about hunting in Ciego de Ávila province was not worth knowing. He was almost sixty, wore old tennis shoes, and walked with long springing strides an unconscionable number of miles through mangrove swamps or around milo fields in the course of a day. Men half his age had tried to keep pace with him and barely lived to regret it. One time during duck season, the story went, he had led a young Cuban, who wished to learn the art of guiding American sportsmen, on a peppy little shakedown jaunt through the swamp to test his mettle. Pausing periodically to allow the much younger man to catch up, Mariño took an occasional shot at a teal or wood duck slipping through the trees. He then slipped the dead bird's head through a leather strap tied to his belt, the bird hanging down along his leg. Once when the young man slogged his way up to him, he reported to Mariño of having heard something "back there" among the trees.

Crocodile, Mariño reassured him.

Crocodile? the young man squeaked.

Yes, but only the females during the nesting season were really dangerous.

And, uh, the nesting season . . . ? the young man just hated to ask.

Oh, Mariño supposed, right about now. But only if there were some blood in the water, or the like, would there be any risk of an attack, he further explained, turning to continue on through the knee-deep swamp, a red billow trailing behind him as he towed along his raft of dead ducks.

After half an hour of travel on the Laguna in the afternoon our big boat turned and made its way through a narrow gut between two reefs, the channel marked by long sticks driven into the mud of the lagoon bottom. On rare early-morning hunts, or at night on the way out, a jollyboat would have to be sent ahead to mark this passage with a light or the big boat would run aground—and sometimes did anyway. Now we made straight through the gut for the edge of the mangrove forest surrounding the lagoon and anchored just outside it. Transferring to the jollyboat, we bounced across the chop, the salt water misting over us.

The jollyboat's motor slowed as we drew up to the mangroves, and we perceived then the long tunnel that had been cut and dug out of the dense green tangle. We churned slowly through this tunnel's oily water, listening to the sounds of unseen jungle birds, until we came to a bank where the small flat-bottomed hunting boats, what Cubans called *chalanas*, were stacked and waiting. The boats were placed in the water and the hunters and guides paired off, each of us hunters, with his guide poling, moving in his boat into a smaller, shallow inner lagoon of brackish water with isolated mangrove trees scattered in it. Every few yards as we traveled, the chalana would skid up onto a submerged snag, the guide grunting, "*Muchos truncos*," as he heaved us off and drove his wooden pole into the mud again, propelling us forward.

By now it was late afternoon, and the heat of the glowing tropical sun in the windless lagoon pressed on our backs like a great hand. The sweating guide poled me into the cool shade under one of the lagoon's mangroves, and I looked up to find a handmade ladder rising up to a railed wooden shooting platform built far up in the tree's branches.

After I ascended into the stand with my Wingmaster and shells, the guide poled back out and chucked his weary bunch of decoys onto the water—the only rules of decoy placement in Cuba, where the very idea of decoys for ducks brought on something like acute risibility in the Cubans, seemed to be a loose set in the morning and a tight set in the afternoon, somewhere where the shooter would not have to look directly into the rising or setting sun, with perhaps just the barest of ripples to give the dekes some action and lend credibility to the subterfuge. The dekes thus placed according to afternoon rules, the guide poled the chalana back under the mangrove, tied it off to the ladder, and climbed up a few rungs himself to sit and light a smoke, waiting along with me for the birds to fly.

It was not until after the sun went down that the birds really flew, the large flights coming into the lagoon for the night, silhouetted against the twilight. While you waited during the afternoon, you watched herons, very white, feeding in a shaded corner of the lagoon, or a flight of black skimmers passing near you, their bodies inches above the water, their long bills ripping it like scissors run across a sheet of satin.

At times in the afternoon you heard Mariño as he made his way around the perimeter of the lagoon, a section or more in area, hooting and firing off his *escopeta* to drive birds already on the water or the roost back into the air. Sometimes he emerged from the mangrove forest to wade across the lagoon, and if he passed near your stand he paused to lift the duck hanging from his leather strap and spread open the feathers to show you.

"Blue. Weeng," he pronounced in the only English I ever remember him venturing, smiling like the Bodhisattva of pass shooting.

Very often Mariño's walking in the mangroves sent up flights of ducks, and as they came in, you hunkered in your stand behind the branches' green leaves, your guide looking up expectantly. The ducks came in extremely low and at high speeds, merely dipping a wing toward the decoys in salute, and you found yourself shooting down at them as they passed, your shot string pearling the water a good yard or two behind. This would be of invaluable assistance to your next shot, letting you know how much to pick up your lead when another skein of ducks skidded by under your stand, enabling you, with luck, to make a nice double on Bahama pintails—one cartwheeling into the water as the other dropped with his wings down and his head thrown back, both of them drakes with bloodred patches of color on their bills.

Also in the late afternoon you might get a high shot at the large white-crowned pigeons coming over on their way to their roosts, but it was not until

last light that the ducks—and mostly wood ducks at that—put in a serious appearance. The air by then was thick with mosquitoes and a little *pinche* sandfly
that could not be seen or felt—but if he made it past your repellent and got to
your skin, late at night as you lay in your bed in the hotel, listening to the band
playing below in the courtyard by the pool, your ankles and wrists would begin
to blaze with candescent heat from his bites, sending you padding off into the
bathroom to run cold tap water over them for twenty minutes and only tem-
porarily slacken the pain. At last light in your stand you breathed in a vapor of
such insects, but it would not matter as the black shapes of ducks began hurtling
across the sky.

I shot three-quarters of my birds in that last half hour before nightfall. Not a
few I took at eye level as they came right at me. It gave me pause to consider
whether some dying wood duck, in all All-Star Tribute to Irony, was going to
sail on into my head and crack my skull into pieces like the white shards of a
shattered coffee mug.

As my guide poled out to retrieve a downed bird, I would drop one or two or
three more on all sides of my stand and have to direct him to the marks in my
scrambled Spanish. Finally, the next duck I shot would be the one neither of us
could find. I called the guide in then.

We poled back under the warm stars, the ducks laid out in the bow like a row
of feathered mandolins. I slapped at a mosquito on my neck, then lifted a wood
duck to feel its weight, turning it over in my hand as the boat sighed across the
water. We reentered the mangrove tunnel and the stars disappeared and the
guide whispered to the darkness, "'*Scuro.*"

As we rode back out to the cruiser in the jollyboat, the water of the tunnel was
filled with the pulsing green lights of spawning animals, the stars below us. Then
the bright lights of the cruiser at anchor came into view, highlighting the pitch
and toss of the large lagoon's surface as we drew across it to the cruiser's stern. On
board the big boat would be waiting rum and ice and cold fresh lobster in a hol-
landaise sauce made with eggs bartered from an old black man who lived alone
on an island in the Laguna where he made charcoal—no one on board able, or
willing, to venture an opinion as to exactly what manner of eggs they might be,
not wanting to spoil the enjoyment of the sauce. As we made our way back across
the dark water to the dock, we sipped rum while watching on the land the fiery
lights of the harvested cane fields as they burned into the night.

Mornings in Cuba were for doves. The shooting came not right at first light
but usually after the sun was well risen. The shooting was over cut rice fields,
and it drew in flights of mourning doves in numbers better suited to astronomy
than to natural history. It was not a little daunting, with your bird boy squatting
beside you, pointing at this gray swarm and shouting, "¡*Ahí, ahí!*"—in the same

lyric way I remembered Turkana gun bearers in Kenya pointing up at incoming flights of sandgrouse and shouting, "*N'dio, n'dio!*"—to rise up and empty your 12-gauge of all the Italian low-brass 9s you were now shooting and not hit a thing. The difficulty with so many birds in a single wad was trying to select which one to shoot. It seemed that just when you locked onto a dove, he'd perform some kind of barrel roll or an Immelmann turn—lacking only a colored smoke trail and a pylon to loop around to make his act complete—and you ended up blowing out a chunk of blue sky.

"O," your bird boy in his camo shirt and billed cap with adjustable plastic tabs on the back and the name of an Indiana coal company printed on the crown would say softly.

My lifetime batting average on mourning doves stands around .370, but I did not begin to shoot at that level until later in the morning when the birds thinned out enough to cease looking like a blizzard of major-league screwballs and began flying straight and strong in singles and pairs and triples. Then they began to fall and my bird boy would be up and running through the yellow rice stubble after them. I can't remember him ever losing one.

One morning I killed more doves than I had ever killed in a single day in my life before. I went through two hundred shotgun shells before noon and was still well shy of the limit. That's when I handed my shotgun to my bird boy and let him shoot. He shot deftly, considering that hunting is a great luxury for Cubans, though an enthusiastically, and often illicitly, pursued one. As he shot—and when I wasn't retrieving his birds for him in what I suppose could be interpreted as a show of solidarity with the workers—I went through the pile of doves, holding them up, turning them over in my hand, examining their violet-gray plumage. There was a monumental pile of dead doves there, and maybe I should have felt bad about killing them all. I felt merely taxed, though, the sport having been transmuted into a task. At dinner that night in the hotel, when the heaped platters of fresh dove breasts, broiled under strips of bacon, were brought to the table and I created another pile of dead doves, this one of bones stripped clean of their dark, wild flesh, that particular task did seem well rewarded. Even so, I now have trouble remembering more than a few of the shots I made on all those mourning doves that morning, and don't need to take that many shots in one place at birds ever again.

The local variation on the flu found me in Cuba. It was a minor ailment, no more than a few days of disorientation and angst, accompanied by mild fever at night. After dinner I waited politely for the fever in the hotel bar, drinking rum and listening to the bartender in the white shirt and black tie, his hair the color of steel shavings, his jowls quivering, tell me about the old days in Havana when drinks would be christened for Mary Pickford—"a great artiste," the barkeep assured me. On top of the stainless-steel refrigerator behind him sat a mammoth largemouth bass mounted red-gilled on a piece of driftwood with bottles of *ron* and whiskey and Soviet pepper vodka arrayed in front of it. Leaning on the bar, the barman ticked off on his fingers the batting order of the great St. Louis *Cardinales* of 1933 as I poured more straight Havana Club into my cocktail glass.

"Leo Durocher," he intoned. "Dizzy Dean."

With burlesqued paranoia, the bartender quickly searched the room for spies and informers, then slid his plump hand across the bar and grasped my cocktail glass by its stem. Raising it, he adroitly flipped the rum down his hatch, the gesture in its way probably not unlike the great Dean's as he picked up a slow roller back to the mound and flipped it to first. The bartender smiled Cheshirely as he set the empty glass down. Then the fever arrived and washed over me in a heated wave.

Back in my room that smelled overpoweringly of insecticide and air-conditioning, I lay on my dorm bed and listened to the band in the courtyard strike up a Kenny Rogers hit, sung in English, while the many Cubans in attendance danced the steps of American dances, wearing American boots and jeans and cowboy hats—gotten ahold of somehow—maybe even dreaming American dreams—or at least Miami ones. Then the music switched to something disco— Afro-Cuban rhythms shipped north to be powdered and sintered and homogenized before running the embargo back south again. The only chances I had in Cuba for hearing real Cuban music, and tasting real Cuban food (the hotel fare being simulated American commissary cuisine), came on my last Saturday in Ciego de Ávila province when we had a farewell picnic in a grove of broadleafed banana trees by the shore of a lake. We were served an entire barbecued pig, black beans and rice, boiled yuca, sweating bottles of Hatuey beer, and dishes of the richest ice cream yet concocted by the hand of man, while a local band of black and mulatto men in simple guayaberas played hot merengue licks on guitars and brass and a big stand-up bass.

On the last Saturday night, when the fever subsided, I went to the hotel's lightless disco to find the guides and bird boys who would be there in their weekend best—and with *novias* rather than *esposas*—to buy them bottles of rum that I could purchase for a tourist price that was one-sixth of what they had to pay. After the bottle came and we shared a drink, I excused myself and crossed the packed dance floor, the laboring air conditioner trying valiantly to lay an arctic breeze across it, to another table spread with a white cloth. I talked with the Cuban girl sitting there, one who spoke English and for some reason found my jokes funny—"You are, eh, *muy cómico*." We danced; and when the waiter came to the table again to ask me if I would have another drink, I declined.

Outside the disco at midnight, walking across the courtyard to the hotel lobby, skirting the band and dancers by the pool, I smelled the smoke of the burning cane fields. Old Mariño, *Mariño viejo*, made his evening constitutional at times such as this, traveling over wide sweeps of the countryside, stepping briskly mile after mile. Perhaps he is, I thought, at this moment on the move.

I had to be on the move myself in the morning, aboard the DC-3 in Camagüey, leaving Cuba. I kept the white-and-green registration card that had boldly identified me as once having been a "distinguished guest" of the "Hotel MORON," and for some time after returning home found it amusing to pick it up and read it. I lost it, though, and if I found it again, after twenty-two years without feeling the warm night air of Cuba, I doubt I'd find it amusing at all.

# Chapter 29

*On a hard hunting trip in mid-winter civilized man learns once more*

*1. To earn his food and eat it with a hearty appetite;*

*2. To feel the delicious comfort of warmth and shelter after extreme exposure;*

*3. To enjoy the life-renewing qualities of sound sleep after utter exhaustion; and incidentally*

*4. To appreciate a respite from the eternal temptations of sex.*

—J. Wong-Quincey, *Chinese Hunter*

# CHINESE BLUE

**Maybe it has** *to do with lingering questions about how they should be classified, other than as the prey of choice of snow leopard and Asian wolf. Maybe it is because they live at such a height, above almost anything else that walks or crawls. Or maybe it is because they are found only in a place on earth that is as far as you can get, a place where it could be today or two hundred years ago, there being no way to tell, that made me want, from the first time I ever saw a photo of one with its thick curving horns and cobalt markings on a slate hide, to go to high lands to find the blue sheep,[1] going first to the "northern capital" of Beijing, then beyond, and beyond even that, to what has always been known, not so simply, as "the back of beyond."*

Three miles above the level of the sea, on the treeless northern Tibetan-Qinghai Plateau of China, the sky was yellow with the fine silt of loess soil thrown up by the northwest winds of March; and there was a feeling of being very, very far away. Spotted eagles and Himalayan griffons hung in the thin air, somehow, sailing over the occasional skulking fox and the white speeding smudges of nearly microscopic Tibetan gazelle. The gazelle ran, among rounded sparsely

---

[1]A "colorful sheep of a bluish-gray-brown, with whitish under parts and lower legs," according to the late James L. Clark, author of *The Great Arc of the Wild Sheep*, the blue sheep is, in fact, not a sheep, and not a goat. Its horns, "dark-olive color and quite smooth . . . especially so when the insignificant corrugations become worn down, as they usually do in fully mature rams," again according to Clark, are supracervical, that is, they sweep back over the neck, like some mouflon sheep horns, while spiraling, however slightly, "heteronymously"—the right horn spirals left; the left, right—like a goat's (a sheep's spiral "homonymously"—right to right, left to left). Yet the blue sheep lacks the goat's beard, while looking stockier (a male weighs about 150 pounds) than a wild sheep. The blue sheep, called *bharal* in the Himalayas and *yan yang*, "rock sheep," on the Tibetan-Qinghai Plateau, shares the same subfamily and tribe as the sheep; but while the sheep occupies the genus *Ovis*, and the goat, *Capra*, the blue sheep has been given a third, *Pseudois*, all to itself.

Blue sheep live in large bands of fifty to sixty animals, and often into the hundreds. They live above timberline, above *everything*, from ten thousand feet up, in country often rougher, steeper, and more blasted than that inhabited by the huge argali sheep. Still, they manage to find grazing and safety, safety in numbers as well as in their sharp eyesight matched to the open terrain and in their sense of smell that can seemingly detect scent from hundreds of yards away. Blue sheep seem little threatened by humans, particularly Tibetans, whose regard for karma tempers their hunting instinct. The greatest threats the sheep face are snow leopard, wolf, and the simple mercilessness of the climate.

grassed mountains[2], on land that was flat and bare (a monument to millennia of overgrazing). Here only a few people, ethnic Tibetans mostly, somehow managed to live, the way the eagles and griffons managed to fly.

Inside the adobe-walled yard of a Buddhist *zhang*, tattered prayer flags[3] beat like the wings of birds in the wind as a nun turned the bright brass prayer wheels that sent the prayers out and packsaddled yaks waited, shaggy and stolid. Around the zhang the adobe homes of herdsmen were far-flung, thrown up miles apart. The flat-roofed houses were built low with no west-facing windows. They, too, had walled yards on their east sides to bring the flocks of sheep and yaks into, while around the perimeter, like the cardinal points of a compass, were chained no less than four great, black-and-brown Tibetan mastiffs,[4] silent during the day except at the approach of strangers, but ready to bark out an alert at anything at night.

Inside one of the houses, new curly-coated lambs slept beneath a dung-fired metal stove. Behind the stove was a large raised wooden sleeping platform the

---

[2]These mountains were already here long before the island India drifted into the Eurasian continent forty-million years ago and piled up the Himalayas, pushing the old peaks back as it levered the land beneath them. To the west of the hunting ground lies the great Qaidam Pendi, the "endless grassland basin," one of the highest basins on earth. The hunting ground itself is defined by a rough triangle of three mountain ranges: the Buran Budai Shan to the west; the Bayan Har Shan, or "fertile black mountain," to the south; and the A'nyêmaqêm Shan, the "holy mountain" (in the local tellings its shining white slopes formed from the shards of a princess' shattered mirror), to the east.

To the south lies Tibet, known to Tibetans (who trace their ancestry to the coupling of a monkey with a she-demon) as Bod and as the Tibet Autonomous Region or Xizang Zizhiqu to the occupying Chinese. To Mongols it was Thubbet, while Arabs knew it as Tubbet. "Qinghai," the name of the adjoining Chinese province in which the hunting area is located, comes from Qinghai Hu, the "blue-green lake," the name of the largest salt lake in all of China, as well as a primary nesting site for migratory birds in Asia. The plateau as a whole is regarded, rightly, as the "Roof of the World."

[3]In some parts of the Buddhist world, such prayer flags are known as "wind horses," and the galloping of hooves may be heard in them as clearly as the flapping of wings.

[4]The Tibetan mastiff, the legendary guardian of temples, homes, herds, and caravans, should more correctly be called the "large dog of Tibet" (which, as *Zang'ao*, is how the Chinese know it) or by the Tibetan name *Do-Khyi*, "gate dog" or "tied dog." Fanciers call it simply TM, though some identify the decidedly ursine, largest type of the breed (dogs nearly three feet high at the shoulder) as *Tsang-Khyi* (which, for some reason, is theorized to mean "bone-line dog" or "penis-line dog," though it may also mean "pure dog" or may be only a recognition of the fact that the finest TMs come from the Tsang district of Tibet). This highly intelligent and independent dog is thickly furred with deep-set eyes and a curled-over, feathered tail, its hoarse, grunting bark (having been variously described as "sepulchral and 'far away'" and like a "copper gong") apparently not worse than its bite. No one goes for a stroll at night around Tibetan houses or encampments because the seemingly more than half-wild 120- to 160-pound dogs are unchained then to form roaming packs that warn of the presence of snow leopard, wolf, and human intruders, and to assault them if called upon (Marco Polo wrote that the TM was "so fierce and bold that two of them together will attack" a tiger). As you are welcomed into a Tibetan home, someone, usually a small child (the dogs preternaturally tolerant of children and women, and infinitely suspicious of strange men), hauls at the nearest dog by its heavy chain and yak-hair collar while someone else, usually an adult, stands in front of it, keeping it at bay with a raised cudgel so you may enter; and yet, the TM is apparently capable of displaying boundless affection toward anyone it knows and who has displayed even the slightest affection toward it.

entire family shared on cold nights. Sacks of rice and barley were stacked to the smoke-blackened ceiling, the wattle in places showing through the daub. Used packing cases, festively painted bright orange and yellow, held the household goods, and it was from a wooden box that the woman of the house, with a gold tooth that showed when she smiled (and if anything only made her more beautiful; all Tibetan women being beautiful), added a full half-pound hunk of partially rancid yak butter to a bowl of salted tea to pass around. Then raised the ante by offering a platter of grease-soaked fry bread with it.

The men of the house, their faces from a lifetime's exposure to cold, wind, and high-altitude sun the color of certain burgundies or heartwoods, dressed in hats of fox fur and long, fur-lined coats that wrapped well around their waists and were held closed with belts studded with faux firearms cartridges. (The daggers hanging from the belts were real enough, though.) The sleeves of the coats extended a foot too far, but their length made gloves superfluous. In his hat and coat a Tibetan carried a complete yurt.

Outside, the saddled horses looked exceedingly small. The saddles were no more than naked trees padded with thick wool blankets thrown across them. They were hornless with soaring pommels and bare steel stirrups hanging from a single leather thong. Swinging into one, a Western hunter's feet dangled farcically close to the ground. The headman, Yi Wa, in his gold-threaded paisley coat, handed up the reins, but then took ahold of the horse's braided lead rope as he mounted his horse, towing the hunter behind him as they set off for the canyons and mountains, Tibetan horses, apparently, not far tamer than Tibetan dogs. Swiveling in his saddle, the hunter saw that the crupper was fashioned from the skins and hooves of a blue sheep's forelegs, which was good, because blue sheep were, of course, what he thought he was here for. They had begun to hunt.

Although hunting is a rare practice among Tibetans due to the inhibitions of Buddhism, these Tibetans seemed eager enough to be climbing up to where the sheep were. Along with Yi Wa there were five others, including tall Zha Xi who insisted on slinging my rifle across his back. With the ends of the lead ropes they slapped their horses to hurry them along to the mountains and the sheep. My traveling companion Carey and I had thought ourselves a long way from home when, two days before, we reached the hunting camp pitched beside an ice-covered river and been shown by another beautiful Tibetan woman, Happy Lake,[5] the white

---

[5] Names like "Happy Lake"—"Heaven Lake" and "Spring Flower" were the other two women working in the hunting camp—help to explain the beauty of Tibetan women. And then there are quick dark eyes; wide, white smiles and easy laughter; clear, smooth skin despite one the harshest environments on earth; and sleek black hair, either held up in back by a large silver barrette or braided into 108 strands to mirror the enlightened mind's 108 sacred qualities. Or perhaps it is because they seem almost always solicitous, joyous, and filled with what might only be described as grace.

yurt in which we would be sleeping. Today, though, with each trotting step of our
horses, we knew we hadn't seen the half of it, in either space or time.

For the first hour that morning, we rode through tall yellow grass growing
out of sandy soil, then beneath rocky bluffs riddled with caves along the shore of
a large frozen shallow lake, Donggi Cona, the "black sea." In the open water at
the lake's edge, mallards and ruddy shelducks flew up as we passed, while far
out on the ice we saw a black bar of yaks wandering to the other side. Once
around the bluffs, we turned away from the lake, passing through a herd of
horses where an eagle stooped on a colt as the mare kicked up at it with her rear
hooves. The land began to narrow, and soon we were working our way up a
canyon, following the stony bed of a dry mountain stream and seeing the first
synecdochic sign of blue sheep lying in the wash: the bleached skull and wide-
sweeping, rust-colored horns, the part standing in for the whole of a ram killed
by a predator or predatory winter, the rest of the bones nowhere to be seen.

We followed the streambed to where it became too steep and rocky to ride the
horses, and dismounted. As Yi Wa and the other Tibetans led the horses up the
mountainside, I hiked behind, walking ten feet and pausing, catching my
breath, then walking another ten feet, until I caught up with the horses where a
trail switched back and climbed the face of the slope diagonally. Saddling up
again, I rode to the crest, somewhere just this side of sixteen thousand feet;[6] but
instead of all the world, there were only more mountain crests to see.

The wind, broken by the mountains, was less bitter; and while dust still hung
in the air, we had reached the upper limits of it, leaving the sky above our heads

[6]The ancient Chinese wrote of "Headache Mountain" in the Karakorams; and the troops of Alexander the Great suffered "mountain," or high-altitude, sickness, as they marched over passes on their
way to conquer the world. The illness is the result of hypoxia—essentially, oxygen starvation—
brought about not so much by a lack of available oxygen, but by a lack of the atmospheric pressure
required to push oxygen into the blood. It can occur at any elevation above five thousand feet.

While some can venture to extreme heights and suffer no serious effects, others have died after
climbing to only moderate elevations. Almost no one, though, who goes very high does so without
experiencing or displaying at least one of mountain sickness's symptoms or signs, which are legion. These include, beginning with the mildest and most prevalent, but are not limited to short-
ness of breath and increased respiration, cephalalgia, loss of appetite, restless sleep, color-enhanced
dreams, drowsiness, dehydration, fatigue, lethargy, a decrease in mental acuity, impaired judgment, slowed reaction time, adverse mood changes, dimmed memory, nausea, vertigo, fever, increased risk of infection, retinal hemorrhage, loss of coordination, sleep apnea, Cheyne-Stokes
respiration, emotional problems persisting after descent, hallucinations, violent outbursts, subcu-
taneous edema, cerebral edema, and pulmonary edema that can end in racking cough, blood-
tinged sputum, coma, and death.

Gradual ascent—no more than a thousand feet per day above eight thousand feet—is the most
reliable prophylaxis. Absent that, certain drugs, such as acetazolamide that increase the amount of
carbon dioxide given off by the body can sometimes help. But there is only one absolute remedy
that *must* be taken in the severest of cases: immediate descent.

blue. Snow was banked on the shaded sides of the slopes; and the rounded crests were covered in close-cropped grass, the horses walking easily. In front of me, Yi Wa saw something that made him dismount; and we all walked, bent low, to a field of large rocks and from behind them glassed a band of blue sheep grazing up a tall slope, the sheep so far away that their images swam in waves of heat, even in the cold air.

We studied them for a long time but could see no mature rams. Saddling up, we rode in the direction of the sheep (who quickly vanished over a summit as we approached), following the contour around and coming to a bald knob where we could glass across at four different peaks.

Directly across the draw from us, half a mile or more away, their outlines blurred by the dust, was a large band of sheep, a hundred animals or more bedded in a bowl under an outcrop of black rock. There were good rams to be had, but to have them we had to mount up again and ride the contours back around the mountain.

We circled wide and came in above the band, keeping the ridge the black rocks sat on between the sheep and us. The black rocks rested less than a hundred yards above the animals, making for an easy shot. Except the Tibetans did not ride to those rocks. Instead, we dismounted behind another cairn of black rocks at the top of the ridge, some 350 to 400 yards above the sheep.

The wind seemed good, and I didn't understand why we didn't try to get closer. But when I pointed to the lower outcrop, the Tibetans pointed to their noses and shook their heads: The sheep's sense of smell was too good to risk getting any closer. I bellied up to the top of the cairn and peered over, lifting my head no higher than I needed to see the sheep.

They lay scattered over the bowl, resting at midday. It was up to me to pick which one to shoot, or whether to shoot at all, the Tibetans having done their job by getting me here and showing me the sheep. It was something of an outrage to some American hunters that the Tibetans did not select, as was the custom of guides on North American sheep hunts, the finest trophy for them, range the shot for them, tell them where to hold, and then coach them through squeezing off the shot. The Tibetans, instead, were all crowding around me where I lay behind the rocks, all pushing and trying to look over to see the shot and call the hit, even though they had no idea which sheep I might be aiming at, and I had no way of telling them.

I saw a ram lying almost directly below me, his horns sweeping out and back and flaring up at the lamb tips, the sign of a mature animal. He seemed as good as the best in the herd, as far as I could tell, and was relatively the closest. He was curled up on the ground, though, giving me only the top of his spine between the two shoulder blades to shoot at.

I decided to try, anyway. I lay my railroader's cap on the rocks, then rested the .30-06 on top of it. I squirmed around to lock myself in solidly, and had to hiss at a couple of Tibetans not to jostle up against me. The ram looked dishearteningly small in the crosshairs of the 6x scope.

I waited, hoping to get my heart and breathing to slow, hoping the wind would lay down, hoping the haze might clear for just a second, none of which happened. I waited five, six, seven minutes, wanting the crosshairs to be anchored on the ram, but not exactly sure where. Finally I had them right on his spine. I thumbed off the safety and waited another few seconds.

The Tibetans hissed as the bullet hit the dirt just over the ram and he was on his feet along with the rest of the herd before the wind carried away the dust. The blue sheep were streaming out of the bowl, running downslope. We got up and got back on the horses and rode down to the bowl.

We checked for blood and hair, but it had been a clean miss. Following the sheep out of the bowl, one of the Tibetans pointed excitedly across another steep draw at another impossible distance at the sheep now working their way swiftly up a sheer rock wall. I got off the horse and into a sitting position with my rifle, more in deference to the Tibetans' expectations of the way a Western sportsman was supposed to behave than out of any real hope of hitting anything. Still, I thought I might have a chance at one ram standing alone on a rock ledge—right up to the point where I pulled the trigger and sometime later saw a splatter of rock some way below him.

That's it, I told myself. I have just one more shot coming to me on this hunt. I am not going to ride around here like some all-too-stereotypical big-game type, filling the air with lead. And the rest of the day, as we came upon other bands of sheep, none with any big rams in them, I never bolted another round, just studied the sheep carefully and in my mind tried to visualize what the perfect shot would look like. That night, as I lay sleepless in the yurt, listening to the wind snap the roof and the felt wall in and out as yellow dust filled my nose and sifted onto floor like loose flour in the bottom of a baking pan, I visualized it still.

The riding and climbing, as well as the failure to sleep, indifference toward eating, weariness, headache, and general dulling of consciousness that were all a part of trying to function at fifteen thousand feet, kept me in bed till after seven o'clock the next morning, and had me wondering, after walking slowly to the cook tent, drinking a glass of green tea, and staring at a wok-fried egg without touching it before walking slowly back to my yurt, whether I even wanted to go out and look for blue sheep again today. Then "Danny" ("My Chinese name is too hard for you to pronounce"), our Han Chinese interpreter (whose first words to us had been, "My English is not so good," and who did not hunt with us because he did not think that horses "liked" him), opened the felt door[7] of the yurt and said that I could lie on my bed for a while longer because the Tibetans were riding to our camp this morning and we would be hunting in the mountains right above us, rather than having to drive the hour to the Tibetans' home before starting out.

It was almost ten o'clock before we saw the horsemen coming out of the haze on the flats on the other side of the frozen river. We drove out to meet them, then saddled up and turned toward the mountains.

Where we came to the first canyons, there was another adobe house where a giant lived with his family and his herds. He wasn't extremely tall for a giant, but his heavy-browed shaved head was much too large for a fox-fur hat and his fingers were like bunched bananas. As the other Tibetans talked with him, I saw one of his mastiffs slouching toward us. The giant saw him, too, and moved around to keep himself between the dog and us as he spoke. Someone asked where any sheep were, and with a tilt of his huge head, the giant pointed to the slope behind us, where a band of ewes and young rams were feeding near the crest.

We picked the canyon that ran beneath the sheep and started up it, following the stony streambed. This time we were able to ride all the way to the ridgeline, the horses blowing hard but climbing steadily. Glassing to the north, we spotted a herd of rams lying under a peak.

We rode down, then up toward them, Yi Wa, Zha Xi, and I leaving the rest behind. Dismounting, we hiked up a narrow defile (I more than once having to lean on Zha Xi's arm as the altitude sucked all the air from my lungs). Halfway up, Yi Wa kicked at the dust, and we saw it drifting up the canyon toward the sheep, telling us they would not be there when we topped out on a knob across from where they had been lying; and they weren't.

We hiked down and got back on the horses and followed the sheep up another draw, catching them crossing a rock face, but never getting what I was now demanding would be a clear shot. Riding out of the draw and onto another knob, we sent Zha Hu Jin, the youngest and most energetic horseman, to ride around the ridges that encircled us and glass for sheep while we waited, resting. In half an hour he was back, having seen no sheep; and we rode on again, around the backside of the knob, flushing a pair of snowcocks who called loudly as they flurried overhead.

The trail around the knob led us to an old cirque, now grass-covered. As we started the horses up its slope, it was suddenly filled near its snowy top with running blue sheep.

---

[7]The flap, often of heavy wool felt, that covers the entrance to a yurt is known, for reasons made obvious above (see footnote 4), by the imperative, "the dog shall not enter."

I got off my horse and lay on the ground with my '06 as fast as I could, which was not very fast, and the sheep kept running across the cirque, their square-hoofed feet seeming hardly to touch the snow. They weren't far, perhaps two hundred yards, but they never stopped or even slowed, and I did not think of shooting. Then they were gone, and we saddled up and rode to the col at the cirque's top.

There was another natural cairn and we rode the horses up to it, the rocks piled high enough to hide them. Dismounting and looking over, I saw this time not a bowl but two large snow-filled cirques with a herd of blue sheep at the far edge of the farther, a very long way away. I looked at Yi Wa who was lying in the rocks beside me, looking at the sheep through his binocular. He looked at me and nodded, and I sighed.

This time I jammed my cap into a notch in the rocks and rested the rifle on it. I got myself arranged, and everything seemed much more solid than it had the day before. I spotted the ram almost at once, moving through the herd that was working its way off the cirque and over another ridge. He was heading for a chine of bare rock, and I knew at some point he would stand on that chine, broadside to me with no sheep behind him; and it would be nearly the shot I'd visualized, only a good deal farther. When he hopped up onto the chine, the horizontal crosshairs of the duplex reticle seemed to cover a third of his body, but I still held them on him, not lifting the crosshairs above him. I let off the safety, inhaled, released half the air, waited for one more heartbeat, and squeezed the trigger.

I lost him for an instant in the recoil, and by then all the sheep were running over the ridge and going out of sight, to appear on another cirque beyond as they ran for yet another ridge and poured off the mountain. The shot had felt, and even at that range had sounded, right; but there was no sheep lying on the chine, and I'd seen none staggering after the herd. I looked at Yi Wa and Zha Xi, but the odds that they had been looking at the same sheep I'd shot at out of the scores on the cirque were slim; and they seemed to be asking me to tell them if I'd hit the sheep or not. Then someone asked Gu May, the oldest of the Tibetans, and one without a binocular. He nodded once, his face emotionless.

Zha Hu Jin and another younger Tibetan took off at a sheeplike trot across the snow on the face of the cirque, while the rest of us circled the long way around with the horses. When we had gotten far enough around that we could look back at the cirque behind the first ridge the sheep had run over, I saw Zha Hu Jin near its top, looking down. He was looking down at a gray rock in the middle of the cirque's snow, then started to walk down toward it.

I was literally afraid to watch, afraid it was just a rock and he would walk past it; and I'd have to find the energy to go on hunting. But when he stopped and sat down beside it, I sat down, too, and in my binocular saw the blue sheep ram lying on its side, one of its thick horns curving up into the air. I stood and started to whoop as well as I could at that airless height, and Yi Wa and Zha Xi turned and waved to me. By the time we had ridden the horses to the bottom of the cirque, Zha Hu Jin had dragged the ram down, and I could go up to it and put my hands on its heavy, rock-scarred, nine-and-a-half-year-old horns, and feel its dense winter coat.

For the first time in days I was hungry, and we all ate fried Tibetan gazelle and bread beside the dressed carcass of the sheep, as griffons gathered on the rocks and ridges around us. Then we tied the ram onto the saddle of the horse we'd brought for packing and rode off the mountain, the griffons sailing down onto the entrails before we were a hundred yards away.

There would be harsh barley wine, Chinese beer, and French cognac in camp; and then the horsemen, with more bottles of wine tucked inside their fur-lined coats, would ride off at sunset—to be home before the mastiffs were unleashed, I supposed—and we would have blue sheep stew for dinner, and sing in Tibetan, Chinese, and an assumed Irish accent in the cook tent after. Later, Happy Lake would bank the fire in the stove in the yurt, then leave me to lie awake most of the night under heavy blankets, hearing in the pauses of the wind the distant barking of mastiffs, and dreaming in the moments when I did dream that I was climbing on horseback to the top of yet another old mountain, and longing for air.

All that, though, would take place after we found our way back to the white yurts through the dust storm we were now riding in, heads tilted down. I lifted my head and looked around at the Tibetans in their long-sleeved coats and fur hats; at the small tough horses; the blue sheep lashed to the saddle; the skeletons and skulls of sheep, yaks, and horses killed by wolf or leopard, or perhaps eagles, lying on the weathered ground. The wind blew harder, and the more I looked, the more it appeared that time had stopped, or reversed; and it seemed logical that this was what people had always done here, and that what the calendar reported was a matter of conjecture because riding through dust storms was the way they had lived, virtually unaltered, for hundreds, if not thousands of years. And I also realized why I was really here, that this was why I had always wanted to find blue sheep, so I could ride, myself, with wild horsemen, and live as someone who might be part of the back of beyond, if only for a little time.

I turned in the saddle and saw Carey behind me, a silk bandanna tied around his nose and mouth, his knees too high because the stirrups were too short.

"Be sure you look at this carefully," I shouted to him over the wind, "because there's no way to take a picture of it. You're just going to have to remember."

He shouted back, his eyes bright above the Chinese red of the bandanna, "What the hell do you think I'm doing?"[8]

---

[8]Driving off the Tibetan-Qinghai Plateau after the hunt, we traveled for over fifty kilometers through a howling sandstorm that at times cut visibility to mere feet (I had to watch the road out the passenger window to keep track of the shoulder) and our speed to near zero. (After passing through the sandstorm, we then drove down into a snowstorm.)

Wind is one of the few natural forces that moves material uphill, while carrying it farther than other forces. Sandstorms differ from dust storms, like those we rode our horses through, both in the size of the particles they carry and in the heights to which they carry them. Sandstorms remain close to the ground, moving larger material shorter distances, while dust storms can lift towering clouds of tiny particles into the atmosphere and spread them globally.

Weeks after leaving the plateau, I looked out the window of my home in the Rocky Mountain West to see the sky filled with haze and sparkle, sunlight filtered through pale yellow silk. It was like the sky I'd seen at fifteen thousand feet, ten thousand miles away. In fact, it was the very same sky: The dust in the sky outside my window had been borne by the spring winds from across the ocean, raised from the distant and arid pendi of the high lands of China.

# Chapter 30

*Africa has a word for it, the most romantic word that seems to have obsessed me for a lifetime. And along with the word, there was an antelope, my obsession for it not filling a whole lifetime, but long enough.*

Over the millennia native tribes moved throughout Africa, pushing into new territories or being pushed out of old; but they had no universal word for this movement. Itinerant Arab merchants, though, had one. During almost two thousand years of scouring the second largest continent for its gold, jewels, ivory, and human cargo of slaves, they used their word for "expedition, voyage, discovery, and unveiling" to describe their venturing, the word descending to us in its Swahili version: safari.

The connotation of hunting with safari was a long time coming. To find that meaning of the word, you have to look well beyond the early European settlers of the Cape. According to author Bartle Bull in his Safari: A Chronicle of Adventure, "The first travelers to make their way into the interior were missionaries, explorers, traders, stockmen, prospectors, ivory hunters and empire builders," with nary a gentleman sportsman among them. The first who could even remotely be described as such was William Burchell, who landed on the Cape in 1810.

Burchell came to Africa in the hope of mending a heart broken by his fiancée, a Miss Lucia Green, who while sailing to Burchell's colonial posting on St. Helena to marry him, fell in love with the ship's captain and out of love with Burchell. In Africa Burchell, a botanist, was soon distracted by the opulence of the Cape's plant life and resolved to strike farther north than any European before him to catalog Africa's flora and fauna. All of five feet, four inches (as Miss Green was perhaps too aware), and reportedly never having spent a night outdoors in his life before, Burchell journeyed on foot and horseback for four years through forty-five hundred miles of Africa, collecting tens of thousands of botanical specimens, producing hundreds of drawings, identifying several new species of large mammals, and hunting game only incidentally for scientific study or food, or in self-defense, once facing a lion while armed only with a brace of pistols.

Burchell published the record of his journey—not yet a "safari"—under the title Travels in the Interior of Southern Africa *in the early 1820s, just in time to be read by a young military engineer in India. Cornwallis Harris's ambition since childhood was to be the world's foremost hunter. Instantly "haunted" by Burchell's account of the practically limitless game of Africa, Harris concluded that he could accomplish his goal only there. It was not until 1836, though, when Harris was sent to the Cape to recuperate from a bout of "Indian fever," that he was able to turn his convalescence into what was the first actual African hunting trip, lasting five months and recounted in his* The Wild Sport of Southern Africa, *and in a folio of his own color engravings,* Portraits of the Game and Wild Animals of Southern Africa. *He had gone "on safari" in fact, if not by definition.*

*Over the years, both men hunted and explored farther afield in Africa—and in Burchell's case in Amazonia, too. They not only were drawn back to Africa, but also succumbed to the maladies that brought them there to begin with—Cornwallis in his forties from fever in India, and Burchell, never having found another to replace Lucia in his unknitted heart, by his own hand. It would still be more than half a century after their deaths before "safari" would acquire the sense it has today, and then in East, rather than Southern, Africa. But where safariing genuinely commenced was to the south, on the Cape.*

*So that is where I went one August, and like Burchell and Harris struck north. While they used trek-wagons and horses to carry them, I rode in a* bakkie *(a small four-wheel-drive hunting truck) driven by the PH. We crossed the Nuweveld Mountains as Burchell had and traveled into the Western Cape's Great Karoo, called by the now-vanished indigenous San people "Land of the Great Thirst." On the rocky desert veldt in the Karoo were springbok in the hundreds—if nothing like the endless herds the earliest hunters saw, still a fair reminder of what once was. There were also many of the other species that would have been seen almost two centuries earlier: Cape eland, gemsbok, blue wildebeest and the Pleistocene-looking black, red hartebeest, mountain reedbuck, steenbok, Vaal rhebok, Cape mountain zebra, and bontebok. These were the original safari game, well before the East African species we associate with Roosevelt, Hemingway, and Ruark.*

*There was another animal from the beginning, another of the original game of the safari that is considered by many the finest trophy of South Africa: the nyala. For a decade I'd been hunting these 250-pound antelope, in my mind if not on the ground, since they had eluded me the first time I pursued them. To find nyala now, I had to move to the East Cape, crossing the route Harris had taken 166 years before when he hunted his way up to the Limpopo River. Where we had to go was to a piece of African bush, the nyala's true home.*

*Nyala bulls, as with a number of the spiral-horned antelope, can be aggressive, but for the most part they hold tight in the bush, only appearing outside cover early in the day or at its end. It was near day's end when the PH and I started seeing the chocolate-brown bulls, with their spiky white manes and shaggy neck ruffs, coming out into the open flats to join the red, bongo-looking cows. And there was only a quarter hour of sunlight left when we spotted the bull we wanted.*

*We stalked him behind the cover of a tall bush, moving through green heather and stepping around the vicious raw-red stems of the jumping cactus plants that were everywhere on the ground. Closing to 120 yards, we found the bull feeding, quarter-*

*ing toward our right, backlit by the falling sun. I got a good rest on the shooting sticks with my 7mm Weatherby Magnum. When I pressed the trigger I saw dust rise off the bull's shoulder and heard the crack of the 160-grain Nosler Partition striking. The bull ran, dropping from sight in the heather. We ran, too, not caring how much jumping cactus attached itself to our boots. He had gone only a little way from where he'd stood, the arc of one of his twenty-five-and-a-half-inch, ivory-tipped, spiraling horns marking where he lay.*

*As the light went, I looked around, reckoning how far you could see from a flat. It was all a question of perspective: I could see both as far as the nyala at my feet and all the way back to the origin of a word that haunts me to this day as much as it haunted two other men nearly two hundred years ago, before they had even heard the sound of it.*

# "A SUGGESTION OF GRACE AND POISE..."

**A way of** gauging the veracity of a hunter's tale is any admission by him of poor marksmanship ("liars never miss"). Rigorous honesty, though, is no acceptable apology for an aim that is not true; and while shooting is not all there is to hunting, it is the one skill that a hunter cannot be without. When I was in Africa again, I began to wonder if that was a skill I still possessed.

At the start of an August in Africa, I began at the beginning, where the Indian and Atlantic Oceans met at the Cape of Good Hope. The land was covered in heathery *fynbos* (fine bush), the unique flora of the Cape. The fynbos was inhabited by a number of native animal species including zebra, eland, blesbok, mongoose, and the always-annoying Chacma baboon. There used to be buffalo here (the Cape giving them their name), lion, elephant, even two types of rhino, along with the quagga (a larger, partially striped zebra) and the blaaubok (a shorter-horned sablelike antelope), both now extinct. Even without those other animals, I was seeing what had been the premiere of Africa for many of the first travelers there, predating the word "safari."

From the fynbos I traveled the five hundred kilometers east-by-northeast up to the Great Karoo with PH Ralph Köster. It's always "PH," never "professional hunter," though that's what the initials stand for. In other parts of the world you may hunt with a *shikari*, gillie, or guide, all of which carry a certain air of someone's being just a bit of a factotum. In Africa, the PH, in the legends and Hollywood version anyway, has always ranked somewhere between World War I flying ace and Lord Greystoke. Look at a "guide" in the movies: He is invariably unkempt, foulmouthed, cowardly, treacherous, and a rube. It was a part made for Walter Brennan. For the PH the role went to Stewart Granger, Clark Gable, Gregory Peck, or John Wayne (perhaps out of all the jumble of reasons why nobody makes safari movies anymore, one may be the utter absence of an actor even approaching the eminence of any of the above on his worst day). In reality, a good PH is, rather than a matinee idol, a reputable businessperson, strategist, astute maître d', Mr. Fix-It, stickler for details, sociable company around a campfire, and skilled hunter and reliable game shot on top of that. When a good PH calls himself a PH, it sounds at least a little self-deprecating and uncomfortable. When a bad one—one of the few, but still too many, who are phonies, crooks, and assembly-line "truck hunters"—calls himself a PH, it rings with false bravado.

Ralph didn't look a thing like Gregory Peck—he bore an all-too-unsettling resemblance to that twisted Aussie boomerang, The Crocodile Hunter. He was, though, a good PH. He'd been at it for fourteen years, since he was twenty. For the last five years he had hunted near the outpost town of Beaufort West (whose claim to fame was that it was the birthplace of the late heart-transplant pioneer, Dr. Christiaan Barnard) in the Nuweveld Mountains in the Great Karoo. Here Ralph had a forty-five-thousand-acre hunting area where the Lemoenfontein River ran (when it rained hard enough).

Nearly 140 years ago a tubercular English gentleman, having made a long sea voyage to the Cape, made an equally long horseback-and-wagon trek inland and built a large wood-floored, high-ceilinged hunting lodge with wide verandas and wider views of the Karoo veldt, naming it Lemoenfontein Lodge. Each year he would escape the English winter to spend six weeks hunting the varied and abundant game of the area, before returning to England. Over the years, the abundant game had disappeared and the lodge fell into disrepair. Not complete disrepair, though, because the lodge still stood in Ralph's hunting area, fully restored with it.

Ralph's area was a cool clear dry winter country of mesa and rimrock, aproned by scrub plains. It looked like Coues' deer's desert terrain in northern Mexico or the red Hole-in-the-Wall country of Wyoming, with every bit as much wind (Ralph assured me that this was an anomaly). The first morning of my safari there we breakfasted—on whole milk, passion–fruit juice, haddock, eggs, bacon, sausage, cheese, croissants, toast, butter, marmalade, apricot jam: the health menu—then went out first to sight in the rifle, then to look for springbok. *Rowland Ward's African Records of Big Game* describes the springbok as "the well-known national emblem of South Africa" and as "the only gazelle [as opposed to antelope] found south of the Zambezi and in former times its numbers were prodigious." The word Frederick Courteney Selous used was "innumerable." The vast herds would eat out the veldt and swarm over the Boer farmers' lands in biblical-pestilence proportions, in what the Afrikaners called the *trekbokken*, or "buck trek," said to trample underhoof whatever could not get out of the way, including humans. To carry the Wyoming analogy a step farther, they were the pronghorn of South Africa (capable of elegant springs while pronghorn rarely left the ground).

Ralph wanted to get me a best-quality springbok ram, one with heavy-based, question-mark horns that hooked back at the tips—producing greater length. After the rifle was zeroed, we had the luxury of looking at a thousand or more springbok around the base of the mesa. At about midday, Ralph spotted the one.

We left the bakkie and stalked after the buck. Closing to within 150 yards, Ralph set up the tripod shooting sticks (the land is, again like parts of Wyoming, too flat and featureless to find a natural rest), and I set the 7mm Weatherby Magnum on them. The wind was howling and I was fighting to get a steady hold, and there was a distinct feeling of opening-night (or opening-day-in-Africa) jitters. I should have backed off and waited, but I let off the safety and fired. And missed. The springbok was hardly fazed and trotted off a little way and stopped and I shot again and missed again. Matters continued in this manner for a time, the springbok drifting out to 200, 250, 280, and 300 yards, when something worse than missing happened: I wounded him in the hind leg and he was off.

We trailed him for two hours across the rocky plain, I feeling the wounded-animal sickness with each step. He kept ahead of us, but we kept him in sight. At one point Ralph, with the utmost courtesy, advised, "I know you can tell me a lot about writing [*I wondered*], but if you don't mind, try to watch him drop in the scope with the next shot—don't lift your head—or we will be walking for a very much longer time." I knew this, but there seemed to be a disconnect between my consciousness and trigger finger.

We got up on him at 175 yards, another tough shot in the wind, but one that had to be made. This time I kept my head down. The 140-grain bullet took him behind the left shoulder and came out at on the point of the right, and he was dead—at last—before he hit the ground.

He was an older ram, his horns over thirteen inches long with six-inch bases. Ralph told me to kneel and smell the *pronk*, the fan of white hair the springbok carried on its back that "everted" when it was excited. I thought it might be a gag, but I figured I owed him the consideration, after the poor display of shooting I'd made him sit—or hike—through. Kneeling, I put my face against the sheaf of hair and smelled a candy-shop smell. It faded as the springbok cooled, and I felt as if something overheated had cooled in me. It hadn't.

They say the French have a word for it (meaning for *everything*), but it seems that the Afrikaners do, too. In the case of my disconnect it was *bokkoors*, the "buck curse," or just plain-old buck fever. Even though I had hunted big game for seven-tenths of my life, I still get bokkoors, especially in Africa. And sometimes it seemed the harder I tried to press it down, the more it wanted to squeeze out. I suppose if I were looking for consolation I could consider the way Theodore Roosevelt had shot in Africa—many if not most of his rounds fired as range finders, though frequently turning into wound finders. Hemingway, when not having the "braggies" about some string of one-shot kills, admitted to misses and woundings, as did Robert Ruark. I was not even sure that I wanted to be entirely immune to bokkoors (what would the alternative be, nothing but icy indifference?); I just wanted to shoot well, in spite of it.

The next morning turned out cold and cloudy with a "spit" of rain. We drove to the top of the nineteen-hundred-meter mesa towering over the hunting area, looking for black wildebeest. It was a day, on the top, when your breath left you in white billows, but all I could worry about was whether my shooting still sucked.

Grinding up the rock-and-dirt switchback road bladed into the side of the mesa, we passed Cape kudu cows and klipspringer (Africa's miniature version of the chamois, and called *ko-ka-tsara* in the native language) perched on the rocks. On the mesa top the land was more lush, with tufted grass and heavier brush, rockier than the plains below. Almost at once we began seeing the blue-black, white, ring-horned, tan-saddled bontebok. When the quagga and blaaubok were being shot out of existence in the nineteenth century, the elegant little bontebok (reduced at one point to a total of eight animals in the world) nearly went with them. Hunting-based conservation in South Africa brought it back, to the point where, although still technically listed as endangered, it could legally be hunted and the trophy imported into the United States. They were beautiful, but if I hunted one I would have had to have the trophy mounted full-sized to do it justice, which would necessitate a second mortgage, remodeling, and probably appointments with divorce attorneys.

There were eland and gemsbok and blue wildebeest up here, too, in this dra-matic, rugged hunting country, but we had come for the black wildebeest. When the Dutch saw these bizarre-looking antelope (bearded and hairy-muzzled with horns growing down from a heavy wide boss and then hooking straight up; high horse-maned neck and withers sloping Paleolithically to low hindquarters and a white flicking plume of tail), they mistook them for a species of wild ox (*wilde beest*), while their other name, "gnu," was imitative of their raucous snort. There was also probably something off-putting to the Dutch Reformed souls of those early Afrikaners to see those animals cavorting on the plains in anarchic leaping circles, no one coming forth to lead, and everyone refusing to follow. This pro-voked the Afrikaners into labeling the black wildebeest "the old fool of the veldt." In truth, they were hardly fools, just sometimes inquisitive; but mainly they were wild, wary, fast, capable of aggression, and hard to put down unless shot right.

Ralph and I left the bakkie and stalked to the rim of a wide bowl. Ralph knew this place and that there was often a herd of black wildebeest in the bowl. When we crept over the rim, the herd was there, four hundred yards away, with a very good bull in it. We made our way from bush to bush, then angled to a tree to cut the distance to under two hundred. Ralph set up the shooting sticks and I tried to get a rest, remembering about seeing the animal in the scope all the way to the ground. I still felt rocky, but I got on him and tried to hold everything in as I squeezed off the shot. And hit him back, far enough for him to run off with the herd. More than an hour of blood-trailing and stalking went by before he could be caught up with and put down. He was an ancient animal with a massive boss and horns that would have ranked him high up in the record book; and I would have traded any ranking for a shot that was clean and quick, not abysmal.

After we got the wildebeest off the mesa and back to camp, we went out to sight-in the rifle, just to make sure. It shot right enough, of course. Maybe I was the old fool on the veldt; but in order to know that for sure, I would have to hunt again.

In African hunting there was "new school," and there was "old." New school meant picking up a hunting client at the airport and getting him five assorted flavors of representative animals, by whatever means were cheapest and most expeditious, then depositing him back at the airport in seven days and picking up another client. Or make that *group* of clients. Hunting clients bought into this travesty because they were ten thousand miles from home and didn't want to come back empty-handed; nobody in their town was likely to be able to tell a springbok from Johann Sebastian Bach, let alone a good springbok from a mediocre one; and who, other than themselves, was ever going to know the manner in which they hunted in Africa? PHs, for their part, resorted to new school for the money, because they'd lost interest in real hunting (if they ever had any to begin with), because they didn't care whether or not their clients experienced a true safari, and for the money.

Old school was climbing down from the bakkie and going out on foot for however long it took to hunt the best animal you could find. It meant turning down all the immature game and the gimme shots—such as when you drove around a bend in the dirt road and found a better-than-decent gemsbok standing in the middle of it, when what you were out for that day was hartebeest. It meant meeting the animal on his own ground and giving him—to use a phrase antihunters love to sneer at—an actual "sporting chance."

Ralph hunted old school. Shank's mare was what you rode to close the distance to game if you were going to hunt with Ralph, and he was not going to let you kill anything that was less than what he would want to put on the wall of his own house. Certainly, this was all quite admirable, though you did have to wonder if sportsmanship always had to be so damn bloody exhausting.

Today the bets were on red as we headed back up onto the mesa top to hunt red, or Cape, hartebeest. This was the "original" hartebeest, a large antelope that in numerous closely related species and subspecies, such as the tsessebe and topi, can be found almost literally from the Cape to Cairo. The Dutch settlers were the first to name it, identifying it with the stag, or "hart"—though of course by the seventeenth century when they left game-depleted Holland for Africa, none of them had probably seen anything wilder than a milk cow for a couple of centuries. It hardly seemed likely that anyone with any firsthand knowledge of the regal red deer would have confused a hartebeest with one, the most charitable descriptions of the animal tending toward abusive comments about its "miserable, stupid appearance."

What the Dutch did see was a 350-pound antelope with remarkable speed and incredible stamina, so much so that they were flatly baffled by the red hartebeest's ability to remain fresh during a long chase, when a hunter's horse would be badly "blown." The hartebeest galloped in an easy, ground-covering lope, its long mule-faced head held up. The red in its hide was a dusting of cinnamon, going to a brick color in old bulls, with patches of steel blue on the upper legs and face. The horns were maybe some of the most remarkable in Africa, thick-based, thick-ribbed hooks that grew forward and turned back, so that from the side they could look like a quotation mark. And few antelope in the world had better eyes.

In the late morning we spotted a bachelor herd of six bulls, and in the herd Ralph sighted one of the best hartebeest he had ever seen. We went after them, but by the time we got around the side of the hill that the herd had walked over, the animals had run almost a thousand feet above us, near the top of a high ridge on the mesa. There was really no way to approach the hartebeest without their spotting us, and the only thing to do was to wait for them to come down.

We made a *braai*, a barbecue, and ate lunch in acacia shade, and by half past one the hartebeest had fed down onto a small plateau a long way from us. We had to go on foot if we were going to stalk them without being seen.

It took almost two hours for Ralph and me to work our way up to the hartebeest. We were able to use the rolling terrain to hide our approach, the hartebeest preternaturally alert to movement. At one point we lay behind a rock pile for half an hour to keep out of the herd's sight while we waited for it to bed down. The winter sun came down out of the clear sky and beat on us as we waited. Then we got up and went on. The ground was a rock garden of brown stones shining in the heat. They could only be stepped over, around, or on, never simply walked past. More than once I wanted to pick them up and smash them against each other until they were dust.

More than once, Ralph, perhaps sensing my frustration and tiredness, turned to say softly, "Let's keep on. I promise you won't be disappointed."

When we were five hundred yards away, we waited for a short while behind some more rocks, then crouched our way down to a draw and followed it up to the edge of the little plateau that sat on the big plateau of the mesa, with the red hartebeest bedded on it. There was no cover, and we had to move slowly onto the little plateau to get in sight of the herd. We would have a few seconds, once the hartebeest spotted us, for them to get to their feet and stand before starting to run. We eased forward, doubled over in the tall grass that hid even more rocks, Ralph carrying the dreaded shooting sticks—the only possible rest there was to shoot from here.

First we saw their horns, then their red bodies. Ralph set up the sticks and I lay the 7mm Weatherby Magnum on it. We waited. A minute passed, then another. A smaller bull stood and looked at us. Then the big bull stood—hindquarters first, then front quarters—just to the right of the smaller one, about two hundred yards away.

I took a breath, eased off the safety, and held behind the bull's shoulder. At the shot he leapt and the herd was up and running. The big bull swung wide to the right of the others and was going straight away. I didn't wait.

I already had another shell chambered and put the crosshairs on the base of his tail. The 160-grain bullet hit where I aimed, and the bull went down with a kick and lay still, the rest of the herd galloping off.

"What the hell was that?" asked Ralph, surprised to see the hartebeest lying on the ground.

"Portuguese brainshot?" I offered. "Texas heartshot?" I wished I'd had some more clever response, but I was just relieved that the bull was not still running with the others.

When we got to him, even Ralph was stunned. It was the biggest red hartebeest he had ever taken with a hunter, twenty-three-and-a-half-inch horns with thirteen-inch bases—good enough to blow past the minimum measurements for *Rowland Ward's African Records of Big Game*. This hartebeest was definitely old school. The entire hunt had been old school. It was the school from which no hunter should ever allow himself to graduate. Now I wanted one more shot to make it right—one shot only, at a kudu.

"There is nearly always a sardonic touch to the story of a kudu," wrote Robert Ruark. Late on a bright afternoon, Ralph, his tracker and skinner Abram, my son Bryan who was with me on the safari, and I went off to the far north end of Ralph's hunting area, to this "kudu haven" to see if we could find that touch of sardonicism. In the band around his hat, Bryan wore a white ostrich feather I'd found and given him, making him look like a definite Captain Kidd. He rode in the open back of the bakkie with Abram, plume fluttering, all of us looking for kudu. It was past four o'clock, and the winter's sun was falling swiftly toward the rim of the mesa looming above us. This was when, according to Ralph, the kudu "let down their guards," as much as they ever did. As we drove slowly along a sandy road lined on either side with heavy thorn brush, Abram leaned down from the back and softly told Ralph that *there* was a kudu bull.

Ralph and I looked, the bakkie still rolling, and even without binoculars we could see him standing stock-still, the angled sunlight shining on the hard mirror-image helixes of his horns. When we got farther down the road, putting more brush between the bull and us, Ralph stopped the bakkie and we dropped silently out of it while Abram swung down and got behind the wheel, Bryan still in the back. Abram drove the bakkie away; and Ralph and I crouched behind the brush, me with my rifle, and Ralph *without* the shooting sticks.

We had to stay in a crouch and move from bush to bush, Ralph expecting the kudu to ghost away at any second. But he stayed. Maybe it was part of what Ruark called the kudu's "perverseness, his consummate genius for doing the wrong thing always," except that it is almost always the wrong thing for the hunter, not the kudu. Ralph was able to glass him carefully and to tell me that he was an old bull, his horns heavy and symmetrical all the way out to their ivory tips. There were longer horns in the world, he advised, but this was a fully mature kudu—past "mature," truthfully—whose horns would never grow any longer. Was I sure I wanted to take him? I nodded and we crouched farther forward.

In the end we had to get onto hands and knees and crawl through a gap in a bush so I could sit up on the other side and try to get the crosshairs on the bull. It was no good, too much brush in the way and not a steady-enough rest. I told Ralph I wanted to move over to the next bush ahead of me, crisscrossed with thick dead branches and see if I could get a shot from there. Ralph shrugged, telling me to go ahead, but more than ever certain that the bull would not stand. He'd sit where he was, where the kudu could probably see him, on the theory that kudu, like most antelope, don't know how to count.

I made it to the bush and got to my feet, trying to see the kudu without his seeing me, and trying to put away the thoughts of all the bad shots. It was the gleam of his horns that showed him to me again. I lay into the bush, letting it take my weight and support me as I slid the rifle ahead and rested it on one of the branches. I could see the bull, facing me, through a halo of bone-white acacia thorns in the scope. I felt, in its inevitability, the bokkoors rising, but this time I didn't try to overpower it, just waited for it to ease and for everything to feel right. I looked back at Ralph, sitting calmly (unlike his manic Down Under Doppelgänger), and he gave a little nod. I thumbed off the safety and held on the center of the kudu's chest.

This time I saw the kudu rock at the shot, then stumble and dive forward, the white plume of his scut curled convulsively over his rump, saw it all in the scope. He went down behind big iron-colored rocks and green brush, and did not get up. When we got to him, the bright white chevron of the Cape subspecies of greater kudu could be seen on this face, and he was gaunt and nearly toothless, a bull who would not likely have survived the winter. The horns were not long (he was far from "making book," as they say), but they were what he had spent all his life growing and were thick, double-curled, polished, and capped in white. I had taken better kudu "heads," but none that meant quite as much. When Bryan got to us with Abram, I was glad for him to see that his old man could still shoot—sometimes.

As an African sunset of near-Capstickian gaudiness painted the sky, I looked at this kudu bull and thought of the words of Sir Percy Fitzpatrick, written in one of the best of all dog books, *Jock of the Bushveld*: "There is a suggestion of grace and poise in the movement of the koodoo bull's head as he gallops through the bush which is one of his distinctions above the other antelopes." Even in death, you could see that suggestion in this kudu; and maybe he had stood there just long enough so the bokkoors could dissolve in me and I could have my own suggestion of grace and poise, for a change.

# Chapter 31

*They saw the buffalo after killing the elephant. The PH switched off the engine and eased out of the battered olive Land Rover, carrying his binocular. His hunter slipped out on the other side, and one of the trackers in the back, without needing to be told, handed his .300 down to him. The hunter pushed the 200-grain Noslers into the magazine and fed the 220-grain solid into the chamber, locking the bolt as the PH glassed the buff.*

*It was nearly sunset, and already in the back of the Land Rover lay heavy curves of ivory, darkened and checked by decades of life, the roots bloodied. They had found the old bull elephant under a bright acacia late in the afternoon, having tracked him all day on foot. He was being guarded by two younger bulls, his* askaris; *and when the hunter made the brainshot, red dust puffing off the side of the elephant's head, and the old bull dropped, the young ones got between and tried to push him back onto his feet, blocking the insurance rounds. The bullet had just missed the bull's brain, lodging in the honeycomb of bone in the top of his skull, and he came to and regained his feet, and they had to chase him almost a mile, firing on the run, until he went down for good. By then it was too late to butcher out the dark red flesh; they left that task until the morning when they would return with a band of local villagers and carry out everything edible, down to the marrow in the giant bones. They took only the tusks that afternoon; yet when they finally reached the Land Rover again they were very tired, pleased with themselves, and ready only for a long drink back in camp.*

*So when on the way to that drink the PH spotted a bachelor herd of Cape buffalo (with two exceptionally fine bulls in it), it was all a bit much, actually. He motioned his hunter to come around behind the Land Rover to his side, and crouching they worked behind some low cover toward the bulls, the* mbogos.

*The first rule they give you about dangerous game is to get as close as you possibly can—then get a hundred yards closer. When the PH felt they had complied with this stricture, to the extent that they could clearly see yellow-billed oxpeckers hanging beneath the bulls' flicking ears, feeding on ticks, he got his hunter into a kneeling position and told him to take that one bull turned sideways to them: Put the solid into his shoulder, then pour on the Noslers. It was then that the hunter noticed that the PH was backing him up on this bull buffalo with an 8x German binocular instead of his customary .470 Nitro Express double rifle. The PH just shrugged and said, "You should be able to handle this all right by yourself."*

*Taking a breath, the hunter hit the buffalo in the shoulder with the solid and staggered him. The bull turned to face them and the client put two Noslers into the heav-*

*ing chest, aiming right below the chin, and the buffalo collapsed. As the hunter re-*
*loaded, the second fine bull remained where he was, confused and belligerent, and the*
*PH urged the hunter to take him, too: "Oh my yes, him, too." This bull turned also*
*after the first solid slammed into his shoulder, and lifted his head toward them, his*
*scenting nose held high. Looking into a wounded Cape buffalo's discomfortingly in-*
*telligent eyes is something like looking down the barrel of a loaded .45 in the hands of*
*a jealous husband. That is a time when you have to be particularly mindful of what*
*you are doing out there in Africa and make your shots count—especially when your*
*PH, already suspect because of the way he talks English and the fact he wears short*
*pants, who is backing you up now on dangerous game with an 8x German binocular,*
*especially when he leans over and whispers, "Look: He's going to come for us."*

*Another careful breath and the hunter placed two more bullets into the bull's chest*
*beneath his raised chin, just the way he had on the first one, except this bull did not go*
*down. That left the hunter with one round in his rifle, and as he was about to squeeze*
*it off he mused about whether there would be any time left afterward for him either to*
*reload or to make a run for it. Now, though, there was this enraged buffalo who had*
*to be gotten onto the ground somehow, and all the hunter could be concerned about*
*was holding his rifle steady until the sear broke and the cartridge fired and the bullet*
*sped toward the bull—but just before the rifle fired its last round the buffalo lurched*
*forward and fell with a bellow, stretching his black muzzle out in the dirt. Then he*
*was silent.*

*Standing slowly, the hunter and the PH moved cautiously toward the two downed*
*buffalo (the rest of the small herd now fled), to find them both dead. Only then in the*
*dwindling light did they see that one of the first bull's horns, the horn that had been*
*turned away from them when the client first shot, had been broken off in recent com-*
*bat and a splintered stump was all that remained. He had been a magnificent bull at*
*one time, but at least the second bull's horns were perfect, matched sweeps of polished*
*black horn, almost fifty inches across the spread. And there, both men stooping to*
*squint at it, glittered a burnished half-inch steel ball bearing buried in the horn boss*
*covering the bull's head like a conquistador's casco. The ball bearing had served as a*
*musketball fired from an ancient muzzleloader. Whoever the native hunter was who*
*fired it, he must have had an overpowering lust for buffalo meat, and for buffalo*
*hunting. What became of him after he shot and failed to kill with his quixotic weapon*
*at much-too-close range was probably best not speculated upon.*

# OLD NO. 7

**The virtues of** mefloquine as a recreational drug are sorely underappreciated. As I lay tucked asleep in bed, the malaria prophylactic produced phantasmagoric, labyrinthine, radioactive scenarios—Salvador Dalí directed by David Cronenberg—without my having to be surrounded by an auditorium full of Dead Heads. As safe and sound as my hallucinatory sleep might be, it was often disturbed (in a physical sense) by roars, or rumbles and screams, awakening me. But that wasn't the mefloquine's fault.

Remembering where I was, I'd sit up in the dark under the mosquito netting and swing my legs out of the bed—pausing, if it occurred to me, to peer around for the silhouettes of scorpions before setting my feet down. Lifting the net, I'd cross to the tent flap and step into the cool August night air where bats swooped past my face. Sometimes, I would hear the distant roar of the lion that had ended the dream. More frequently, though, from the Songo River flats below camp, the screams would come again, and under the Southern Cross I would see the moon-washed elephant bumping one another as they all tried to crowd around the salt lick. These cows and calves, the "Songo Bitches," expressing their extreme displeasure at being jostled by one another, were not park or wildlife-preserve elephant. They were members of a healthy wild population of legally hunted elephant—a thing far different from the seminarcoleptic attractions found at Africa's finer game lodges. These elephant were much too wide awake ever to permit one of those zebra vans to drive up to them. Either they would vanish into the brush, like ectoplasm dissolving at the end of a séance, before the van could get anywhere near; or they would let it get near, then "*stuffing* try to kill" the van and all its occupants, as Zimbabwean PH Rory Muil would put it.

Where my tent was pitched, and where I hunted with Rory, was in a million-acre hunting concession spread across the Tonga tribe's Binga Communal Lands up from the Kariba Lake shore in northwestern Zimbabwe. The place was called Songo Camp, and the elephant were the almost-nightly entertainment. Some nights they might be accompanied by the bellowing of Cape buffalo, but by morning they, and the buff, would be gone from sight, and I would have to go looking for them, the buffalo in particular.

If mefloquine gave me bizarre but relatively harmless dreams, it was *nyati*, the buffalo, who produced another sort of delirium—one that carried a serious threat of addiction, as I knew too well.

Not everyone necessarily gets hooked on nyati. In terms of side effects, the first one is usually free. A hunter may get "lucky" and stumble onto a bull in open terrain and make a practically anticlimactic one-shot kill, and wonder what all the fuss was about. Another hunter, after chasing snorting, stampeding buffalo around in the bush for days, may be so unnerved by the experience that he will happily make his first buffalo hunt his only buffalo hunt, and from then on stick to less distressing game, like grizzly bear. It is only after a person deliberately hunts Cape buffalo a second time, or a third, that he makes a crossing to being something, and someone, distinctly different from whatever he was before.

Once over the line, it is a fact that such people will hunt buffalo whenever they are in Africa and there are buffalo to hunt. Robert Ruark quoted his (then) youthful PH Harry Selby: "You will always hunt buff. It's a disease. You've killed a lion and you don't care whether you take another. But you will hunt buff until you are dead, because there is something about them that makes intelligent people into complete idiots. Like me."

Even as I watched those elephant like white hills in the moonlight below the camp, I was thinking about the six Cape buffalo I had killed in twenty-eight years—because that was how many buffalo there had been for me to *hunt* in twenty-eight years. (One, a Nile buffalo up in the Central African Republic, had been more a matter of my counting coup after a PH and his hunter had wounded the bull and we tracked it and found it waiting for us, gathering itself for a charge; but I counted it all the same.) I was back again in Zimbabwe after many years, in the hardly best of times for the country, for the sole purpose of hunting buffalo some more. I had, in short, a buffalo on my back; and after six of them, served straight, the only possible cure for my jones was a shot of Old No. 7.

I don't know if it requires a special darkness or a heart of clear radiance to be drawn to the hunting of Cape buffalo. The only thing I do know is that is unlike all the other hunting of all the other game I have given chase to in Africa. The glamour species such as sable, kudu, and nyala can regularly be spotted from a vehicle and stalked. Lion and leopard are almost invariably baited into rifle range. The pursuit of giant eland, or bongo, can be grueling to the point of heartbreak; but only the bongo, reportedly, has even a slight tendency toward aggressive behavior if confronted. Black rhino, though no longer hunted, are belligerent by disposition, but are also intractable simpletons. White rhino are similarly heedless *and* exceedingly docile. Elephant are five times the size of buffalo, arguably smarter, and hunting them is never anything less than a long, hard, throat-tightened slog. Their charge is nearly always bluff, though, and a bullet through a flared ear—no more to an elephant than a piercing to a teenage girl—can turn them.

Buffalo seldom charge unless made to, but they never bluff. Their sight and hearing, while not acute, are far from poor (having few "natural" enemies, they haven't had to evolve those senses to the level of the smaller prey species'); their sense of smell is astounding; and all their senses are wired into a large brain and a redoubtable, decidedly uncowlike intellect. You have to hunt them on foot, you have to get close, you have to use a heavy rifle, and you have to shoot straight the first time.

Among Cape buffalo, the dugga boys are the most unadulterated form of the buffalo drug. *Dugga* boys (the word means "mud" in Zimbabwe's native Shona language) behave as if they belong to the Skull & Bones society of the wallows. Either bullies or grandees, they lay claim to the mudholes by seeming divine right; and their attitude toward much of the rest of the world, including humans, is about on a par. That, and all of the above, is what makes them so interesting.

If you hunt dugga boys, you want a PH you can rely on, first, not to take you (too) unnecessarily into harm's way, but, second, to be there to lend an assist if a "situation" needs sorting out. Until you really learn how a PH will react during a buffalo incident, you look to external signs for a clue. It might be his eyes—if he meets yours directly—or his posture or how much rubbish he may or may not talk. Or you can look at his wrists.

There are PHs who collect all variety of native good-luck string, copper, elephant-hair, ivory, or rhino-cartilage bracelets (the last only on an old-timer, a *mzee*, these day—one PH who hunted into his late seventies affected such a hoop for a time as a young man, till he found that it rubbed uncomfortably on the backs of others in intimate circumstances). The suspicion arises that bedizened PHs may just fancy themselves Masai *Morani* (who tend to wear wooden bracelets that look an awful lot like the black-rubber drive belts off vacuum cleaners), bent on proving, or hiding, something. As a rule: The gaudier the bangles, the more dubious the competence of the PH. Rory, who resembled a shopworn version of the actor Patrick Stewart, wore a Timex, with a cloth strap.

This seemed to matter when we found ourselves trailing a dugga boy whose track showed he was dragging a right hind hoof. He had likely been caught in a poacher's wire snare and pulled free—no mean feat, considering that the snares were generally constructed from double strands of twelve-and-a-half-gauge high-tensile fence wire. (Three days prior to my arrival in camp, a poacher and several of his associates went down to the Sengwa, the area's main river, in order to spear a buffalo who had tangled a snare around his head and horns and had the poor manners not to strangle himself to death. As the spearmen approached what they took to be a harmless, neck-roped buffalo, the bull was filled with a surge of adrenaline and snapped the snare—with a breaking strength twice his body weight—and proceeded to butt, gore, and stamp the poacher into the ground while the poacher's cohort fled. Then the buffalo walked off, still wearing his crown of wire.)

We trailed the skidding track through the open jess (as the thickets of bushwillow are known) down to a dry creek bottom where the tracks played out. A mopane tree grew out of a dense clump of bushwillow, and we spread out around and above it, hoping to pick up the trail again. One of the trackers, Tino, was down in the creek bottom when a pair of oxpeckers flew out of the bushwillow. Everyone, and everything, froze.

Rory and I were on the creekbank above the bushwillow. Rory slid to my side when the birds flew.

"If he charges," he whispered, his eyes on the bush, "he's coming, and we'll have to *grab* him." As he said this, he held up his free hand (the one not wrapped around the barrel of the .458 Model 70 with iron sights and the bluing worn off) and closed it on the air.

"Do you know where he is?" I asked, so I would know where to reach—with my .450 Nitro Express 3¼-inch Ruger No. 1.

He shrugged.

"Haven't a clue."

As it turned out, the buffalo was twenty yards away, lying in the bushwillow under the mopane, watching. It took us a quarter hour to verify that as we moved side to side and in and out to try to get a look at him. The best that could be seen, with a binocular, was an eye and a segment of horn.

"This buffalo should have been gone by now," Rory said, unease and excitement rising in his hushed voice.

Do you think there's fear to be seen in a handful of dust? Imagine a bush, yards away, where a dugga boy waits, having decided not to run.

As long as we stayed downwind of the buffalo, he was not going to show himself, so we crossed (rapidly) the rocks and sand of the creek bottom and circled upwind of where the buffalo lay on the opposite bank. As our wind drifted into the bushwillow, and we waited with our rifles, we heard the buffalo getting to his feet. Then we saw his gray-blackness moving. Then he walked into the open.

He was a young dugga boy, packing his hind hoof. His hipbones showed, and he'd been fortunate not have been taken by lion. He moved slowly, obviously uncomfortably, under the slanting afternoon sun, looking at us levelly as he drew off from us. We watched him go. He could still survive and in time mend—maturing into a bull who did not run. Rory calmly consulted his Timex and said we should head for the Land Rover.

In the days after that the buffalo hunting was a matter of old tracks, no tracks, blown stalks, wrong buffalo. In the middle of the bush, another tracker, John, found a 1961 Rhodesia and Nyassaland penny, with a hole in the center and dancing elephant on the obverse. I bought it off him and strung it through the band of my hat, hoping it would change our luck; but we went on hunting without any noticeable improvement in our fortunes.

We were not without buffalo meat in camp, though. Whenever a buffalo was killed, the trackers cut it in two with their tribal axes and knives and took everything from the body cavity—even stabbing handholds in the bulging white wall of the stomach to roll it out onto the ground and cut it up into tripe. When they were done, all of the buffalo, except the two-hundred-pound bale of grazed grass from the stomach and the contents of the lower intestines (what Lewis and Clark's "wrighthand" cook Charbonneau would have described as *"not good to eat"*), was loaded into the Land Rover and transported back to camp. There was abundant, virtually fat-free meat in camp from buffalo killed by previous hunters, and we ate it as rolled fillet; braised oxtail; steaks; biltong; cold in sandwiches; the liver, fried; testicles, likewise (Buffalo McNuggets); in traditional *muriro* stew with onions and rape greens, scooped from the pot with stiff corn-meal *sadza* (the main staple of Zimbabwe) rolled into a ball in the hand; and once for lunch as a poignant, handcrafted cheeseburger—the cheese Zimbabwean cheddar, the onion and tomato from the camp's small vegetable garden behind the wattle-and-daub cook hut, the homemade bun baked in the hut's woodstove, the mustard stirred up from dry powder—as if someone was placing a call to you on a telephone he had carved from wood. But eating yesterday's buffalo only made me want to find tomorrow's even more.

The routine of the hunt was to check waterholes for a track that was not *nezuro* (yesterday). Today's track, if not up-to-the-minute, could still be used to judge what the bull would be doing in an hour, in the afternoon, tomorrow. If shiny and sharply outlined, we would be on it on foot.

We were indifferent to a great deal as we tracked, whether the bounding escape of a big kudu or the gray apparition of a rare roan bull galloping off. We weren't blind to our surroundings, though. Once, Rory picked up a small tortoise, fast asleep under the grass, showed it to me, then placed it back carefully into the cover. Snowy flashes caught our eyes, and looking we saw *marangwonda*, scattered bones, the immense broken skeletons of elephant, too heavy to have been dragged off by scavengers. We would also find wide sandy elephant beds where the giants laid on their sides, a lesser indent up at the head where a tusk furrowed a resting spot. (In marula season, the fruit fermented in the elephant's stomachs and they flopped down, snoring, sleeping one off.)

The buffalo knew too well, though, where to lead us to make the tracking of them, if not impossible, then at least dubious: unbroken dry shoals of quartz pebbles, tall thick grass, shelves of flat bare rock, and across noisy acres of fallen leaves.

"Like walking around in a crisp factory," Rory would say, taking a fatalistic drag on his Newbury cigarette.

Mentally translating "crisp" into "potato chip," I thought of "a dangerous man," Floyd Thursby, in *The Maltese Falcon* who "never went to sleep without covering the floor around his bed with crumpled newspaper." Cape buffalo were nothing if not the Floyd Thursbys of the African bush. With thoughts like that—especially at moments when the trackers halted in voiceless unison, like a synchronized swim team practicing out of the pool, all of them staring at the same (for me) unidentifiable object in the bush—I had to remind myself that I was coming for the buffalo, not he for me (except for that unpredictable, but statistically significant, instance when he actually could be coming for me).

For six days we hunted like that. Far from frustrating, it was six days of valuable practice—I even began to find tracks myself when we had lost them. As the days went by, I also began to develop a premonitory awareness. At the end of a long fifth day, I told Rory my secret prediction: We would find the dugga boy, Old No. 7, on the seventh day. Rory did not argue.

On the seventh morning we looked for buffalo on a high grassy flat where we had seen tracks heading the evening before, klipspringer bounding out of the kopjes ahead of us. The buffalo had already moved on, though. I didn't have to ask Rory where we were going next: We would go to his favorite area for buffalo, Kapinda, a distant part of the concession where stands of mopane trees grew up to the bottoms of rock ridges, the bushwillow jess could be thick, and long-yellow-grassed woodland parks rolled out over broad ridgelines.

The morning grew warm as we drove the more-than-twenty kilometers to Kapinda. Reaching the area, we rolled slowly down the indistinct dirt roads, looking for tracks, and at midmorning found large round ones—those of two dugga boys together.

We parked the white Land Rover in the shade of a tree. I took my soft case down from the rifle rack welded to the rollbar behind the front seats, unzipped it, and slipped out the .450. Sliding in a snap cap, I levered the action closed and dry-fired offhand at fifty, thirty, fifteen yards, keeping my eye on the unripened turquoise monkey orange or yellow leaf I held in the crosshairs of the 1.75–6x32mm scope, keeping it steady through the shot, the power ring turned down to 1.75x. I ejected the snap cap and chambered a 500-grain soft-nosed bullet, loaded to twenty-one-hundred-feet-per-second velocity, and set the safety. I took a long drink of water (but not enough to slosh in my belly) from one of the canteens John carried in his day pack. It was time to go.

The track led across all the usual dubious terrain. We lost, and found, the dugga boys' trail time and again until we tracked them into a keep of tall crenulated rocks on a high ridge. We knew they had to be just ahead; and they were, bedded.

What gets buffalo killed, above all else, is the wind; but it is also what keeps them from getting killed. This time the wind swirled in their favor. We heard thunderous crashing, like three-quarter-ton mule deer busting from cover, unseen. Hunkering in silence in the rocks, we waited to see if the buffalo would tell us what to do next.

Fifteen minutes later, Samuel, Rory's head tracker, spotted the two good, old dugga boys feeding among the mopane out on the flat ground below the rocks, as if all had been forgiven. They had not been irreparably spooked and drifted back toward the rocks.

"How far can that rifle shoot?" Rory asked. It was not a question I liked.

"Not that far."

"Two hundred yards?"

"One hundred. Less."

Rory was calculating. We had the wind up here and could see the buffalo well. If we went down, we would lose sight of them and did not know how the wind was there. A low ridge ran near the buffalo with large rocks piled on it. If we went down in a wide circle, using the rocks as landmarks, we could get within a hundred yards or less of the bulls—if it all went right. Rory knew I didn't want to do this at sniping ranges: Oddly, I felt better the closer I got to buffalo, even glint-of-the-eye distance—as long as I was seeing more of a buffalo than just that glint. There was also something fundamentally unseemly about trying to "fell" Cape buffalo "at a venture." Hunting buffalo was, at least for me, ultimately a highly personal matter, and therefore ought to be carried out up close. There wasn't really a choice.

Rory decided and we crawled out of the rocks and when we were away from the buffalo's line of sight stood and worked our way off the ridge. I stumbled more than once on the way down (either from simple clumsiness or excited tension), and I was certain I had started the bulls. We couldn't know, so we went on with the stalk.

On the flat ground, moving toward the low ridge and the landmarks, Rory asked me what I had chambered. I told him soft.

"Solid," he whispered, and I reloaded the single-shot quietly.

Reaching the low ridge, we left the other trackers behind, and Samuel, Rory, and I climbed it and moved along the crest. The rock we had singled out to navigate by (black and wind-carved) was just ahead. I could see off the other side of the ridge, and I saw a black shape standing beneath the low branches of a mopane. I reached out and touched Rory, and he whistled softly to Samuel and we all stopped.

We lined up three trees and used them for concealment as we worked closer, until the dugga boy was sixty yards away, slightly downhill. There was no cover or any place to get a rest, and I slid out alone from behind the last tree and set the fore-end of the .450 in a leather-covered cradle on the top of the hiking staff I used. I found the buffalo in the scope. I turned the power ring up to 4x. The bull had his head in the branches and leaves, but I could see a blocky rump, slightly swayed back, and heavy belly, his real weight carried in the bulked hump of his shoulder. He was quartering toward me, and as I looked among the branches and leaves of the tree, I saw a boss and the curve of a horn and a glint: He saw something where I stood, but he waited for the wind to tell him what it was.

The buffalo's left ear drooped and below its tattered fringe I could see his chest and the base of his neck. I whispered to Rory that there were twigs in the way, and he whispered back, "Not enough to bother that bullet; all quite thin stuff."

I looked back through the crosshairs and saw that he was right. I found a place on the bull's chest that looked open.

"I'm going to shoot him in the chest, just below his left ear."

"That's a good place."

I held a little longer, making sure that what I was seeing in the blackness in the scope really was the bull's chest. I slid the tang safety forward.

"Don't shoot unless you're absolutely happy," Rory warned.

I was tense, concentrated, and yes, happy—nearly euphoric in a semiterrified sort of way. My finger pressed the trigger and the rifle fired.

The bull spun out from beneath the tree in a splintering of branches. He ran counterclockwise in a half circle, placing himself fifteen yards farther out along the line of fire, but partially covered by the mopane's trunk. His head was up, domed by the heavy boss, his Roman nose scenting for the source of the bullet that had struck him. Out of nowhere the second dugga boy pounded past and turned into the wind, drawing along the wounded bull. They went straight away, making for a second, lower ridge. I had another solid in the chamber and threw the scope on the wounded bull (clearly the rear one of the two), a hundred yards away now. I scarcely felt the powerful roll of the gun as it fired and the second 500-grain solid broke the buffalo's left hip. It didn't seem to slow him, but the first solid was finishing its work as he ran.

As I reloaded once more, the two bulls went out of sight over the second ridge. Then the first reappeared, going away from sight; and I saw the horns and boss of the second, lit from above by the harsh noon sun. I mused about whether I would have to try an even farther, unseemly shot, when the second bull lurched to his right. His head twisted down, and his body dropped, dust rising from where he fell from view, two hundred yards from where I stood.

We hurried down off the first ridge, heading for the second. Before we were halfway there, we heard a mourning bellow from the other side.

"He is dead," announced John with a solemn nod. Not quite.

Coming over the second low ridge, we found the buffalo lying on his right side, his back to us, his bellow faint and his head wobbling feebly on the ground. As a grace I walked up close behind him and gave him a third solid in the back of his deeply creased neck.

It almost seems a requirement of hunting stories, especially ones about "dangerous game," to offer a ballistics formula. There is the one describing kinetic energy or "Pondoro" Taylor's (sadly, rather questionable) "Knockout Value" for large calibers. Looking at this old dugga boy, the formula I came up with was:

$$\text{Ruger No. 1} \cdot [(.458" + 500\text{grs.}) \cdot 2100\text{fps} \cdot \{(1 @ 60\text{m}) + (1 @ 100\text{m}) + (1 @ 2\text{m})\}] + 1700\text{ lbs.} = \text{Old No. 7}$$

It would take more than a formula, though, to define this buffalo's wide boss, embedded with pale green cambium from his butting and rubbing his way through tree bark. Or horns that were worn back to where the thickness carried all the way out to the blunted tips. (The most elderly bulls could batter their horns back to stumps, so they looked as if they wore Wehrmacht helmets; this bull's horns, though, were an honest badge of at least fifteen years in good standing as a dugga boy.) Or define why, even as "he lay in death," as Theodore Roosevelt wrote in *African Game Trails*, he still "looked what he was, a formidable beast."

By the time a road had been hacked through the bush so that Tino could bring the Land Rover up to retrieve the carcass, the buffalo had exacted his own final revenge by dying in a spot remarkable for its infestation by mopane flies, a small stingless bee that sups on sweat and tears and other human and animal liquid excreta and is said for all that to produce exquisite honey. The flies soon had Rory beside himself (though a native Zimbabwean, he'd never acquired an indifference to the tiny insect). He gathered up cabbage-sized lumps of dry elephant dung and set them alight to smolder in an almost incense-scented cloud of smoke, in the vain hope that the flies would be driven off by it. They weren't, and they became so annoying to him that he resorted to stopping up his ear canals with his old cigarette butts to keep them out—or maybe just so he could keep from hearing them.

Meanwhile, the trackers, working away with axes and knives, had opened the buffalo and let run out a rivulet of blood, drained into his body cavity by the first 500-grain solid through the veins and arteries at the top of the heart—

which nonetheless had not stopped him from running as far as he did. Trying to step around the blood and other fluids, they laughed and horsed with one another, nobody showing so much as a hint that "*in the depths of his conscience*" he felt the unease that José Ortega y Gasset claimed all hunters experienced (and these men were nothing if not among the truest hunters I had ever known). The killing of other animals might very well bring unease and regret; but no one was ever really unhappy after finding a big Cape buffalo, dead.

Paying the mopane flies no mind, I opened a warm beer from the cooler in the Land Rover, to propose a silent toast here among the trees and brush. The beer wasn't bad, but I realized that my drug of choice was neither it nor mefloquine, but the object of my salute: dugga boy. To find the pure dugga boy you had to get as far away as you could from the Africa of a million UPF-rated sun hats and photographic opportunities during game drives across clean, well-lighted plains. That was the kind of Africa the last decent parts were swiftly turning into; and there was nothing genuinely wrong with that, if you were satisfied with "Africa Lite."

Where I wanted to be, though, as long as it continued to exist, was an older place, where things worked out harsher, even crueler—though no more so than the continent's natural background level of cruelty. At this moment, that place was located approximately twenty-eight-degrees east of Greenwich and seventeen-degrees south of the equator. It was located with these men and mopane flies, heavy rifles, smoldering dung, bright fresh blood, and always, a dugga boy. It was where I had come for my ancient, savage fix, my shot of Old No. 7, neat. If it meant troubled sleep, that was all right because it also meant that it was not Africa Lite out there, not yet. It was still Africa Dark. Let there be dark.

# Chapter 32

*I remember that hunt, for before that time I had only killed a calf. I was 13 years old and supposed to be a man, so I made up my mind I'd get a yearling. One of them went down a draw and I raced after him on my pony. My first shot did not seem to hurt him at all; but my pony kept right after him, and the second arrow went in half way. I think I hit his heart, for he began to wobble as he ran and blood came out of his nose. Hunters cried "Yuhoo!" once when they killed, but this was my first big bison, and I just kept yelling "Yuhoo!" People must have thought I was killing a whole herd the way I yelled. When he went down, I got off my horse and began butchering him myself, and I was very happy. All over the flat, as far as I could see, there were men butchering bison now, and the women and the old men who could not hunt were coming up to help. And all the women were making the tremolo of joy for what the warriors had given them. That was in the Moon of Red Cherries. It was a great killing.*

—Standing Bear, Oglala warrior, *Black Elk Speaks*

# DUST AND SHADOW: A SHORT STORY

**Haardt hazed the** little bunch of cows and calves out of the draw toward the Double Fork and a hot iron. They were skittish as a turkey flock when he found them that morning, the calves without a brand or earmark among them. It wasn't till midday that he got them all rounded up and pointed home.

It was a year of yellow clover, and in places locoweed marked the green of the hills in lush pads of purple. The sun stood straight overhead, but to the northwest a line of snow clouds was coming, running over the land and hiding the tall blue mountains behind. Riding to the top of the rise, Haardt felt the bite of the wind above the stubble of his gray-shot beard. The little bay tossed her black mane like a squaw shaking out her hair when Haardt reined her in, swiveling in his saddle to untie his oil slicker. As he did, he swept his eyes across the country out of old habit. And sighted the buffalo.

He lay six hundred yards distant where Haardt would have never looked for a buffalo in the old days, in the shadow of a redrock outcrop, never once having seen a buffalo shade up, not even on the hottest plains day. At first Haardt was not certain he wasn't all shadow—wouldn't he have to be?—and cursed himself for not having his field glasses. But the more he looked, the more of a buffalo he saw: A head of black, bowl-cut wool, thick hump high, hipbone old-bull sharp, and long beard, the horns black gleams, all of it lying solid against sheer impossibility. The buffalo turned its head, big as a keg, and looked Haardt's way. In that instant Haardt was certain and wanted to abandon all these cows and calves and run after him, this feeling not just old habit, but old being, long given up. Before he could touch his spurs to the mare's flanks, snow drove against him; and then the storm was all around, hiding everything but the cockleburred tails of the cattle in front of him as he shrugged into his slicker.

Snow, wet and heavy, filled the crown of his hat when he pushed open the bunkhouse door hung on rawhide hinges, the cattle all round-penned.

"Evening, Haardt," said Blond Jones, not looking up from his hand of cards.

"Evening," said Haardt. He shook his hat off outside the door, then hung it to dry along with his slicker on a peg set into one of the logs of the bunkhouse wall near the iron stove. He poured himself a cup from the sooted pot sitting on the stovetop. Lowering himself to the edge of his bunk, Haardt held the cup in both hands and watched the steam wisp up from the oily black coffee. Every man in the room had a price on his head: $32.50 and found each month.

"What's the matter?" asked Red Jones, looking over at Haardt as he slapped a queen of spades down to take the trick. "You look as if you seen a haint." Red Jones came from Baton Rouge and Blond Jones from somewhere back in Minnesota. No one asked what their names used to be.

Pidgeon, the half-Negro, half-Choctaw contract buster, exhaled a cloud of blue pipe smoke as he pondered his cards. Now he looked over at Haardt, too.

"Yeah," he asked, "you happen across old Crazy Horse out there?"

Before Haardt could answer, towheaded Wicher spoke.

"Cerman says we're all going to Cuba to fight the Spanish," he crooned. Everyone concurred that Wicher's benign idiocy was likely congenital, probably involving cousins-german.

Haardt looked at Wicher's beaming, child's face and close-set eyes and said, "That a fact."

"Tell him, Cerman," said Wicher, smiling and nodding like a panting hound.

Well-fed Claude Cerman, Princeton University class of '96, lay on the bunk next to Haardt's, reading a two-week-old copy of the *New York World*, a pair of green-velvet carpet slippers on his feet.

"The assistant secretrary of the navy, Roosevelt," said Cerman, not lifting his eyes from the newsprint, "is organizing a First Volunteer Cavalry to free Cuba from Spain—"

"Says we're all going to San Antone to sign up," Wicher jumped in, squirming on the three-legged stool he sat on, impatient for the story to be told. "Soon's branding's done."

"That so," said Haardt, wondering what any of these boys might know about free, about how pure and terrible a thing it could be. Something the sight of the buffalo had reminded Haardt of.

"So what was it you saw?" asked Pidgeon, tamping the tobacco in the bowl of his clay pipe with the square head of a nail. "Whose ghost."

"No one's," said Haardt, lifting his coffee cup and breathing away the steam, knowing better than to try to tell them.

When the calves were cut and branded and notched and dehorned and turned back out, bawling, with their mamas, the hands pulled their good boots up over their trouser legs and knotted red silk kerchiefs around their brown necks and, smelling of pomade and bay rum, headed for town, cheering "Remember the *Maine!* / To hell with Spain!" as they rode. They all went, even Pidgeon, who (despite being a gentleman of color, or perhaps because of it) had a distinct following among the blue-eyed girls and widowed (and sometimes not) ladies of the town. They all went, except Haardt.

Haardt stood in the open doorway of the bunkhouse and watched them go until they were hidden by a bend in the muddy rutted road. Stepping back inside, he slid a tin trunk out from under his bunk and opened the lid. On top lay the .38–56 Marlin he carried for a saddle gun these days, when he was hunting meat or alert to grizzly in the spring in the cottonwoods along the creeks. He leaned it against the wall, then took out the white-and-red Indian blanket folded under it. Beneath the blanket lay a bundle, wrapped in brain-tanned elk hide. He lifted the bundle out and placed it on his bunk. Within the elk hide were the tools of Haardt's former trade.

A pair of stained chinks lay there, still carrying the smell of buffalo fat soured in the sun. The Wilson skinning knife, its handle rubbed black with buffalo blood, was in a flat sheath of Mexican leather along with the long ripping knife and sharpening steel. A set of crossed-sticks was joined by a thong binding. The loops of a belt held necked cartridges. And there was the Sharps Sporting Rifle.

Dubious of innovation, Haardt had left the vernier sight on the tang of the sixteen-and-a-half-pound .44–2⅞-inch rifle when he'd mounted the full-length brass Malcolm scope on its barrel the first year the telescopic sights had come onto the market. He had not hesitated to add the cap of German silver to the fore-end when he had the money, and on the bottom of the stock Haardt had made a notch, fine as a line of checkering, for every ten of buffalo he had killed with it—one day, north of the Yellowstone in '81, making nine notches. Finally, he'd grown tired of marking down dead buffalo and just went on killing them, no longer bothering to cut notches.

Before the Sharps there had been a .50 Springfield with iron sights and army-issue cartridges. Back then before he'd been old enough to be able to see the end of it all, the killing, as well as the rifle, had been different. There'd actually been less hunting to it—the buffalo too many and still too unwary—but at least when he killed for the railroad it seemed to mean something more. He was feeding men who were laying steel rails across the prairies, leading to grand places he had dreamed of as a boy back on a failed forty-acre Ohio farm.

With the Sharps the killing changed. Now it was just for hides and he would have to crawl sometimes half a mile with the heavy rifle and two belts of shells, his knees and hands filling with cactus thorns, to make a stand. Setting the Sharps on the crossed-sticks and laying out shells on the ground beside him, Haardt would find the herd's biggest, oldest cow in the glass of his telescope and kill her first, white cloud of breath exiting the wound in her side, then heart-and-lung blood following. As the other buffalo gathered, scenting her hot claret that steamed onto the frozen ground in a solid stream, he would make one shot a minute, killing every buffalo he could, pausing between to pick a thorn from his palm with his teeth and thinking, for some left-handed reason, of a hymn about being washed in the blood of the Lamb.

If Haardt had buffalo enough for a load, he wouldn't wait for the skinning wagon but would lay his searing rifle down and begin to take the hides himself. He left his mustache long, even after fly season, and kept his knife so sharp that he never felt it if he cut himself, even to the bone. When he got the robe free, he spread it out on the ground and marked it with his initials, cut into the flesh side. Stretching the kink out of his back, Haardt looked at the starkly naked tallow-white body of the buffalo, with its somehow indecent unskinned head still attached, and saw something he felt should not be looked upon. This was, he knew, what true freedom looked like, even if at best it only amounted to the freedom to travel as far as the hide traders in Miles City. And still he missed it.

The wind had licked away most of the snow, leaving only patches in north-facing hollows and pockets below the ridgelines. This morning Haardt had his field glasses in his saddle bag, and his knives and steel, his cartridge belt and crossed-sticks, and the Sharps balanced across the pommel of his saddle, the old feel of it coming back to him as soon as he laid it there. Before dawn, as the other hands snored through their hangovers in the bunkhouse, Haardt had run a rod with ticking down the barrel of the rifle, wiping it clean of grease.

Haardt had seen his last buffalo fifteen years before. And out of all the ones he'd killed he'd never kept a single part for himself, not a robe or a horn or a scalp. This time he meant to keep it all, hide, head, horns, hooves, meat, bones. Even drink the buffalo cider, if he took a notion. He didn't know how he would do all this, and didn't much care that as soon as he pulled the trigger he would be a felon.

For a time after the buffalo, before his life had became a slow drift to no place in particular, he'd dreamed of Africa and hunting ivory, and even heard there were endless herds of buffalo down in Australia. Once he gave some considera-tion to a grass widow with a quarter section along a spring creek. He had always meant to be more than a hand, meant to have more than the ceiling of a bunkhouse to lie on his back and stare at, and never meant for the buffalo hunting, at least parts of it, to be the best memories he would ever know.

Here he was, though, nearer fifty than forty, and things had just gotten away. He knew there would never be any Africa or Australia. Nor a woman or a child or a home. There was not even a buffalo. There ought to be a buffalo.

As Haardt rode through a little valley, he passed grouse cocks on the dancing ground, tails erect and wings spread, facing one another with drumming and coos, the air sacs on their necks puffed out and purple as the locoweed. Coming out on the rise where he'd been the day the snow came, Haardt whoa-ed the mare and pulled out his field glasses. There was the red outcrop, and though he didn't expect to find the buffalo still lying under it, he wanted to study it before riding up on it.

Today the shadow was only shadow. Haardt dismounted and led the mare to the outcrop, hunting sign as he went. Beneath the outcrop the rock had unquestionably been worn smooth by buffalo rubbing, but most big rocks in this country had. Searching, he found not a strand of hair on the rock nor any track nor dung on the ground, not even an old dried chip. But there had been a buffalo here, Haardt knew. He tried to think where the bull could have traveled. He looked toward the blue mountains.

Haardt rode all day, into the foothills, along the edge of the timber, and into the timber itself. He found deer and elk in velvet, the old track of a grizzly in a bank of rotting snow, and once thought he caught a glimpse of a lion, moving between trees. He saw no buffalo, no tracks, no dung. He rode till near sunset, then turned the mare back toward the Double Fork.

Dark was coming on when Haardt crossed a creek, the water running fast and muddy, then turned away from it and rode up a long ridge that led to a high flattop where he might get one last look around the country. The mare climbed with her head down, steadily, hardly breathing. When they came onto the top, Haardt's eye was caught by something on the ground.

It looked at first like a large river stone, rounded and white, but Haardt, who'd ridden onto this flat hundreds of times before, had never seen a river stone up here and knew of no way for one to get here, unless carried. The mare halted, seeming not to want to go any closer, and he had to nudge her with his spurs. The sky had gotten darker faster than Haardt had expected and it took him a moment to recognize what it was, lying on the ground. He sat in the saddle, studying it.

The horn sheaths, and the rest of the skeleton, were gone long ago, tooth marks showing on the bone. But the hollow eye sockets and bare horn cores, the smooth broad flat of the forehead—all were intact. It lay on some small rocks, tilted up on one side, like a horned moon racing over a mountain peak. Buffalo would be drawn to the highest ground in a storm, Haardt knew, and there they often met up with lightning. Haardt sat in the growing dark, wondering if that was the way this bull had come to be here sometime long ago—felled by electricity instead of lead—and he had simply not seen it until now. Haardt sat until the real moon rose and the sight of his own long shadow falling across the skull started him back for the ranch again, nowhere else for him to go.

"Last time I hire a remittance man," said old man MacQuie, standing in the doorway of the bunkhouse, talking somewhere past Haardt, the bunkhouse's sole occupant, who stood on the opposite side of the iron stove. Eight days after branding, all of the hands, except Haardt, and except Pidgeon, had asked for their pay and headed for San Antone, following Cerman. Pidgeon had seen enough of army life when he'd served with Coppenger's Tenth to decline, as he put it, to participate in "Cerman's march to the sea." But he had gotten another contract to break horses for an outfit out around Recluse, and so he waited one day more, then asked for his pay, too. Haardt, of course, had no other contracts, or intentions.

" '. . . We shall give the world a progeny yet more corrupt,' " quoted Mac-Quie, then looked at Haardt. "I don't suppose you know Horace."

Haardt looked down at the toe of his boot. The only Horace he'd ever known had been a teamster in Glendive who'd been born without ears. And he'd been called "Ho'ace."

"No," concluded old man MacQuie, looking past Haardt once again, "I don't suppose so.

"Well," said MacQuie, "I guess you and I will have to push the herd up to summer range ourselves. Then all I'm going to have for you till the fall's riding fence. That do?"

Haardt studied his boot a moment longer. Looking out the open door, past MacQuie, Haardt answered, "It will."

Old man MacQuie nodded. As he turned and walked out of the doorway, he said to himself, "Lord, let me find just one fair hand before I depart this world."

Old man MacQuie and he, along with two cow dogs, got the cattle moved to summer range, then MacQuie set Haardt to mending fence. He carried a sewed boot-top pouch with wire, cutters, staples, and a hatchet hung over the horn of his saddle. And he carried the Sharps, following wooden posts and barbed wire to the horizon as spring changed to summer and summer moved toward fall.

In August word came back about the boys who'd left for Cuba. Cerman died of yellow fever without ever firing a shot, while Wicher had gone on to win a medal on a silk ribbon. As for the two Joneses, they both deserted when the volunteers were transferred to the staging area outside Tampa. And Pidgeon got bucked off over by Recluse and broke an arm that knitted peculiar.

Haardt went on hunting the buffalo, seeing him twice that summer, once moving through the edge of the timber at noon on a breathless, baking day and once walking down into a gully in an early morning. Haardt rode hell-for-leather after him each time, showers of pale green hoppers clacketing up as he galloped the bay through the tall clover; but no matter how fast he rode, each time he got to the place where the buffalo had been, he could find no buffalo nor any spoor.

On an afternoon at the end of August, Haardt sat on the back of his bay and watched the thunderheads build and their tops flatten against the blue mountains. He still swept the country as he sat. And this time through the heat shimmer he saw, not the bull buffalo, but a pronghorn buck crossing over a rise half a mile off.

Haardt reined his pony around and started her toward the pronghorn. He wasn't sure what he was going to do, but he had an inkling he'd grown weary of Double Fork beef.

He trotted the bay the half mile, then dropped the reins and left her under the rise, swinging his right leg over the saddle horn and dropping to the ground with the Sharps. Haardt lifted the flap on his saddle bag and pulled one extra shell out of the belt coiled up inside, took out two clean-washed flour sacks also rolled up in there and meant for carrying buffalo straps, and pulled the pair of crossed-sticks from behind the saddle where he had them tied on. He slipped the extra shell into his trouser pocket, feeling the jackknife lying there, then jogged toward the rise.

Haardt made himself lower and lower as he got to the rise, making sure he never peeked over it, until he got down on hands and knees and crawled. Older, if not wiser, he got away without picking up any cactus thorns.

He knew the wind was right without having to think about it. Taking off his hat, he pushed it onto the top of the rise ahead of him, then lay the Sharps across it, deciding not to put up the crossed-sticks. Bellying up through the short dry grass, Haardt fit himself behind the stock of the heavy rifle. Now he looked over the rise and saw the buck feeding on green grass in the bottom of the draw, 150 yards away.

The pronghorn was about as big as any Haardt had ever seen. As he settled the telescope sight on it, it occurred to him, as it had not at all during the time he had been hunting the buffalo all summer, that these old cartridges probably wouldn't even fire anymore, and he had no idea if the telescope was still on target. As he cocked back the side hammer on the Sharps, it almost made him laugh to think that all this time he'd been chasing a shadow with a gun that would not shoot.

It surprised him when the Sharps went off as cleanly as it used to in the buffalo days. The buck had been quartering toward Haardt and the 470-grain bullet struck true with a dull slap just to the left of the right shoulder and angled through to the point of the left hip. The buck sank onto its haunches, then got back up, turning in a tight circle and wobbling off a dozen yards before collapsing.

Haardt got to his feet slowly. He picked up his hat and sacks and sticks and rifle and walked down to the antelope. The pronghorn lay on its side. Haardt kept looking at the place it lay, as if there was something about it he should be able to recognize. It took him a minute to regain a past way of seeing, and then it was clear that the pronghorn had fallen inside the circled stones of a long-abandoned tipi ring. Haardt hardly dare let himself imagine the life that had been led when a lodge of fine buffalo hides had stood here.

Haardt lay his gear down and opened the jackknife. He rolled the pronghorn onto its back and was about to open it when he hesitated. Outside, he thought. Haardt dragged the pronghorn beyond the stone circle and began to dress it.

When he had the guts out, he looked through them and took the liver—the heart blown to flinders—though he ordinarily had no taste for organ meat. He planned to rip the hide quickly off the antelope because of the heat and carry the quartered-up meat back in the clean flour sacks; but now he found himself skinning with extreme care, leaving no meat or fat on the hide. With the hide spread out on the ground under the antelope, Haardt unrolled the clean flour sacks and started removing the quarters. When he disjointed the lower legs he lay them carefully off to one side on the ground, rather than just flinging them away. Soon he had the four quarters, backstraps, and tenderloins lying on the sacks. Then he rolled up the hide, taking it, too, even though it made poor leather. At last he looked at the head and decided he would not leave it, either, too much already having gone to waste.

When Haardt turned from the antelope to go back for his horse, the buffalo was coming up the rise toward him. The bull looked six foot high at the hump and walked head-down in the sore-footed way Haardt had seen big buffalo walk. His horns were heavy at the bases, turning up to ends blunted by wear, and as he came a warm breeze rustled the long black wool of his scalp.

Haardt stepped slowly backward into the tipi ring, not taking his eye off the buffalo. He could see as the bull walked how old he was both by his stubbed horns and the way his bony hips showed through the thin summer coat. Inside the ring, Haardt lowered himself to a sitting position and picked up the Sharps and the crossed-sticks. He found the second cartridge in his pocket and slid it into the breech, closing the action.

The buffalo walked on until he was directly in front of the place on the rise where Haardt had killed the antelope from, and stopped. Bending his front legs, he lowered his chest to the ground, then his hindquarters, dust rising off his hide as he settled. He leaned his body into the slope of the rise and turned a round, calm eye upon Haardt.

Haardt could never say how long he sat there, cradling the Sharps in the crotch of the sticks. (Till the last morning of his life—when he awoke to stare, not at a bunkhouse ceiling, but at the ceiling of a room in the Occidental Hotel in Buffalo, Wyoming, heard the call of a meadowlark outside the window, and got out of bed to put a bullet from the Sharps he'd never given up through his heart—he never spoke a word of the buffalo to anyone.) He only knew that in time the sun went down and no moon rose, and in the darkness he was no longer able to see the buffalo. The bull was there, though, Haardt hearing the rasp of the buffalo's breath as he went on sitting. He also began to hear the rumble of thunder, like the old sound of a buffalo herd passing, lifting huge drifting clouds of dust into the sky as they went. Inside the far storm clouds lightning burst, like a light flaring behind the shade of a lamp; and Haardt was certain he could see the outline of the buffalo for that instant.

The storm came on, moving across the hills toward them. The wind rose and Haardt smelled the buffalo in it. A bolt of lightning at last showed before the clouds and made a jagged fissure across the dark plate of the sky, letting in a flash of the light the night held back. For one second it was a strange, black-skied day, everything perfectly visible. And there, directly in front of him where the bull had been, stood the bay, wandered over from behind the rise with her reins trailing, her ears up and head tossing, ready for Haardt to saddle up and ride her back to where the day had begun, to head back before the clouds opened and washed everything clean, the buffalo, it seemed, having climbed some time ago to higher ground. Leaving Haardt behind.

# AFTERWORD: . . . OR NOT TO KILL

**What is the** expiration date on life's passions?

I began wondering about this after leaving L.A. some years ago. In Los Angeles, where much of what matters most in life somehow comes to be viewed through a glass, darkly, I was hardly ever surprised to hear from yet another friend that he had given up hunting. It was social pressure, or maybe just L.A.'s ability to blunt the human desire to hunt as easily as it subverted most people's innate affection for clean air, open space, and calm.

Then I moved to the heart of hunting country, and even here I found people—albeit not many—who after years of hunting had also given it up, for no better reason, it seemed, than that they just no longer cared for it, the love between them and hunting having died, to get perilously close to paraphrasing Evelyn Waugh.

Certainly, the long-range trend is toward a decline in hunters; simple demographics explain that. As the overall population ages, so too does the hunting cohort: Knees give out, eyesight dims, reflexes slow, the hills become taller and steeper, and in the end, we die. Death makes nonhunters of us all. But that isn't what I'm talking about or what, frankly, troubles me.

What does trouble me is not hunters in their sixties or seventies who decide they've grown too old, but hunters who quit before they even turn forty. Why does someone, young and healthy, living in decent game country, give up hunting, especially when it is an activity he has seemingly enjoyed for many years, often since childhood? Conventional wisdom offers a variety of answers.

A lack of land to hunt on is said to be what compels many to quit. This is particularly true out in the once Wild West, where an awful lot of it has now metamorphosed into the Soccer-Mom West, sage supplanted by Bermuda grass, deer trails converted to bicycle paths. Every day more POSTED signs appear and more landowners want to be paid before they will forgive hunters their trespasses (something unheard of Out West not long ago). On the acres that do remain open, in the supposed words of Yogi Berra, nobody goes there anymore because they're too crowded.

Then there is a panoply of pop-psych reasons, enough for a week of talk shows: single mothers unable to pass on a hunting tradition to their sons; a geometric expansion in sensitivity toward our fellow sentient beings brought about by the enlightenment spread by the animal-rights movement; the changing relationship between the sexes; blah-blah-blah, yackety-schmackety. There may even be something to that last one. ("Hunting [is a form] of institutionalized escape," wrote Doug Stanton some years ago in *Esquire* magazine, and as such allows men to light out for the territories without wrecking their marriages. Or at least it once did. "It's funny," he continued, "and maybe no coincidence that hunting [has] never seemed less reputable than [it does] today.") Hunting, an overwhelmingly male activity dating back to the undated origin of the species, may now, for some, exemplify a man's disrespect for the partnership he has formed with the woman in his life by his purposely abandoning her, even if only for a matter of days. Yet when someone says he has given up hunting to be closer to his wife (to "spend more time" with his family), you do have to wonder exactly how sound that marriage is if she feels so threatened by his week or two in the woods each year, especially when you come to find out (usually after the divorce) that she never actually gave a damn about it, perhaps even welcoming his temporary absences—How, indeed, can I miss you if you won't go away?

Then we come to an extremely popular and fondly held theory, especially among animal-rightists and the general run of opinion makers—who do seem to listen attentively to animal-rightists when it comes to jumping to conclusions about hunters and hunting—that most experienced hunters finally "hang up their weapons because they have simply grown sick of killing." Although the "sick of killing" theme is one found extensively throughout popular fiction, films, television, et cetera (as we shall see), it strikes me as quite an odd state for any true hunter to find himself in. I do know some (very lucky) hunters who believe they have reached a personal quota when it comes to certain species or classes of game—usually very large, somewhat rare animals such as lion or even elk—concluding that they've killed their fair share. But in my own case, I recall the last bobwhite hunt I went on at the very end of the Kansas season: Five days and some twenty-five miles of muddy slogging for a personal bag of four quail, plus three misses. Overall, much of my hunting—much of most *everybody's* "rough shooting" (as the British call it)—tallies up about like that. At approximately three and a half miles per bird flushed, it was, I can assure you, not the killing that made me sick; it was the missing. So when I hear someone say he has killed enough, it strikes me as a case of what Ortega y Gasset labeled "the height of affected piety," a form of loathsome crypto-braggadocio (*gosh*, just no more worlds to conquer), or the lament of someone who's never done a lick of real hunting in his life.

Yet another hypothesis for why some quit has to do with a change in mental status. "Because hunters have trouble articulating and defending their motives, non-hunters often conclude that they are simply crazy," proclaims one anthropologist with an animal-rights ax to grind—never mind that much of the trouble may lie with the way nonhunters have been schooled to listen to what hunters articulate. And if not crazed, then hunting is considered an immature, or perhaps even infantile, activity.

In the first instance, the consensus seems to be that those who give up hunting have finally regained their sanity; while in the latter, hunting is reckoned something that rational individuals eventually mature out of. (Peter Matthiessen, in *The Tree Where Man Was Born*, even proposes an average age for when such transformations occur, quoting a Tanzanian parks official to the effect that thirty-five is "the age when most men outgrow hunting big animals.") These, and that *mal de massacre* thing, are served up lavishly in our popular culture as reasons why people choose no longer to hunt, creating a definite public sentiment that venerates quitting.

Throughout popular culture, the former (or "reformed," or maybe it's even "recovered") hunter is held in far greater esteem than the unreconstructed one. Atticus Finch in the novel *To Kill a Mockingbird* is laudable not for his being "the deadest shot in Maycomb County," but rather for his not having fired a shot at an animal in thirty years. Robert DeNiro's character in *The Deer Hunter* finally "gets it" when he lays down his rifle and chooses not to kill that buck (when did Pennsylvania acquire eleven-thousand-foot mountain peaks and European red deer, by the way?—you had to see the movie). Walt Disney, of course, made sure that Davy Crockett apologized for all them b'ar he kilt once upon a time, even though the historical Crockett did so primarily to salt away meat for his family and neighbors to enable them to survive the frontier winter, for which no apology would seem to be in order. Even Hemingway, in his posthumous novel *The Garden of Eden*, has a young boy repeatedly curse elephant hunting, as a sign of his having gained the knowledge of good and evil.

Yet for all the customary reasons put forth for why people quit hunting, I'm afraid that none rings true, at least not for me. They do not because they all, at their root, seem to depend on an acceptance of there being something essentially corrupt about hunting. Now, we can hunt well, or we can hunt badly, but neither is a reflection upon the nature of hunting itself, just as the behavior of sinners or saints (being fallibly human) has, ultimately, nothing to do with the ultimate nature of faith. There's no question, though, that people do quit hunting, and the real reason for that, I believe, has far more to do with the real reason for why they began.

There is nothing that prevents people from becoming hunters for any number of extremely shallow reasons: parental coercion, social conformity, an intense sense of competitiveness, a desperate need to assert their masculinity, and so on. Those are also the people who seem most likely to quit hunting. When someone says he once loved, or even enjoyed hunting, but has now lost his taste for it, I wonder what it is he has in fact lost his taste for.

To be sick of killing, to come to one's senses, or to "grow out of it" is not what becomes of the true hunter, the one who was drawn to hunting because he found in it something—in the way it let him bind with the wild, exercise senses and instincts that had lain in hibernation too long, and don the psychic skin of his brother animal as he went in pursuit of him—that he could find nowhere else. Hunting is not something that can be "taken up" like court games or golf, or so easily laid aside. The only reason the true hunter has for hunting is that it is what he loves—and in a sense, is what he is. How do we quit being what we are?

So I would contend that when people stop hunting, hunting is not what they are stopping at all. For them, "hunting" is about something else all together, about pastimes and conventionalisms and compulsions that involve only transitorily the mystery of wild animals and the chase, and in the name of something whose meaning is far less than the sum of its parts. With only superficial motives to justify it, the death of any animal would appear an obscenity. Who, in his right mind, would not be sickened, feel he has risked his sanity, or put away "childish" things after sufficient exposure to such a killing joke?

I would hold that those who quit hunting outright never knew what true hunting was all about, and never genuinely came to love it. It's like the way we forget. When we forget, it is not because we have lost our cherished memory of something. We forget only what we never really knew to begin with.

I go on hunting even though I am by definition no longer young, and "healthy" is such an ambiguous term. As I've put these stories together I've remembered,

once again, all that hunting—in its cloudless arduousness and sometimes startling ease; cold and heat, dry and wet; predawn darkness, midday glare, and
evening time that is actual gloaming; most excellent toys and the exercise of
empty-handed animal cunning; flashes of danger and interludes of absurdity;
the brotherhood of fellow hunters and the lonesomeness of waiting on stand or
stalking silently; wry sadness and bittersweet joy; in short, the whole fabulous
mess—has meant to me. These stories have made me want to get out as soon as
possible to hunt down new memories. Maybe, if I have been lucky rather than
good, at least one of the stories, or even a paragraph or sentence, has given you
the same feeling. I'd like to hope so. At some point, memories are all there are—
conscious life itself, at heart, merely an excuse for creating them—and hunting
memories are plainly the best.